AMERICA OBSERVED

America Observed

On an International Anthropology of the United States

Edited by

Virginia R. Dominguez and Jasmin Habib

berghahn

NEW YORK · OXFORD

www.berghahnbooks.com

Published in 2017 by

Berghahn Books

www.berghahnbooks.com

Library of Congress Cataloging-in-Publication Data

Names: Dominguez, Virginia R., editor. | Habib, Jasmin, editor.
Title: America observed : on an international anthropology of the United States /
    edited by Virginia R. Dominguez and Jasmin Habib.
Description: New York : Berghahn Books, [2017] | Includes bibliographical
    references and index.
Identifiers: LCCN 2016026096 | ISBN 9781785333606 (hardback : alk. paper)|
    ISBN 9781785334351 (paperback : alk. paper)| ISBN 9781785333613 (ebook)
Subjects: LCSH: Ethnology--Fieldwork--United States | Anthropology--
    Fieldwork--United States. | United States--Civilization.
Classification: LCC GN346 .A57 2017 | DDC 301.0973--dc23
LC record available at https://lccn.loc.gov/2016026096

British Library Cataloguing in Publication Data

A catalogue record for this book is available from the British Library

ISBN 978-1-78533-360-6 (hardback)
ISBN 978-1-78533-435-1 (paperback)
ISBN 978-1-78533-361-3 (ebook)

Virginia:

For Jane, who understands the issues and shares my vision of a world in which we all learn about each other and from each other; and for the many who enter our lives in different ways, make us smile, cry, think, argue, and laugh.

Jasmin:

For Jim, who shares my fascination with America and for Mark Behr ("Markus") who indulged me in this pursuit from 1992 until his untimely passing in 2015.

Contents

Introduction: Can the US Be "Othered" Usefully? On an International
Anthropology of the United States   1
Virginia R. Dominguez and Jasmin Habib

Part I. On the Outside Looking In? The US As Fieldsite

1. Manhattan as a Magnet: Place and Circulation among Young Swedes   31
Helena Wulff

2. Is It Un-American to Be Critical of Israel? Criticism and Fear in the
US Context   51
Jasmin Habib

3. Biosecurity in the US: "The Scientific" and "the American" in Critical
Perspective   79
Limor Samimian-Darash

4. American Theater State: Reflections on Political Culture   103
Ulf Hannerz

5. Observing US Gay Organizations and Voluntary Associations: An
Outsider's Exposition   120
Moshe Shokeid

Part II. From the Inside Out? Reflections on
an International Anthropology of the US

6. Who Cares? Why It's Odd and Why It's Not   143
Geoffrey White

7. Power and Trafficking of Scholarship in International American Studies 155
Keiko Ikeda

Afterword: The Sounds of Silence: Commissions, Omissions, and
Particularity in the Global Anthropology of the United States   164
Jane C. Desmond

Index   173

Introduction

Can the US Be "Othered" Usefully?
On an International Anthropology of the United States

Virginia R. Dominguez and Jasmin Habib

This book raises a question and addresses a mystery. The primary question is whether the United States can be usefully "Othered," and the mystery is why few social or cultural anthropologists outside the US seem to do long-term fieldwork in the US or consider the US their primary area of specialization. Since anthropologists as a whole study human groupings and cultures throughout the planet, and this is true in many different locations around the world, the question is why not study the US? And since scholars in a number of other disciplines in many different parts of the world do indeed specialize in the study of the people and things of the US—literature, foreign policy, and history, for example—the question in part becomes one about anthropology itself. To put it directly, if not quite bluntly, here, we ask whether there is something about contemporary anthropology that this absence reveals.[1]

We consider this to be an issue of some importance and not just for anthropology. As we have explored this phenomenon over the past several years, it has become clear that a country of over 300 million people ought to command the curiosity and attention of more than a small number of colleagues, and that the colleagues who have indeed done extensive ethnographic fieldwork in the US deserve much more attention both inside and outside the US as specialists on the US than they seem to get, especially inside the US. In exploring the phenomenon and choosing colleagues to feature in this volume, we have been guided by the desire to lead readers to the issue of the US as a fascinating place, country, space, society, and

Notes for this chapter begin on page 24.

location that is definitely "Other" to most people on this planet and that could well use the careful and long-term insights of the worldwide anthropological community, and not just the insights of those anthropologists who live and work within it.

In this introduction we want to address a set of issues that no doubt arise when people we talk to first hear of this phenomenon—since we anticipate that such issues will arise in the minds of readers who come across this book. The issues are (1) whether this is not just about money, the costs of doing long-term research in the US, and the difficulty of getting visas to do such research in the US; (2) whether we are not actually objectifying colleagues as "Other" and assuming that their research, analysis, and interpretations are automatically different from those produced by anthropologists in the US itself; (3) whether we are not ignoring significant bodies of scholarship (including anthropological scholarship on the US) produced and consumed over long periods of time outside the US about the US; and (4) whether we are not fetishizing "fieldwork" as our marker of value in determining who is and is not an expert on the US. Each one of these issues deserves exploration, and we have obviously considered them with care, so we begin by addressing them here.

The Practicalities—Money, Cost, and Visas

The question of money and visas comes up frequently whenever we first broach the topic. Indeed we frequently hear that it costs money to do ten, twelve, or fifteen months of fieldwork in the US. The problem is that this does not explain why a number of anthropologists—anthropologists in other countries, including rather prosperous ones—become specialists in, and on, other parts of the world and spend a good deal of money getting to those places, living in those places, hiring field assistants with more skill or familiarity with those local languages, and so forth. There are, for example, numerous serious Latin Americanists in France (including in anthropology/ethnologie) and they do lengthy fieldwork in, among other countries, Brazil, Colombia, and Mexico. There are also numerous excellent anthropologists in Germany who specialize in sub-Saharan Africa, and there are numerous important anthropologists in Japan who work in and on Southeast Asia. Money does not seem to be the obstacle in those long-term field projects. Yet money comes up as an obstacle when one asks colleagues in many settings, including those who work in and on the US, why there are not more anthropologists choosing to do the same.

An answer—hence an argument put forth—economizes the issue by invoking the cost of doing long-term fieldwork in the US. But we do not believe that this is the main factor, not even for colleagues in middle-economy countries or even poorer ones (since many of those still come on scholarships to the US to complete their graduate studies or they find their way to European states). There is something else. As one colleague in Germany put it just a few years ago, "I was told that there is no culture in the US so why am I wasting my time doing research there?" And another colleague, this time in France, put it also very recently: "I think I am the only anthropologist in France working on the US . . . Some have studied Native American/AmerIndian societies but they don't really see them as part of the US . . ." And then there are the sort-of travelogues like Baudrillard's *America* (1988) or even de Tocqueville's old *Democracy in America* (1835), which seem to imply that one can travel through the US and write reflections on what one sees and hears (which become bestsellers) or one can study societies in the US, though they are not considered to be a part of the US. To the extent that there is indeed something else going on that is not really about the cost or difficulty of getting into the US to do long-term anthropological fieldwork, we ask ourselves, and our readers, what that might be and whether the implication is not that the US is uninteresting or even, at the risk of raising postcolonial critiques of anthropology, not exotic enough to hold our interest.

As we contemplate this question of practicalities, and the perception that it is the primary explanation for the mystery we have uncovered, we ask readers to consider the following, even if the thought of money or cost is initially disturbing or off-putting:

(1) Scholars and students often invoke money/cost/funding demands when explaining why few, indeed very few, social/cultural anthropologists normally located outside the US study the US, work on the US, or specialize on the US. But these are acts of invocation. Are they indeed explanations that account for most of the absences we note here?

(2) Scholars and students (both in the US and in many other countries) often spend a good deal of money going elsewhere, learning other languages, and specializing in other regions or societies. When these issues come up in conversation, they have no explanation for those choices. Is something so taken-for-granted, tacit or, to invoke Pierre Bourdieu (1977), doxic in the world of social, cultural, or linguistic anthropology that it remains unnoticed or unremarked upon until someone (like us) takes it out of the "universe of the undisputed"? Yes, of course, there are now quite a few social/cultural anthropologists in the US who do not go abroad for their fieldwork, but many still do, and many do in countries other than the US (though not typically to, or in, the US).

(3) In at least some regions of the world, and certainly apparently France
     and Germany, one does not need to do much more than scratch the
     surface to be then given a different explanation (or at least to get such
     a view from those few who do study the US who are discouraged
     from doing so by their professional home communities). When chal-
     lenged or questioned, other possibilities emerge, but are they the
     deeper issues rather than the first line of explanation that tends to be
     given?

Objectifying Colleagues outside the US as Other

An uncomfortable question also typically arises when we bring up this
topic, and we assume that it will also come up when readers come to
think of it. Hence, we consider it important to address here and to explain
what our focus is. The issue is why we think that the absence of non-US
anthropological research on the US matters. Indeed we sometimes hear
from colleagues inside the US that our question makes little sense to them
because there has, in fact, been quite a bit of anthropological fieldwork
done in the US since the 1970s, and that our pointing out that the great
majority of that work is done by people who live and work in the US means
that we assume our colleagues outside the US somehow automatically
see and perceive US things differently by virtue of being foreign. It is, of
course, an important matter to address, even if it is an uncomfortable one
for us as well as perhaps for some of our readers.

If we were indeed to assume that the issue was a cultural one and that
we sought to point out that we would automatically get different insights
on the US if we promoted the anthropological study of the US on cultural
grounds, our skeptics would probably have a point. But that is not what we
are interested in pointing out here. We are interested in why so few social/
cultural anthropologists outside the US actually do long-term fieldwork
in (and on) the US. There is a very noteworthy pattern, and we argue that
this needs to be noticed, acknowledged, and changed. For example, we
are just as interested in whether there are perceptions of the US elsewhere
and perceptions or practices within the anthropological community in
the US itself that lead many anthropologists away from studying the US.
These need not be the same, but it is clear that there is something (or some
set of factors) that lead the US not to be studied by many anthropologists
regularly living, teaching, writing, and working outside the US. Are these
matters of access? Are they forms of anti-Americanism? Are these the
product of interesting "imagined geographies" that work simultaneously
to see the US as uninteresting or as "already known" or as less interesting

than societies more traditionally (or conventionally) within the purview of social/cultural anthropology?

The issue we bring up does not assume that anthropological colleagues outside the US would naturally or automatically see things in the US differently. It does, however, ask why it is that so few of the many thousands of social/cultural anthropologists who live and work outside the US do long-term anthropological fieldwork in the US. We note that some people may initially think of this as a question of access (and hence of the power of the US government to keep them out), but colleagues from quite a few parts of the world could enter the US with relative ease and do not. We understand that this is not the case with colleagues from certain regions or countries that the US agencies tasked with "homeland security" are most concerned about in 2016. In those cases indeed, the gatekeeping power of the US government and its agencies looms large. Yet many other countries and their nationals are seen as allies or at least not as threatening to the US and few anthropologists in those countries seem to do long-term fieldwork in the US or even to specialize on the US.

It seems to us that the issue is not the objectification of anthropological colleagues as either "American" or "foreign" but, rather, an interesting, if odd, combination of factors—some are perceptions of US society apparently held by numerous colleagues outside the US and some are perceptions of US society held by colleagues inside the US—that seem to make the US a very infrequent site of contemporary anthropological fieldwork except by people who already live and work in the US regardless of where they were born or raised.

We are tempted to say that these are questions of power, not of culture, but we recognize that they may well be perceptions of culture and society that presume the power of the US in the early twenty-first century. If so, they are indeed questions of power—but we are interested in the fact that these are not necessarily matters of foreign policy or military power. They may instead be examples of the ways US power is perceived and approached by anthropologists both inside and outside the US.

Scholarship on the United States

There is indeed anthropological scholarship on the US in the US itself. There did not always seem to be, or when there was it was often received with doubt, even suspicion. Good examples are the work of Hortense Powdermaker on Hollywood (1950) and Zora Neale Hurston (1937) on African-American life. That has changed since the 1970s, although it is not clear to us that much of that fieldwork claims high prestige (especially when it is the result of not getting a major grant to go abroad). There are, of course, exceptions. In some cases, fieldwork on the US is conducted after a scholar in the US establishes his or her credentials based on long-term fieldwork outside the US, and arguably that reputation carries over to the fieldwork they later do on the US. Excellent examples of that are Catherine Lutz, Marshall Sahlins, and Chaise LaDousa. Lutz's original fieldwork focused on emotions in Micronesia (1988), but she has gone on to do insightful fieldwork in and on the National Geographic Society (Lutz and Collins 1993) and, more recently, on the US military and militarization, with long-term fieldwork in Fort Bragg, North Carolina, and the surrounding community (Lutz 2002). Sahlins' earliest work was in and on Fiji (1962), but he went on to do influential research and fieldwork in and on history and historiography in Hawai'i (1981) as well as a book critiquing the use and abuse of biology in US scientific and educational contexts (1977). Chaise LaDousa did long-term fieldwork in and on educational practices and institutions in India for his doctoral dissertation (eventually publishing it as a book in 2014) but wrote a wonderful book on house signs and their meanings in Oxford, Ohio, long after working in India (2011).

There are, of course, others. Some like Stefan Helmreich do fieldwork in and on scientific communities in the US and carry that defamiliarizing (but learning) orientation in and out of those circles (cf. Helmreich 2000 and 2009). Still others tend to work in and on underprivileged and under-empowered social circles—often migrant populations or populations racialized in the US as non-normative/non-white and often low-income. Some of that work has been highly regarded and cited—such as Karen Brodkin's *How Jews Became White Folks and What That Says about Race in America* (1998), Nina Glick Schiller et al.'s *Nations Unbound* (1993), Carol Stack's *All Our Kin* (1975), and Arlene Davila's *Latinos, Inc.* (2001) and *Barrio Dreams* (2004). Much of this work has resulted in doctoral dissertations, academic and non-academic jobs, and some journal articles, but still not a great deal of intellectual prestige. This may be a controversial point but we are not sure how many US-based anthropologists would disagree with us. It is "anthropology at home" (cf. Jackson 1987; and DiLeonardo 2000), and it may be defended and endorsed as a way of countering primitivism and (neo)colonialism but it is still not the prime orientation of most US graduate training departments or the "area studies" centers that often count on social/cultural anthropologists to provide them with substance, language skills, knowledge, and dedication.

This view of the anthropology of the US may not be universally shared but we believe that it resonates with a great deal of the actual teaching, mentoring, and hiring practices among anthropologists in the US. Looking at introductory anthropology textbooks produced and used in the US can be telling. They all make a point of presenting anthropology as global in its reach and applicable as well to the US. And we should not forget the interesting original, but also continuing, appeal of Horace Miner's 1956 article ("Body Ritual among the Nacirema") published in the *American Anthropologist* and republished multiple times since then—a spoof of sorts but frequently included in introductory courses and readers as a way of reminding entry-level students of the applicability of social/cultural anthropology "at home."

In this context, it is useful to consider Jessica Cattelino's recent (2010) and thoughtful review of anthropology in and of the US. In "Anthropologies of the United States," she states that she shows:

> that anthropologists of the United States have been concerned to locate the anthropological field (as discipline, ethnographic site, and theoretical domain) in three ways. First, they have undertaken spatial projects that include regional ethnographies, community studies, and explorations of America's power at and beyond US borders. Second, epistemological and methodological projects have located Americanist anthropology in cultural critique and defamiliarization. A third area is emergent: ethnographic research that locates Native North America not as distinct from the Anthropology of the United States but rather as critical to it. (2010: 276)

True enough, yet it is worthwhile noting that the work referred to, discussed, invoked, and noticed (even when not the most prestigious in the profession) is nearly all done by anthropologists who live and work in the US. They may not all have been born and raised in the US, and at times they are consumed (even billed) as representatives of those countries or regions of the world, but they largely live in the US, are employed by US institutions, and are (de facto) US anthropologists.

Interestingly this is not a point made by Jessica Cattelino. In fact, she offers no comment at all on the fieldwork experiences of, or writing by, anthropologists who study the US but who live outside its territory. We do not find it surprising, but we still find it noteworthy. Clearly there is a pattern there, an expectation, an understanding that she shares—namely, that the only anthropologists who might be engaged in Americanist anthropology in the contemporary period would be those living in the US. Reworking a point that Cattelino makes in the same article (2010: 280)—but for reasons that are different from our own—we also contemplate (and want readers to contemplate) if an anthropology *in* the US necessarily adds up to an anthropology *of* the US.

This is an issue that SANA (the section of the American Anthropological Association called the Society for the Anthropology of North America) has struggled with for some time. It struggled to gain recognition in the

last decades of the twentieth century, and it remains an issue today. That
Canadian colleagues have recently become leaders of SANA is an interesting development, though SANA has "North America" in its title and
this has always meant to include Canada. Yet, who is doing anthropological fieldwork in the US and does SANA really reach out to sociocultural
anthropological colleagues normally located outside the US who specialize on the US?

On Fieldwork and Why It (Still) Matters

As we ponder the phenomenon, perhaps we should address the questions
that truly stare us in the face: Why study the US as an anthropologist?
What might we gain in our understandings of the US from an ethno-
graphic/anthropological perspective? How might we supplement and/
or critique the work of those in the fields of Cultural Studies, American
Studies, political science, or history where the study of the US is considered important, even essential? What is it that anthropologists bring to
the study of the US and what is it that anthropology itself might learn
about itself?

We realize that when Jasmin Habib (normally in Canada) speaks about
this project in general, she tends to get a puzzled look that suggests the
person is really asking: "Why would you want to do *that*?" As we contemplate this frequent reaction, we ask ourselves what lies behind it. Is
it that some anthropologists in Canada (and other parts of the world) are
so repelled by the thought of the US that they do not want to go anywhere near it? Can it be that there is—underlying all of this—a form of
anti-Americanism that in/forms or rather de/forms this particular field
of analysis? It is no surprise that Jasmin Habib finds herself asking why
"those of us living outside the US [are not] compelled to study such issues
as street violence, gun use, the high rates of incarceration, shopping zones
and practices, street fashion, television viewing, family vacations, among
many, many other cultural practices and concerns?"

It is important to ask about where one might find the "America" one is
looking at, and for, in the US. Many of the non-US-based anthropologists
who have done their research in the US have tended to conduct fieldwork
in big cities—for example, in New York (Helena Wulff and Moshe Shokeid,
in this volume); Washington, DC (Ulf Hannerz in his earlier work); the San
Francisco Bay Area (Christina Garsten), but some have worked in rural
areas and small towns (Eva Mackey in upstate New York; Lucy Pickering
on the "big" island of Hawai'i), and others in smaller cities and metropolitan areas (such as Jasmin Habib, Keiko Ikeda, and Hyang-Jin Jung in
the Midwest, and Sara LeMenestrel in southern Louisiana) (cf. Wulff 1998;

Shokeid 1988, 1995, and 2002; Hannerz 1969 and 2004; Garsten 1994 and 2008; Mackey 2005; Pickering 2009, 2010a and 2010b; Habib 2004 and 2007; Ikeda 1999; Jung 2007; LeMenestrel 1999). Of course, there are others, but the question is both about the type of location they have chosen and the "America" they have (or have had) in mind.

Is there an "America" that is imagined and then sought in particular types of locations, and is this more prominent when speaking of colleagues outside the US, or does that not matter? The country is big, after all, and many types of projects seem to us worthy of study. At a minimum we would expect to see a mix of US-based anthropologists doing research and non-US-based anthropologists doing research in the US. Yet the fact is that there are very few anthropologists based outside the US who do fieldwork in the US and the question remains: why do they not?

Is it that too many people feel they actually *know* the US by virtue of the fact that so much of *it* is everywhere and all the time (in film, fashion, television, the Internet, news, books, music, alternative media, just to name all the kinds of things that blanket and circulate around the globe)? If so, we would need to contemplate what they are assuming and how this contrasts with the long-received wisdom drilled into most anthropologists around the world about the importance of deriving knowledge from long-term fieldwork and not just from media, circulating retail products and ads, or news reports. To say that the US might repel some people (or even many people) may not be important in and of itself, but it is important when we consider key aspects of anthropological practice, namely, our relationships and the wide-ranging commitments we make to those we study.

As Ulf Hannerz noted in a piece he wrote on multi-sited ethnography entitled "Being There and There and There!":

> Anthropologists often take a rather romantic view of their fields and their relationships to people there. They find it difficult to describe their informants as informants because they would rather see them as friends, and they may be proud to announce that they have been adopted into families and kin groups— not only because it suggests something about their skills as fieldworkers but also *because it carries a moral value*. They have surrendered to the field, and have been in a way absorbed by it. (Evans Pritchard [1951: 79] shared similar sentiments: "An anthropologist has failed unless, when he says goodbye to the natives, there is on both sides the sorrow of parting.") (2003: 208–9; Habib's emphasis)

There is something to this point. Some of Jasmin Habib's colleagues are disturbed—really disturbed—that she would choose to do any research in the US. They think it is a place that is "on the decline," "a disaster zone," "dangerous," and, ultimately, even "uninteresting" and "unimportant." It is not simply because they think the US is all of those things; rather any relationship to the US seems a waste of her time and, just as importantly, her efforts. They seem less interested to hear her stories upon her return— as compared to their response when she returns from Israel, or even after meeting with indigenous leaders in Montreal or Ottawa. Against the backdrop of so much US Cultural Studies, literary studies, communication studies, and US American Studies, which are more often than not textual in their analyses, one also has to wonder why there is not also the appeal or call to anthropologists to become more engaged in experience-based fieldwork.

In *Being There* (2009), John Borneman and Abdellah Hammoudi write that

> [h]owever creatively we might interpret documents, a textualist approach is often duplicative of literary studies and, in insistence on power as the core substance of all experience, overlaps with political science. By insisting on it, we ignore what anthropology can bring to literary scholars and to political scientists, what other scholars cannot produce or intuit from the study of documents: the diverse forms of social action and interaction, interlocution in experience. (2009: 16)

We think they make an excellent point about what fieldwork brings to the world of knowledge, research, interpretation, and education, and why we believe it does matter that so few of our anthropological colleagues outside the US seem to engage in field studies in the US. While Borneman and Hammoudi may not have had the US in mind when they wrote their piece, much of their argument for fieldwork works here as well. "It is certainly true," they write,

> that an encounter and an exchange, verbal and nonverbal—Being There, in short—guarantee nothing. And indeed, discrepancies between what is said and what is meant, in interaction, in writing, in reading, can play out ad infinitum; ambivalence, contradictory meanings, tensions cling to every word and utterance. Such is the predicament of discourse that every meaning implies a deferral. It is also certainly true, however, that the more one shares time and speaks with people, the better acquainted one becomes with the texture of other life, making it more probable there will be a closer fit between the order of orders and the order of things. (Ibid.: 14)

This is definitely an argument for long-term engagement with people in the field and it is one of the key reasons we stress work that is based on long-term fieldwork.

A book that is often-referred to in reference to "outsider" perspectives on the US is *Distant Mirrors: America as a Foreign Culture* (DeVita and Armstrong 2002). However, it does not draw on long-term professional anthropological field experience. Of the nineteen essays included in that collection (whose third edition was published in 2002), the great majority are short essays based on encounters and observations but not long-term anthropological fieldwork. It is true that fifteen of the essays were written by people born and/or raised outside the US, but many wrote these as reflections or observations they made as university students or professors in the course of their everyday lives in the US. Two examples will suffice here.

Amparo B. Ojeda, born and raised in the Philippines, described in the book as "now an anthropologist and linguist" and identified as retired from Loyola University in Chicago, wrote a four-page essay for the book titled "Growing Up American: Doing the Right Thing" (2002). Her biography states that she "conducted fieldwork in the Philippines and is involved in ongoing research on the adjustment of Filipino immigrants in Metropolitan Chicago," yet the essay's abstract refers to her early encounters with the US and her reactions to it. She writes:

> As a young student on her first visit to America, Professor Ojeda, a Fulbright scholar, was reassured that her adjustment to American life and culture would be easy. The orientation survival kit was of minimal help in adjusting to some American customs, especially those involving childrearing. Years later, in returning to the US with a daughter, Professor Ojeda was faced with a crucial conflict of values—American values versus the more familiar values of her own Philippine traditions. (2002: 44)

Likewise, Jin K. Kim, professor in the Department of Communication at SUNY-Plattsburgh, born and raised in South Korea but trained at the graduate level at Syracuse University and the University of Iowa, contributed an eight-page essay that is basically a letter to an old friend in South Korea after the friend calls Kim "an American"—presumably a letter from a "Korean cultural perspective" about US issues of "privacy, manners, sexual mores, individuality, interpersonal relations, and doublespeak" (2002).

Distant Mirrors: America as a Foreign Culture makes a point of addressing anthropological history and expectations and is valuable as a teaching tool in that respect. Yet it clearly does not rely on the kind of long-term professional fieldwork that we have come to expect of social/cultural anthropologists. The message is clear on the back cover as well as in their editorial introduction. "This book," the back cover notes, "features intriguing essays, written by anthropologists and other scholars, that are selected for their captivating and often humorous views of American culture. Each essay helps you understand yourself better by focusing on your own culture and seeing it from a new perspective." And in the editorial introduction ("Understanding Ourselves: About the Third Edition") the editors write appropriately:

> Anthropology has a long history of concern with the "other," the different, the strange. This focus on others and their cultures gives anthropology a comparative perspective that provides a reflective lens for understanding ourselves and our own immediate world. However, the ethnographic spaces of today differ a great deal from the ones inhabited by exotic people seemingly untouched by Western influence who are considered by many to be the main subjects of anthropological scrutiny . . . We are, therefore, compelled to look closer to home for the strangeness and similarity that is the compelling part of the ethnographic enterprise. (DeVita and Armstrong 2002: xi)

This is pedagogically useful but it does little to address the mystery it contemplates. The question remains: why are more anthropologists from the very large community of professional and doctoral-level anthropologists all over the world not doing fieldwork in and on the US? While US-based anthropologists offer us a very rich ethnographic literature ranging from, and on, the effects of the attacks on 9/11, the wars on Iraq and Afghanistan, a collapsing "middle class," the rising rates of incarceration in the inner city as well as along the US-Mexican border, finance and the financial markets, the rise of gated communities and wealth, and the like—all subjects that we would imagine could be of great interest to non-US-based anthropologists—little to no anthropological attention has been paid to these or other important issues by those living outside its borders.

Factors or Fudges?

To put this in broader perspective, we ask readers to consider the fact that many anthropologists indeed come to the massive Annual Meetings of the American Anthropological Association toward the end of each year, and that it is not rare to find anthropologists spending some of their sabbatical time (or some kind of postdoctoral or research period) connected to a university in the US. Yet it has become clear that this does not lead to many actively doing fieldwork/long-term research in the US. Examples that comes to mind are Indian anthropologist Nandini Sundar coming to the DC area for a number of months to write and use the US/DC-area libraries or Shinji Yamashita, Professor of Cultural Anthropology and Human Security Program, University of Tokyo, who held the Terasaki Chair in US-Japan Relations at UCLA in 2013–14. Earlier examples include noted French anthropologist Claude Levi-Strauss in New York during World War II and noted Norwegian anthropologist Fredrik Barth (as a visitor at Johns Hopkins and later at Emory and at Boston University). Rather,

Nandini Sundar's (1997) work is about "sectarian"/ gender/communal violence in India, while Shinji Yamashita's work is on tourism, globalization, and migration in Southeast Asian contexts (Yamashita 2003; Yamashita, Bosco, and Eades 2004; Yamashita, Haines, and Yamanaka 2012). Claude Levi-Strauss and Fredrik Barth contributed much theory and, especially Barth, fieldwork-based knowledge and theory drawing on parts of the Middle East, Southeast Asia, Yemen, and Norway but not the US (cf. Levi-Strauss 1955; Barth 1962, 1969, 1975, 1987, 1993).

There are some who, of course, come to the US from outside the US to do their graduate studies (master's and/or doctorates), but few of those, to our knowledge, actually choose the US as their "field of study" and therefore very few do their long-term field research for their doctorates in the US. In fact, they tend to come to the US to acquire skills, knowledge, and degrees from US research universities but often choose to specialize in their home country or region (or are encouraged to do so by their US-based faculty advisers). Numerous examples come to mind—many from India, Latin America, Israel, Turkey, South Korea, Egypt, and China, to name just a few countries. In fact, the number of non-US-origin graduate students in past and present US Masters and Ph.D. programs in the US is quite large. Yet this has really not led to the development of US studies as an Area Studies that might be a specialty within world anthropology/ies.

If we broaden the context here, the mystery is even more compelling and noteworthy. Many thousands of people do study the US outside the US but they do so in other disciplines, especially literature and international relations/political science/foreign policy studies but also history (cf. Desmond and Dominguez 1996). It is equally important to note that there are established anthropological communities in many different kinds of societies around the world—and some of them are quite prosperous. Consider Germany, Japan, France, and Australia, to name but a few, and then there is Canada, of course.

In a study that Jasmin Habib conducted in the summer of 2009 (Habib 2009), she found two seemingly contradictory facts. On one hand, a number of Canadian anthropologists have been educated in the US and are (or were) US citizens, yet very few of those teaching in anthropology departments in Canada have conducted any field research in the US. Among those who did conduct such research, several have moved into other departments and/or disciplines (e.g., Eva Mackey and Jasmin Habib, among them).

So Is It Just Anthropology That Is the Problem?

All of this then raises the question of contemporary anthropology, and it is a troubling one. Has anthropology indeed changed all that much since the middle of the twentieth century, all of those postcolonial, subaltern, and postmodern critiques notwithstanding? The phenomenon we have been tracking (and now seek to share with readers) might suggest that there is more conservatism in the profession than most anthropologists either believe or want to believe.

Some years ago Michel-Rolph Trouillot wrote an essay in *Recapturing Anthropology* (1991) in which he named a "space" he called "the savage slot," which he identified with anthropology. As we ponder why so few non-US-based anthropologists specialize in the study of the US, do field-work in the US, or even identify themselves with American Studies abroad, we want to raise the uncomfortable suggestion that some version of "the savage slot" continues to exist in the practice (and training) of anthro-pologists today. When other places, societies, locations, and sites seem much more interesting to anthropologists than the very complicated and powerful US, should we not contemplate the possibility that there is still the lure of the "exotic" (or at least the "exoticized") in the world, or what Anna Tsing (1993) calls the "romance of the primitive" and the "dream space of possibility" associated with small-scale societies that much of the world still thinks of as marginal or "primitive" or frankly unimportant in today's geopolitical makeup? Or, to put it differently, what if there remains a tendency to study people without power and those societies that do not have real economic or military power—power one now most often associates with European and Euro-settler-colonial states?

While we might not be comfortable labeling any societies "primitive" or "marginal" or even "unimportant," and we might even make the point that other disciplines actually primitivize, marginalize, and/or ignore many of these societies, and as such it is our responsibility to continue to do research in and alongside those cultures and communities. But is it pos-sible that all this is behind that very apparent absence of anthropological fieldwork in and on the US outside the US? Another way of putting it could be that there remains a widespread commitment to inclusivity that has long led anthropologists to study, and remain engaged with, those parts of humanity largely ignored by other fields of knowledge in the humani-ties and social sciences, and that this has tended to mean not studying the US? Then perhaps this has amounted to a commitment to a kind of continuation of "the savage slot" even when (or precisely because) power and inequality and the politics and ethics of knowledge production have become highly visible issues for nearly all anthropologists.

We also need to contemplate the idea that the avoidance of fieldwork in the US except by those living in the US might also be an unarticulated response to postcolonial critiques of anthropology—first expressed by Edward Said as the engagement in Othering practices of Orientalism (1978)—that largely lead scholars (and perhaps especially sociocultural and linguistic anthropologists) to avoid the study of "Others" in the world thus unwittingly producing a privileging of an "anthropology at home."

We are clearly not making a point about the US being outside the realm of anthropological research. On the contrary, a great deal of work goes on, and it has especially grown in the past twenty or thirty years, but it is interesting, and ultimately worrisome, to see who is *not* doing that work. Hence, we want to call attention to issues raised through this phenomenon as well as to what may be lost if this pattern persists. Consider, for example, the issues of power and their continuing impact on anthropology. These are related to the attribution of power, the expectation of power, and the very unsettling possibility that this area of knowledge has not, in fact, changed as much as many anthropologists hope or assume.

The issues are both simple and daunting but absolutely worth exploring. It is hard enough to do fieldwork, but what exactly is it like to do fieldwork in the US, and does it help, hurt, or play little role when the fieldworker is (and is seen as) an outsider to the fabric of US society? If we look at who is actually doing the fieldwork, and the kind of fieldwork they are doing, should we not ask anthropologically, sociologically, politically, and, yes, ethically, why so much of it is being done as "anthropology at home" in a field that prides itself in taking all of humanity into account?

A Beginning and an Approach

The essays we chose to include in this volume show both how some anthropologists normally residing outside of the US have contributed substantial insights to anthropological topics through their fieldwork in the US as well as how their "outsiderness" matters.

Helena Wulff's "Manhattan as a Magnet: Place and Circulation among Young Swedes" addresses the role of Manhattan in the imaginary of some (perhaps many) normally outside the US, but it also points to a habit (common to the social sciences and many in the general public in the US) of thinking that the US is a magnet for people in poor (or poorer) countries who see in the US a path to upward mobility and, hence, that the issue of immigration and illegality is always one concerning the US's relations with the poorer countries in the world. Drawing on ethnographic fieldwork with Swedes living in New York City throughout the

1980s and 1990s, Wulff explores how young adults flock to New York to experience the city's expansive economy and culture. Wulff asserts that early in Swedish childhood and, since the end of World War II, the US circulates through popular media as a site of the imaginary, which facilitates an "anticipatory socialization" of young Swedes. Wulff invokes Erik Eriksen's concept of a "psychosocial moratorium" (1968) to describe the young Swedes' sojourns to New York: a delay of adult commitments and a prolonging of their youth. Interestingly, the experience that young Swedes acquire during their sojourn in New York is not merely understood as a transnational experience but, rather, a global one in large part because, for Swedish sojourners, living in the culturally diverse, economic powerhouse, and cosmopolitan city of New York is described as "reaching across the world."

For many, New York City is its own separate country, distinct from Swedish society as well as the larger US society. Stays in New York, according to these travelers, have taught them more about the world than about the rest of "America," providing them with global competence and sensibility rather than deep knowledge of the US per se. At the same time that New York is regarded as culturally apart from the US, it remains a product of the US: Manhattan is only Manhattan because it is located and locatable as a US city. Living in New York is also a means of acquiring social and cultural capital, providing some travelers the opportunity for career enhancement and personal development as well as "temporary opening of imaginary opportunities."

Here Wulff reflects on the common theme of experimentation—wherein the Swedes shared how they felt they could play with their identities and "try on another possible life." Drawing on Arjun Appadurai's work on fantasy as social practice (1996), Wulff describes how young Swedes see their current lives through the New York imaginaries they created in response to the mass media–created "America" they had been exposed to in their childhood. Swedish travelers, Wulff tells us, prepared themselves for the exceptional to occur during their Manhattan experiences—largely based on the notion that New York was the city where anything was possible. Whether the travelers were entirely successful or rather unremarkable did not seem to be the point. Given that their journey to New York served as a method of attaining social and cultural capital and not economic benefit, even the lack of success in New York was translated into cultural capital upon returning to Sweden.

While some Swedish transplants to New York stayed in the city on a permanent basis, Wulff focuses her attention in her chapter on those who returned to Sweden and asserts that the return completes the psychosocial moratorium. Young Swedes describe returning to Sweden with a new identity formed out of their global experience. Many complained they faced difficulties relating to old friends who lacked the Manhattan experience. In fact, Wulff writes: "The Manhattan experience is not completed until afterwards, when it is recreated through the young Swedes' recollections, both individually and collectively in groups." Borne out of their Manhattan nostalgia, returnees have contributed to the creation of Little Manhattan in Stockholm. Despite their attempts to recreate their former experiences of young adulthood, Wulff emphasizes the inseparability of sense from place. In this chapter, Wulff has traced the effects of a physical mobility—to and from the US—as well as how what circulates is also an imaginary US both in the US and abroad.

Jasmin Habib's chapter considers the "global" imaginary within. Drawing on Amy Kaplan's work, she examines how US global power and empire have affected US Jewish activism. She focuses on US Jewish activism in the context of the Israel/Palestine conflict, particularly for those living outside cosmopolitan cities and centers. The point of Habib's essay is not to idealize or romanticize the efforts of such activists but, rather, to understand and appreciate the extent to which their lives are marked by their difference as Jews living in the US. She is especially interested in the fact that they speak against empire and produce a counter-narrative, but that this also often reveals a rather complex crisis of belonging. Habib's contribution in this volume shows activists supporting nonviolence, criticizing Israel's military occupation of the West Bank and the settlement project, opposing all forms of militarism, and publicizing Israeli human rights abuses. It also shows them involved in criticizing US inaction on the peace process, and promoting Palestinian autonomy and self-determination, in a range of forms from support for non-state autonomous regions to advocacy for one democratic state.

Habib is also interested in apparent contradictions and struggles. For example, she shows that during periods of extreme violence activists call for a ceasefire and the immediate return to negotiations and that, to a large extent, these activists rely on Israeli Jewish peace and human rights organizations for information and calls to action. Jewish activists she interviewed in the US surprised her when they spoke of US anti-Semitism while talking about their views regarding Israel and Palestine. They invoked a long history of US anti-Semitism as the backdrop for some of their fear of speaking out. But they also invoked it when talking about the extent to which criticizing the US was problematic, particularly in the post-9/11 period. As Kaplan notes, empire frames the terms for engagement with "the foreign" as well as "the domestic." Therefore, a focus on "the homeland" has an exclusionary effect that underwrites a resurgent nativism and fear of "the other within." Habib examines the difficulties of these critics and takes the topic to heart, yet we note that she does so both with compassion and worry.

Criticizing the US takes on a much greater weight when the lens—in search of enemies within—turns inward to the "domestic front." As such, Habib points to how US Jewish activists convey the sense that they are carrying a double burden: those who are critical of US policy vis-à-vis Israel/Palestine are also critical of US foreign policy more generally. Criticizing US policy toward Israel, which is a policy developed out of empire, is tantamount to being critical of the US and, as such, could be considered "un-American." That this is a label that "tarnished" those who criticized past wars, particularly in Vietnam and Iraq, becomes an important point here. Habib asserts that US Jewish activists alert us to an imperial presence in the country, and that their perspective leads us to see important political and cultural processes and institutions that are shaped by, and within, the context of empire. This chapter highlights how empire is alive in institutional life, how heroic narratives are developed and incorporated into US history, and how militaristic and masculinist/patriotic citizenship may be embodied. Habib pinpoints paradoxes of contemporary US Jewry's relations to their "Americanness" while shedding light on broad questions of nationness and belonging.

Limor Samimian-Darash's "Biosecurity in the US: The 'Scientific' and the 'American' in Critical Perspective" raises questions about biosecurity in general but also about those taken-for-granted elements of STS (Science and Technology Studies) scholarship that background the Americanness of much of the biosecurity talk in both the US and STS. Samimian-Darash analyzes the problem of biosecurity in the US in an effort to highlight the contradictions that exist when "one sees science and the US as both global and non-cultural." She details the perceptual framing of this disconnect in two ways. First, she asserts that there is a disconnect between science and security, resulting in "the social" implications of biosecurity research being regarded as outside of the "domain of scientific research and responsibility." And, second, she observes that US scientists involved in biosecurity issues refer to themselves as engaging with a manifestation of a global problem, rather than with a local problem. Samimian-Darash's intention is to disconnect these contradictions through the use of a US case study, namely, Fouchier and Kawaoka's 2011 research on the H5N1 virus (Enserink 2011; Enserink and Malakoff 2012), which science regards as a "global case" meaning that it is beyond culture and society. By detailing the history of biosecurity in the US and calling attention to the dramatic increase in US government spending on defense since 9/11, Samimian-Darash provides us with an interesting case study as US and international scientific communities' positions on the dissemination of this research diverged on the most fundamental of levels: while US discourse on the issue centered on the deadliness of H5N1 and thus its potentially deadly uses and on matters of biosecurity, scientists in the "international" arena were instead concerned with public health preparedness and the advancement of treatment in non-Western (Euro-American) zones. Their concern lay in what they believed would be constraints and limitations on the dissemination of information that could have negative global impacts. Samimian-Darash asserts that the US discourse on biosecurity decontextualized the problem, identifying it as a primarily national-local concern and that could have a global impact or reach. To foreign actors, the US problematization of the issue represented US dominion/control over global public health discourse. Lastly, Samimian-Darash argues that when one conceptualizes the US field and scientific profession and its interests as global, one actually drastically minimizes (or even causes the disappearance of) the extent to which scientific concerns about and attention on biosecurity is a matter that has a social context and field.

In some unexpected ways, then, Habib and Samimian-Darash's pieces point to the role of domination and the power of empire to frame, as well as establish, the taken-for-granted or politically normative. Both also shed light on the broad questions that are of interest to contemporary anthropologists: on the silences, imaginaries, and occlusions of power.

Ulf Hannerz's "American Theater State: Reflections on Political Culture" explores theatricality in US political practice and culture but also raises questions about what counts as fieldwork and how temporality matters. Born and raised in Sweden, Hannerz describes himself as an "ethnographer at large" who has engaged in observing the US beginning as an exchange student and visiting scholar throughout his long career. Hannerz suggests that this long-term, low-intensity method of fieldwork is fairly unconventional in the field of anthropology. As an outsider, Hannerz asserts that there are two main ways in which his perspectives are useful: first, it fulfills "an intellectual niche for perceptive outsidership," providing "consciousness raising in relation to what is usually taken for granted"; and second, the outsider may become a "cultural broker" who can interpret foreign places to the people of their home country upon their return, and in this way foster greater global understanding.

Hannerz identifies the connection between contemporary US political culture and the entertainment industry, arguing that performance, commentary, humor, satire, and politics are all interwoven into US political culture. This is evidenced by the fact that several Hollywood stars have achieved great success in the US, with former President Ronald Reagan and California Governor Arnold Schwarzenegger two of the most prominent and well-known examples, although Donald Trump's multi-year experience on television and effects on 2016 electoral politics clearly continues the tradition, too. In the same vein, former politicians can go on to achieve success in entertainment and media, with Al Gore winning an Academy Award for his film, *An Inconvenient Truth*. Hannerz notes that studies have shown that most Americans prefer to get their political news and commentary not from traditional news programming but instead from satirical programs such as *The Daily Show with Jon Stewart* and *Saturday Night Live's* "Weekend Update."

Hannerz draws attention to the theatricality of US politics by invoking the concept of "politics as theater." Following Clifford Geertz (1980) and citing Fareed Zakaria's work *The Post-American World*, Hannerz asserts that the US political system has been "captured by money, special interests, a sensationalist media, and ideological attack groups" (Zakaria 2008). In the US, he argues, political theater is an important way for a politician to present himself (or herself) as a well-rounded, likable public personality, one who can play more than an official role and who is personable. This remarkable interpenetration between politics and theatricality is of interest to Hannerz, who is also concerned with difficulties faced by reputable print media. On another plane, Hannerz speculates on the relationship between "the sense of politics as entertainment and a certain weakness for conspiracy theory" and, in this context, recalls historian Richard Hofstadter's description of the "paranoid style" of American politics that emerged in 1965. To Hannerz this still describes the paranoia and suspicion that have found new expressions in contemporary US politics.

Of course, Hannerz recognizes that elements of theatricality also exist in European politics, both historically and more recently. The scandals surrounding Italy's Silvio Berlusconi provide a contemporary and vibrant example. Yet Hannerz concludes his chapter highlighting how US political culture is perceived and received abroad. Invoking Joseph Nye's concept of "soft power" (2002, 2004), Hannerz stresses that US political values— democracy, personal freedom, and upward mobility—are projected onto the global stage using education, foreign policy, and, most importantly, popular culture. The global circulation of US political values and culture is reinforced by the political system's strong attachment to the entertainment industry, which has achieved remarkable success around the globe.

Moshe Shokeid's chapter reflects on ethnographic research that he conducted in Greenwich Village, New York City, throughout the 1990s and 2000s. Early ethnographic studies of gay communities in the US focused largely on the field of anonymous sexual relationships in commercial sites and public spaces. Shokeid's observations presented in this study expose another reality of gay life. Intrigued by the diversity and expansion of new voluntary associations among gay communities, Shokeid employed

fieldwork based on the "extended case method." He observed the operation of various voluntary organizations in Greenwich Village Center. In
this chapter, Shokeid begins by calling our attention to the historical
importance of voluntary associations in US culture. Such civil organizations have sustained importance in US urban life, providing the means by
which individuals may identify and engage. Reflecting on his upbringing
in Israeli society, Shokeid asserts that the extensive role that voluntary
organizations play in society is a distinctly US phenomenon.

In this essay, Shokeid makes a point of tracing the proliferation of voluntary associations within non-heterosexual communities in New York and
describes the extent to which these organizations have expanded beyond
their traditional tasks of sociality, national improvement, and reform, and
in this way have become part of the "mainstream." They have expanded
their roles to provide spaces for their members to engage in therapeutic
models of civic engagement. Throughout the essay, Shokeid emphasizes
his "outsider" status stressing that his Israeli upbringing did not prepare
him to divulge intimate personal stories to strangers, a common practice
for all those engaged in these organizations in New York.

Among those of Shokeid's generation, indeed a common Israeli attitude
has been that therapy should only be for those with severe emotional
problems, and that such issues should be kept a secret. While clinicians
often dismiss the role of such practices in gatherings as simply "curing,"
Shokeid objects to such simplistic descriptions noting that these voluntary
organizations were not support groups led by professionals working with
traumatized individuals. Instead, he explains, dedicated individuals who
catered to their communities' needs in the midst of liberation activism,
and who worked toward the expansion of gay rights and institutions ran
these groups. Although Shokeid reports that the various gatherings did
not assume the structure of support groups, the style of discourse at these
meetings displayed a therapeutic approach. The author attributes this
to the "therapeutic culture in America," spawned by the long tradition
and success of Freudian psychoanalytic theories. We note here as well
that Shokeid draws heavily on Robert Putnam's work on social capital,
Bowling Alone (2000). It is work that emphasizes that the existential conditions of modern urban living in the US have weakened what were once
very strong community bonds and organizations. Yet we see in Shokeid's
chapter that, at the same time, and in point of fact, voluntary organizations that cater to specific communities continue to fortify certain ties. The
Greenwich Village Center provided safe spaces for gay social gatherings
that allowed for community-building in the course of discussions about
existential issues while also helping to found and advance the development of a gamut of important institutions in New York City.

In the second half of the chapter, Shokeid contrasts the nature and scope of gay voluntary associations in New York with those in Israel. He contemplates developments in US society and culture that circulate and impact other parts of the Euro-American world, and he considers the expansion of gay voluntary associations to be no exception. Israel, a country that orients itself both toward the "modern" democratic world and the more conservative Jewish mainstream, embarked on its journey toward gay liberation at a much slower pace. Shokeid points out that homosexuality remained a criminal offense in Israel until 1988, and that gay Israeli men still occupy a conflicted position in Israel. They aspire, Shokeid argues, to become a part of the "Western" gay community, yet they also confront unrelenting pressures from traditional religious and family-oriented norms and values in Israel. Before 1983, when Uzi Even, a prominent chemistry professor publicly came out and spoke about the "demedicalization and depathologizing" of homosexuality at a meeting of the Knesset Committee on Social Affairs, gay life was essentially invisible. Even's speech in the Knesset helped to usher in the era of advancement and the promotion of equality. Yet despite this progress, Shokeid observes, efforts made by gay institutions in Israel to engage gay men in voluntary associations based on the US model have been unsuccessful. Unlike the Greenwich Village experiences, it is professionals in Israel who ensure that biweekly meetings are held, counseling and medical services are offered, and lecturers and events are facilitated.

One of the most poignant observations Shokeid makes here is that, although the Israeli gay community has adopted discourse and descriptive terms typical of the American gay community, their narratives reflect disparate cultural codes: "the Americans expressing the individuals' solitary heroic journey, as against the Israelis striving to present themselves as participants in a collective battle." The fact that gay voluntary associations are more limited in Israel than in the US should come as no surprise, as this is also true of many other types of associational organizations in Israeli society. The therapeutic model that has formed the basis of gay life in the US simply does not translate well within Israeli societal perceptions of therapy and its discourse. Shokeid asserts that the circulation of the US therapeutic model has run into obstacles in other societies that hold a similar disregard for this approach. In this way, Moshe Shokeid's "Observing US Gay Organizations and Voluntary Associations: An Outsider's Exposition" not only sheds light on self-help groups and organizations in the US, but also compels us to (1) revisit gay (and LGBTQ) scholarship and the way it tends to frame the topic as on or around "identity," and (2) revisit older scholarship on voluntary associations as hallmarks of US society.

In each of these chapters, one learns how the ethnographer's understanding of a topic has been made richer over the course of their long-term research in the US, and in each case the topic under investigation itself becomes ever more complex because each contributor made the most of being (normally and over many years) an outsider in the US, and an ethnographer of the US. We also note that these colleagues come from specific countries, arguably countries with established anthropological communities with broad field experience and in which English is a language people either speak at home or learn early in school.

All of those who have contributed to this volume express a critical reflexivity that exposes their complex relationship to the US. Most have spent an extensive period of time in the US as students, teachers, and researchers, and thus their identities vis-à-vis the US are more complicated than a strict insider/outsider, native/foreigner dichotomy would suppose. The production of knowledge they are engaged in should not be cast so simply as an "outsider" perspective on the US and, yet, their perspectives cannot be understood as representative of all Swedes/Canadians/Israelis/Japanese.

To round out the picture we paint here—of very good anthropological work on the US being done by these few colleagues outside the US—we also include three other essays that contextualize the pattern, the challenges, and the points made in these essays, as well as in the struggle to alter expectations both at "home" and "abroad." Geoffrey White's essay is an excellent exploration of the papers included here. Keiko Ikeda's essay is a troubling account of her own struggles both in the US and in Japan, struggles with people's expectations that she is a specialist on Japan when she is, in fact, a specialist on the US. Jane Desmond writes about the efforts of the International Forum for US Studies and the International American Studies Association to counter a very tacit, largely unnoticed pattern in which US scholars (especially in American Studies) privilege scholarship produced in the US even when many thousands of scholars outside the US (though not in anthropology) make a point of studying the US. The contradictions raised by juxtaposing perceptions and practices, proclamations and de facto exclusions, collusions, and complicity make this volume a necessary, if troubling, one.

Virginia R. Dominguez is the Edward William and Jane Marr Gutgsell Professor of Anthropology, Jewish Studies, Global Studies, Caribbean Studies, and Middle Eastern Studies at the University of Illinois at Urbana-Champaign in the US. She is recent past president of the American Anthropological Association, recent past editor of *American Ethnologist*, and cofounder of The International Forum for US Studies. She is best known as the author of *White By Definition: Social Classification in Creole Louisiana* (Rutgers 1986) and *People As Subject, People As Object: Selfhood and Peoplehood in Contemporary Israel* (Wisconsin 1989), and associate editor of the World Anthropology Section of *American Anthropologist*.

Jasmin Habib is an associate professor of political science at the University of Waterloo and the Global Governance Program at the Balsillie School of International Affairs. She is the editor-in-chief of *Anthropologica* (the journal of the Canadian Anthropology Society) and series editor of *Cultural Spaces*, University of Toronto Press. Among her honors is an Outstanding Teaching and Research Award from the University of Waterloo. A second edition of her book *Israel, Diaspora and the Routes of National Belonging* is due out in print in 2016 (University of Toronto Press, [2004] 2016).

Acknowledgments

We would like to thank the contributors to this volume, along with Jim Novak and the anonymous reviewers at Berghahn Press who helped us to strengthen this chapter. Jasmin Habib's research was generously supported by the International Forum for US Studies and the Robert Harding Award/SSHRC, University of Waterloo. Virginia R. Dominguez's work here has also been made possible by her named professorship at the University of Illinois at Urbana-Champaign, so she especially thanks Edward William and Jane Marr Gutgsell for their continued support.

Note

1. Some panels exploring aspects of this issue have taken place in recent years in both anthropological and international American Studies circles. One was the Central States Anthropology Association Annual Meetings at the University of Illinois at Urbana-Champaign in 2009. The second was the American Anthropological Association Annual Meetings in New Orleans in 2010. The third was the Canadian Association

for American Studies in 2013. A fourth setting was the sixth World Congress of the International American Studies Association, held in Szczesin, Poland, also in 2013. And a fifth setting was the May 2014 Inter-Congress of the IUAES (International Union of Anthropological and Ethnological Sciences) held jointly with JASCA (the Japanese Association of Social and Cultural Anthropology). Invited and/or participating in one or more of these were Jane C. Desmond (University of Illinois at Urbana-Champaign, US), Virginia Dominguez (University of Illinois at Urbana-Champaign, US), Christina Garsten (University of Stockholm, Sweden), Jasmin Habib (University of Waterloo, Canada), Dieter Haller (University of Dortmund, Germany), Ulf Hannerz (University of Stockholm, Sweden), Keiko Ikeda (Doshisha University, Japan), Gustavo Lins Ribeiro (University of Brasilia, Brazil), Limor Samimian-Darash (Hebrew University of Jerusalem, Israel), Roger Sanjek (City University of New York, US), Moshe Shokeid (University of Tel Aviv, Israel), and Helena Wulff (University of Stockholm, Sweden).

References

Appadurai, Arjun. 1996. *Modernity at Large: Cultural Dimensions of Globalization.* Minneapolis: University of Minnesota Press.

Barth, Fredrik. 1962. *Nomads of South Persia: The Basseri Tribe of the Khamseh Confederacy.* Oslo: Universitetsforlaget.

———. 1975. *Ritual and Knowledge among the Baktaman of New Guinea.* Oslo: Universitetsforlaget.

———. 1987. *Cosmologies in the Making: A Generative Approach to Cultural Variation in Inner New Guinea.* Cambridge: Cambridge University Press.

———. 1993. *Balinese Worlds.* Chicago: University of Chicago Press.

Barth, Fredrik, ed. 1969. *Ethnic Groups and Boundaries: The Social Organization of Culture Difference.* Oslo: Universitetsforlaget and New York: Little, Brown, and Company.

Baudrillard, Jean. 1988. *America.* London and New York: Verso Books. Originally published in French in 1986 as *Amerique.* Paris: Editions Grasset & Fasquelle.

Borneman, John, and Abdellah Hammoudi, eds. 2009. *Being There: The Fieldwork Encounter and the Making of Truth.* Berkeley: The University of California Press.

Bourdieu, Pierre. 1977. *Outline of a Theory of Practice.* Cambridge: Cambridge University Press (English translation of French original published in Paris).

Brodkin, Karen. 1998. *How Jews Became White Folks, and What That Says about Race in America.* New Brunswick, NJ: Rutgers University Press.

Cattelino, Jessica. 2008. *High Stakes: Florida Seminole Gaming and Sovereignty.* Durham, NC: Duke University Press.

———. 2010. "Anthropologies of the United States." *Annual Review of Anthropology* 39(1): 275–92.

Davila, Arlene. 2001. *Latinos, Inc: The Marketing and Making of a People.* Berkeley: University of California Press.

Davila, Arlene. 2004. *Barrio Dreams: Puerto Ricans, Latinos, and the Neoliberal City.* Berkeley: University of California Press.

De Tocqueville, Alexis. 1835. *Democracy in America.* First published in France as *La democratie en Amerique.* Recent edition: 2003 Penguin Classics.

Desmond, Jane C. and Virginia R. Dominguez. 1996. "Resituating American Studies in a Critical Internationalism." *American Quarterly* 48 (September): 475–90.

DeVita, Philip R. and James D. Armstrong, eds. 2002. *Distant Mirrors: America as a Foreign Culture.* 3rd ed. New York: Cengage Learning (the first and second editions were published by Wadsworth in 1993 and 1997).

DiLeonardo, Micaela. 2000. *Exotics at Home: Anthropologies, Others, and American Modernity.* Chicago: University of Chicago Press.

Enserink, Martin. 2011. "Scientists Brace for Media Storm Around Controversial Flu Studies." *Science Insider.* Retrieved 20 February 2013 from http://news.sciencemag.org/scienceinsider/2011/11/scientists-brace-for-media-storm.html.

Enserink, Martin and David Malakoff. 2012. "Will Flu Papers Lead to New Research Oversight?" *Science* 335: 20–22.

Eriksen, Erik Homburger. 1968. *Youth and Crisis.* New York: Norton.

Evans-Pritchard, E.V. 1951. *Kinship and Marriage among the Nuer.* Oxford: Clarendon Press.

Garsten, Christina. 1994. *Apple World: Core and Periphery in a Transnational Organizational Culture.* Stockholm Studies in Social Anthropology. London: Coronet Books Inc.

———. 2008. *Workplace Vagabonds.* London: Palgrave Macmillan.

Geertz, Clifford. 1980. *Negara.* Princeton, NJ: Princeton University Press.

Glick Schiller, Nina, Linda Basch and Cristina Szanton-Blanc. 1993. *Nations Unbound: Transnational Projects, Postcolonial Predicaments, and Deterritorialized Nation-States.* New York: Routledge.

Habib, Jasmin. 2004. *Israel, Diaspora, and the Routes of National Belonging.* Toronto: University of Toronto Press.

———. 2007. "Memorializing the Holocaust: Diasporic Encounters." *Anthropologica* 49(2): 245–56.

———. 2009. "Canadian Anthropologists Who Have Conducted Fieldwork in the United States." Unpublished report prepared for the International Forum for US Studies (IFUSS). September.

Hannerz, Ulf. 1969. *Soulside: Inquiries into Ghetto Culture and Community.* New York: Columbia University Press.

———. 2003. "Being There and There and There." *Ethnography* 4(2): 201–16.

———. 2004. *Foreign News: Exploring the World of Foreign Correspondents.* Chicago: University of Chicago Press.

Helmreich, Stefan. 2000. *Silicon Second Nature: Culturing Artificial Life in a Digital World.* Berkeley: University of California Press.

———. 2009. *Alien Ocean: Anthropological Voyages in Microbial Seas.* Berkeley: University of California Press.

Hofstadter, Richard. 1965. *The Paranoid Style in American Politics.* Cambridge, MA: Harvard University Press.

Hurston, Zora Neale. 1937. *Their Eyes Were Watching God*. New York: J.B. Lippincott.

Ikeda, Keiko. 1999. *A Room Full of Mirrors: High School Reunions in Middle America*. Stanford, CA: Stanford University Press.

Jackson, Anthony, ed. 1987. *Anthropology at Home*. ASA Monograph. London: Tavistock Publications.

Jung, Hyang-Jin. 2007. *Learning to Be an Individual: Emotion and Person in an American Junior High School*. New York: Peter Lang.

Kim, Jin K. 2002. "American Graffiti: Curious Derivatives of Individualism." In *Distant Mirrors: America as a Foreign Culture*, ed. Philip R. DeVita and James D. Armstrong, 59–67. 3rd ed. New York: Cengage Learning.

LaDousa, Chaise. 2011. *House Signs and Collegiate Fun: Sex, Race, and Faith in a College Town*. Bloomington: Indiana University Press.

———. 2014. *Hindi Is Our Ground, English Is Our Sky: Education, Language, and Social Class in Contemporary India*. New York: Berghahn Books.

LeMenestrel, Sara. 1999. *La voie des Cadiens: Tourisme et identité en Louisiane*. Paris: Editions Belin.

Levi-Strauss, Claude. 1955. *Tristes Tropiques*. Paris: Plon. English translation, 1963, New York: Atheneum.

Lutz, Catherine. 1988. *Unnatural Emotions: Everyday Sentiments on a Micronesian Atoll and Their Challenge to Western Theory*. Chicago: University of Chicago Press.

———. 2002. *Homefront: A Military City and the American Twentieth Century*. Boston: Beacon Press.

Lutz, Catherine and Jane Collins. 1993. *Reading National Geographic*. Chicago: University of
Chicago Press.

Mackey, Eva. 2005. "'Universal' Rights in National and Local Conflicts: 'Backlash' and 'Benevolent Resistance' to Indigenous Land Rights." *Anthropology Today* 21(2): 14–20.

Miner, Horace. 1956. "Body Ritual among the Nacirema." *American Anthropologist* 58(3): 503–7.

Nye, Joseph. 2002. *The Paradox of American Power*. New York: Oxford University Press.

———. 2004. *Soft Power*. New York: Public Affairs.

Ojeda, Amparo B. 2002. "Growing Up American: Doing the Right Thing." In *Distant Mirrors: America as a Foreign Culture*, ed. Philip R. DeVita and James D. Armstrong, 44–49. 3rd ed. New York: Cengage Learning.

Pickering, Lucy. 2009. "Dancing My True Dance: Reflections on Learning to Express Myself through Ecstatic Dance in Hawai'i." *Anthropology Matters* 11(1): 1–12.

———. 2010a. "Past Imperfect: Displacing Hawaiians as Hosts in a 'Drop Out' Community in Hawai'i." In *Loves Lives: Migration and the Micropolitics of Place*, ed. C. Trundle and B. Bonisch-Brednich, 49–63. Ashgate: Farnham.

———. 2010b. "Toilets, Bodies, Selves: Enacting Composting as Counterculture in Hawai'i." *Body and Society* 16(4): 33–55.

Powdermaker, Hortense. 1950. *Hollywood, the Dream Factory.* New York: Little, Brown, and Company.

Putnam, D. Robert. 2000. *Bowling Alone: The Collapse and Revival of American Community.* New York: Simon & Schuster.

Sahlins, Marshall. 1962. *Moala: Culture and Nature on a Fijian Island.* Ann Arbor: University of Michigan Press.

———. 1977. *The Use and Abuse of Biology: An Anthropological Critique of Sociobiology.* Ann Arbor: University of Michigan Press.

———. 1981. *Historical Metaphors and Mythical Realities.* Ann Arbor: University of Michigan Press.

Said, Edward. 1978. *Orientalism.* New York: Random House.

Scheper-Hughes, Nancy. 1977. *Saints, Scholars, and Schizophrenics: Mental Illness in Rural Ireland.* Berkeley: University of California Press.

———. 1993. *Death without Weeping: The Violence of Everyday Life in Brazil.* Berkeley: University of California Press.

Shokeid, Moshe. 1988. *Children of Circumstances: Israeli Emigrants in New York.* Ithaca, NY: Cornell University Press.

———. 1995. *A Gay Synagogue in New York.* New York: Columbia University Press.

———. 2002. *An Israeli's Voyage: Tel Aviv, New York and Between.* [In Hebrew.] Tel Aviv: Yediot Books.

Stack, Carol. 1975. *All Our Kin: Strategies for Survival in a Black Community.* New York: Harper.

Sundar, Nandini. 1997 [1999/2007]. *Subalterns and Sovereigns: An Anthropological History of Bastar, 1854–2006.* Delhi: Oxford University Press.

Trouillot, Michel-Rolph. 1991. "Anthropology and the Savage Slot: The Poetics and Politics of Otherness." In *Recapturing Anthropology: Working the Present,* ed. Richard Fox, 17–44. Santa Fe, NM: School of American Research Press.

Tsing, Anna L. 1993. *In the Realm of the Diamond Queen: Marginality in an Out-of-the-Way Place.* Princeton, NJ: Princeton University Press.

Wulff, Helena. 1998. *Ballet across Borders: Career and Culture in the World of Dancers.* London: Bloomsbury Academic. Reprinted in 2001, Oxford: Berg Publishers.

Yamashita, Shinji. 2003. *Bali and Beyond: Explorations in the Anthropology of Tourism,* trans. J.S. Eades. Oxford and New York: Berghahn Books.

Yamashita, Shinji, Joseph Bosco and Jerry S. Eades. ed. 2004. *The Making of Anthropology in East and Southeast Asia.* Oxford and New York: Berghahn Books.

Yamashita, Shinji, David W. Haines and Keiko Yamanaka, eds. 2012. *Wind over Water: Migration in an East Asian Context.* Oxford and New York: Berghahn Books.

Zakaria, Fareed. 2008. *The Post-American World.* New York: W.W. Norton and Company Ltd.

Part I

On the Outside Looking In?
The US as Fieldsite

Chapter One

Manhattan as a Magnet
Place and Circulation among Young Swedes

Helena Wulff

Since World War II, children in Sweden have grown up with an increasing exposure to American culture through the media. It started with the arrival of the magazine *Donald Duck* translated as *Kalle Anka*[1] in the late 1940s, and continued when television was introduced in Sweden with sitcoms such as *Father Knows Best* and *I Love Lucy*. For six decades, on Christmas Eve, the day when Christmas is celebrated in Protestant Sweden, a Disney cavalcade entitled *Donald Duck and His Friends Wishing a Merry Christmas*—"from all of us to all of you"—has been broadcast on primetime television. For many Swedish children, teenagers, and for those of us adults who started watching it when we were children, watching *Donald Duck* with its rhythmic music and Schubert's military march on Christmas Eve is as much a compulsory part of the Christmas ritual as a decorated tree, dinner, and presents (cf. Löfgren 1989). This is when Sweden comes to a halt. Streets are deserted as the program is allegedly watched every year by between three and four million people,[2] which is almost half of Sweden's population. The voice of a vicar's wife on the subject is quite unusual, but to the point. As Christmas was approaching one year, she remarked drily: "Yes, it's time to commemorate the birth of Donald Duck again!"

The Schubert March featured in *Donald Duck* was as much as a young Swede living in New York in the 1980s was able to get live—via the telephone. This was why Sven, a musician, called home when the program was on, and had his brother holding the receiver close to the television

Notes for this chapter begin on page 48.

set, to allow Sven to share the Christmas experience with his family. Sven was one of the young Swedes in New York City I researched in the late 1980s (Wulff 1991, 1992, 1994). They often identified New York as "a city where anything seemed possible," which incidentally was exactly how Lévi-Strauss once described New York (Clifford 1988: 238).

With ethnographic examples from this field study of young Swedes conducted in Manhattan in New York, in this chapter I will discuss Manhattan as a magnet for young people. The Swedes were artists, business executives, and au pair girls who were attracted to Manhattan in the expansive economy and culture of the 1980s,[3] after that particular time period this trend has been reduced but it is still there. (In the 1980s, young Swedes used the designation New York more often when they had Manhattan in mind than native New Yorkers and other Americans seemed to do.) There were Americans, Europeans, Asians, and young people from other parts of the world as well. The young Swedes described how they were "taking in impulses from all over the world" not only from people they met, but also from work routines and opportunities. Working as a photographer or a bank executive in Stockholm entailed having Sweden as a working habitat, while in New York, they liked to tell me, they had a sense of reaching across the world, and often did. This is why I will argue that the young Swedes acquired a global experience, rather than merely a transnational one.

As virtually everyone in my study was a newcomer, and sojourner in New York, this is an ethnography of how the United States is observed by outsiders. It also matters that the ethnographer is an outsider in New York, but has a similar background as the Swedes. On an auto-ethnographic note (Reed-Danahay 1997), this study was inspired by my first visit to New York in the summer of 1980. I then realized that there were a vast number of young Swedes in Manhattan who spent a few years in the city including, to a varying extent, in formal structures and institutions.

Arriving in New York in the early hours of a hot July morning, I was enthralled (and somewhat frightened) by the height of the skyscrapers, the ethnic diversity, and the fast pace. As I stood there on the pavement, I heard cars honking. There was the smell of a dry cleaner's chemicals mingling with garlic fried in oil. Later that first day, the noise would increase: the traffic becoming aggressive and conversations loud, the heat heavy. Within weeks, I would get used to the taste of weak coffee and to people not knowing where in Europe my home country is located.

On a New York Quest

Before delving deeper into the lives of the young Swedes in Manhattan, let me identify two pivotal points that inform this study. The first point is that it is a well-known fact in transnational urbanization that different types of immigrants are drawn to world cities. Most of them are poor and uneducated people. They are an expected topic of research on social injustice, as well as of government policy. This is certainly the case with immigrants in Manhattan and New York. The second point is that New York tends to be regarded as culturally apart from the rest of the US. The young Swedes were referring to this, and to New York, as if it was a separate country, and so would many native New Yorkers. It is the special combination of a cosmopolitan city with a long history as an economic center that has enabled cultural diversity and activity to flourish. Also New York is still a place where many immigrants, tourists, and other visitors first arrive in the US. Having noted that New York is different from the rest of the US, it is necessary to add that this city remains a product of the US. It is not generically cosmopolitan. Manhattan could not have happened anywhere else. What is typical of New York from the outsider's point of view, such as frontier spirit and diversity, is typical of the US, but to varying and lesser extents in other cities and towns, let alone in rural areas. It is my contention that an analytical observation of the US is incomplete without New York and its social and cultural diversity, which includes middle-class Europeans.

There was an emic term, a New York term, for young middle-class Europeans who were conspicuously present in Manhattan, especially in the nightlife: native New Yorkers called them "Eurotrash." The young Swedes were aware that they were running the risk of being classified as "Eurotrash," and when they talked about this slightly jokingly derogatory designation, they pointed out that it referred to others, not themselves, and that it might contain an element of envy from the New Yorkers. Typical "Eurotrash" dressed in "flashy clothes," they were predominantly men who came to New York with the sole intention of sparkling in the nightlife. They were mostly around in the 1970s and 1980s, and lacked any hint of serious commitment to improving their education or career. Still, there were certain similarities between "Eurotrash" and the young Swedes since the latter were educated people, rather comfortable economically, and were visible in that nightlife.

About two hundred Swedes were included in my study, thirty of whom were in focus, aged between 19 and 30. There were as many artists and executives as au pairs, but altogether only one-third were men while two-thirds were women. Among the executives, the majority were men, while artists and au pairs tended to be women. I conducted fieldwork for six months in New York, which consisted of participant observation and interviews. In addition, I interviewed returnees in Stockholm; some were the same individuals as in New York, some were not. I was able to engage in participant observation with the young Swedes when they were at work in studios, at galleries, at banks, and in homes. I also joined them when they were at play in the evenings at bars, restaurants, and clubs. I spent some time at social activities at the Swedish Church, which was a meeting place with ethnic—not religious—significance to the Swedes. It should be pointed out that they were all ethnic Swedes. This would be different now, as the population of Sweden has changed rapidly and become quite diverse, a circumstance that is noticeable not least when Swedes go abroad to represent Sweden at international competitions in sports, music, or even film.

I visited quite a few of the young Swedes in their homes ranging from tiny one-room apartments to classical studios and lofts. Many of the artists, but also executives, were sharing apartments. Most of the au pairs lived in suburban houses outside Manhattan with the families they worked for, but they were oriented toward Manhattan, spending most of their free time there. Some au pairs did live in Manhattan, though, in small rooms behind the kitchens of grand apartments on the Upper West Side.

The majority of the young Swedes were middle class, that is artists and executives, who tended to be of upper middle class background. Some of them were upper class, from well-known business families in Sweden. A few were from the aristocracy. The au pairs were mainly of lower middle class origin—more of them had working class parents than artists or executives—but there were some from upper-class homes. Many of the artists were supported economically by their parents, and still they rarely had enough money, and it did happen that they survived on very little food. They then borrowed money from friends, had dinner with people they knew would pay for them, ran away from checks, or lived on popcorn for days. None of them were able to make a living on their art, at least not yet, which was their criteria of success. Almost all of them made extra money by waiting tables or working in ice-cream parlors or supermarkets. If these jobs had anything to do with their artistic ambitions, such as a makeup artist selling makeup among other goods in a pharmacy, or a dancer working in the box office at a dance theater (which included access to a studio where he could practice), they saw it as a step in their careers. At least they were moving in the right direction (Wulff 1992). Writing about German and Austrian refugee intellectuals and artists who had escaped to New York in the 1930s and early 1940s, Helmut Pfanner (1983) notes that they had problems getting the kinds of jobs they used to have in

Europe. Just like the young Swedes almost five decades later, some of these Europeans took simple jobs in their area of endeavor, hoping that they would be promoted with time. There were thus book dealers who worked as errand-boys for bookstores and film producers working as ushers in cinemas.

The artists worked with painting, photography, jewelry design, graphic design, window decorating, modeling, swing and jazz music, acting, dance, sculpting, and architecture. One woman worked as a makeup artist, another woman attended the Tisch School of the Arts learning filmmaking. Some were involved in more than one pursuit simultaneously, or one after the other. The executives were employed at Swedish or American banks or agencies, or were running small companies doing export or import business with Sweden, or went to business schools.

Among the young Swedes, artists tended to come from Stockholm, while the au pairs and the executives had grown up in small towns, which meant that the majority of the young Swedes had moved from a relatively small town to the global city that New York is. There was an attitudinal difference in how those who were used to Stockholm on one hand, and those who had not lived in a city with at least some kind of cosmopolitanism, related to the intensity and diversity of Manhattan. Those who came from Stockholm were usually uncritically positive, even engrossed— "hungry" as they said themselves—in relation to New York. They were eager to go out on all kinds of visits, to destitute ghettos and to decadent clubs, as well as to learning how to operate in the art world and the business world. This was not the case with those who came from other parts of Sweden, especially the younger ones, who mostly were less comfortable in New York (Wulff 1992). They frequented less spectacular restaurants and clubs that still might provide them with unexpected excitement in the form of romantic encounters.

All the young Swedes were well aware of the fact that they were in the process of acquiring the social and cultural capital that a sojourn in the US tends to entail in Sweden. The artists and executives were above all busy collecting job qualifications, which they were planning to use afterward back in Sweden. Still, they did have many different reasons to make the move to New York when they finally did, and their reasons to stay on might in fact not be those that had urged them to go there in the first place. The artists principally went to New York in order to expose themselves to the opportunity of becoming famous, while the main reason for most of the au pair girls was the nightlife of New York (Wulff 1992). But New York was a place for unlimited opportunities, beyond what any of them would ever experience in Sweden, at the same time it included the possibility that they might settle down permanently in New York.

Moratorium in Manhattan

Erik Homburger Erikson (1968: 156–58, 242), the psychoanalyst, has said
that a psychosocial moratorium, "a delay of adult commitments . . . a
period that is characterized by selective permissiveness on the part of
society and on provocative playfulness on the part of youth," seems to be
inherent in human development. Young adults are allowed to experiment
with different roles; there may even be certain social zones that are meant
to take care of such activity. The young Swedes shared this, and the opportunity to devote themselves to the nightlife of Manhattan. They were all
in the process of prolonging their youth while enjoying the freedom from
responsibilities and long-term personal commitments far away from
parental surveillance and control. Very few were married, not all that
many were living together with a partner, although it was more common
than not to have a boyfriend or a girlfriend. A small number were gay.
None had children. And it was in the roaring nightlife of Manhattan that
artists, au pairs, and executives felt free to meet across class boundaries.

   This they could do, at least the men, at the gentlemen's club Friends
of the Pea (Ärtans *vänner*) to have traditional Swedish pea soup every
Thursday at different restaurants with Swedish connections. The oldest
member was an 85-year-old shipbroker who had been a member for about
half a century, the youngest was on one occasion a 19-year-old man with
his hair in a ponytail who had arrived in New York a week earlier. Like all
cultured gentleman's clubs, Friends of the Pea is partly organized for men
in order to build and cultivate their work networks, but also, and for most
of them, it is above all a reason to party and confirm their Swedishness
in the ethnic diversity of Manhattan. In other words, they formed what
Shokeid (1988) has called affective ethnicity, the kind of ethnicity without
political, economic, or other social interest that relatively invisible ethnic
groups form in a changing situation. Yet, the affective ethnicity at Friends
of the Pea did have an instrumental aspect since it happened that the men
helped each other extend their professional networks, and the setting was
indeed social.

   Soon spirits are running high at Friends of the Pea, and the conversation consists of bolder-and-bolder dirty jokes. It is, to quote one of the
happy young men "the hottest night on earth" (*jordens drag*), not least
because of the sweet alcoholic punch that is served with the pea soup and
pancakes. So what are the girls up to while the boys are enjoying themselves in all-male company? Some of the au pairs, at least, went giggling
to see male striptease as a way to break boundaries.

   Erikson (1968) brings up the importance of pranks during moratorium.
The young Swedes were often involved in pranks on nights on the town:

artists, au pairs and executives, men and women, all together dressed up in black clothing—short leather jackets, black jeans or mini skirts for the women. The identity play, experimentation with different roles, tended to take the form of pranks. One of the au pairs described this, without me having asked about it, by saying "you can play a little with your identity here."

A night on the town might last for twelve hours and take place at three or four locales beginning at a restaurant with dinner, going on to a bar and clubs for dancing until the early hours of the morning when it was time for the "after hour" clubs (Wulff 1992). The city that never sleeps offered opportunities for identity play, "to go out and lie," as the expression was, about who you are, trying on another "possible life" such as that of a fiction writer or a film director. This experimentation with different identities mostly had to do with nationality, occupation, age, sexual orientation, and class. It took place during short conversations with strangers in the anonymity of the Manhattan nightlife. It was a good way to get into contact with people and easily get out, if you did not want to pursue them. But it did happen that people the young Swedes had known for quite some time turned out to be someone else, of a different background, than they had told the Swedes.

Another kind of identity play was performed by executives and other professionals who were doing very well, working extremely hard, making a lot of money, and enjoying splendid career prospects. They also enjoyed the nightlife. Still, I understood that some of them entertained secret dreams about changing their lives completely and turning into artists. An intellectual banker working with currency trade confided in me that he would prefer to spend his time writing novels. A medical researcher said that as long as he was still in New York, he could keep nourishing his dream of becoming a photographer instead. New York was thus, besides the real opportunities, also a temporary opening of imaginary opportunities.

Growing Up through Global Experience

It is quite common among youth and young adults in Europe and the US to be engaged in global experience, a temporary extension of their opportunities in the form of long trips or stays abroad, more or less planned or structured. Such undertakings are similar to the vision quests that American Indians (Norbeck 1961; Lowie 1963) set out on or a "hero's journey" (Campbell 1949). It has also been a part of the last phase of growing up and constructing an adult identity in Western bourgeoisie and aristocratic life for centuries in order to learn of the ways of the world. It goes back to the fifteenth and sixteenth centuries when upper classes sent their sons on the Grand Tour. This came out of two earlier types of travel intended to conclude apprenticeships: the chivalric excursion by young knights to courts and the *peregrinato academica*, the journey of young scholars to places of learning (Leed 1991). Swedish ethnologist Orvar Löfgren (1989) has noted that Swedish noblemen and sons of civil servants traveled to Florence as early as in the seventeenth century where they could gain their worldly polish, not least because there was an elite that offered accommodation and conversation. Löfgren argues that contemporary young train travelers, Eurorailers (*tågluffare*) who are mostly middle class, are modern peregrinators. Just like their predecessors, they develop personally by being exposed to the world. Travelling by train for a summer month in Europe was something many of the young Swedes had done before going to New York, as one way to prepare for a longer stay abroad, to begin to learn self-reliance, and to take initiatives. It happened that the young Swedes went Eurorailing afterwards, though, together with friends they had met in New York. Quite a few of them had moreover done what they referred to as Long Journeys (*långresor*), low-budget trips, for a year or about six months around the world, or through parts of Asia and Australia as backpackers.

There is thus a connection between the young Swedes' New York stay and the earlier chivalric, academic, or educational travels as well as present-day Eurorail and the Long Journeys through Asia. In this context, when the US is being observed, it is significant that there have also been transnational and global movements in this tradition from the US to Europe: the Grand Tour could with time start out in the US and go to cities such as Paris, London, or Berlin. Nowadays, a junior year abroad is a common stage in American college education that is often spent in European cities (Fava and Desena 1984). Another example of a work that discusses possibilities of self-realization through journeys or stays abroad is by Yehuda Jacobson (1987) who writes about young adults from Israel who go on secular pilgrimages to South Africa or the Far East, as a kind of rite of passage, between military service or university studies and settling down into marriage and work. Donald Broady (1987) reminds us that a year in the US for young adult Swedes from the Swedish economic elite contributes to the reproduction of this elite, at the same time as it improves career prospects of individuals belonging to it.

So the young Swedes were not the only sojourners or travellers who return with a new identity formed out of a global experience. Importantly, this return is very much a part of the journey. Still, even though all these different stays and journeys abroad have linkages back to early chivalric and peregrinatory undertakings, the young Swedes do differ in one significant sense that makes their New York stay a contemporary experience. The US is very present in Sweden, not least through the media that, as we saw in the opening vignette, has produced a kind of anticipatory socialization of the young Swedes that soon pushed them into New York life. As a woman artist confessed to me: "I've had a dream about New York since I was a child. You grow up with New York in the media. At school, I was drawing arrows in my Geography book, from Gothenburg, where I was living, to New York." This awareness of New York made the Swedes more involved in the city than their historic predecessors ever were in Florence, Paris, or Berlin. The fact that the young Swedes worked in New York was clearly important for their immersion in the city, and something that contributed to its long-term impact, not least for executives and artists who often relied on professional contacts from New York afterward in Sweden.

The young Swedes talked about the impact of impressions of New York from popular songs, films, television, fiction, newspapers, magazines, and music videos on how they had imagined the city before they came. Despite this preparation through the media, though, they had found them understating matters such as the physical size and the competitiveness of New York, while exaggerating the violence but also the anonymity. They were impressed by being taken into account in a polite manner by strangers (which is highly un-Swedish unless there is an emergency). Many times their pre-images of New York drawn from the media were simply confirmed as they recognized buildings, department stores, avenues, restaurants, and clubs—as if they had been there before!

It is noteworthy that in New York young Swedes had to reconstruct their media behavior; they were not culturally competent media consumers in the American context. At first, they felt at a loss confronting the enormous amount of offerings, but with time they learned to ignore commercials on television and radio, to zap between different television channels, and to switch radio stations to get what they wanted to watch or listen to. It took a while for them to get used to the luxury of watching television in bed, as well as to watching alone, not with the rest of the family or with friends, as many had been in the habit of doing in Sweden. A woman photographer explained to me that she did not really get to watch television in New York, despite the fact that there was a television set in the apartment she was sharing with some fellow students—since there was no couch! This was one sign that she was still dependent on Swedish television consumption behavior, that is, to watch television with one's entire attention focused, whereas Americans often consume television as sociable furniture in the background while they move around the place eating dinner, doing the dishes, or having conversations about other matters.

The young Swedes were not only leisure media consumers, but some of the artists were professional media producers as well. Others were training to become a link in the production process, the one connecting (sometimes with uneasiness) political and economic structures with aesthetics. The photographers belonged here, a filmmaker, the makeup artist: they all worked backstage while an actor, a singer, some dancers, and some models performed on stage, film, video, and records. Some of the young Swedes consumed media for professional reasons, as well as for entertainment and existential reasons. The artists indulged in the many photography, design, and fashion magazines while the executives read up on current economic affairs in the business press. All the young Swedes tended to consume more media in New York than in Sweden, and more varied forms of media, not only because more were available, but also because they were in an expansive phase in their life.

Looking for the Unexpected

The young Swedes were "looking for the unexpected" in career and nightlife as they shared the idea of "opportunities in New York." Some were indeed successful, while others had to leave the city disappointed. There were also those who were said to "be stuck" in New York faced with failure. The young Swedes carved out their different New Yorks among a multitude of landscapes within the city. They were able to make certain choices about what they made of the city, which contrasted painfully with other parts of the city that they knew were inhabited by poor immigrants who had also been drawn to Manhattan in search of opportunities, but were living in destitution, and often humiliated by racism. Coming from Sweden, a welfare state where homelessness is very rare, many of the young Swedes were shocked by the sight of homeless people in the streets. As one woman, Anna, who worked as a model in New York, described the city:

> Life in New York is such a contrast to Swedish life, the boring Swedish life. In Sweden, you're used to getting everything served, not only from family and school, but from authorities, as well. Everything is laid out for you. But arriving in New York—it's like a hurricane! All the different cultures! It's a total stew! Very sad life, too. It's such as contrast between the grim reality and the slightly glamorous life that you live as a Swede.

The circulation of the young Swedes toward New York can be said to have started already when they were children watching *Donald Duck* on Christmas Eve, in the form of imaginary circulation. Influenced by the media, the young Swedes had been rehearsing desired and feared events in their transnational imagination that they experienced as a part of a possible reality. As Appadurai (1996: 54–55) has suggested: "More persons throughout the world see their lives through the prisms of the possible lives offered by mass media in all their forms. That is, fantasy is now a social practice." But he is "quick to note that this is not a cheerful observation, intended to imply that the world is now a happier place with more choices (in the utilitarian sense) for more people, and with more mobility and more happy endings" as this also includes the fact that "the harshest of lived inequalities are now open to the play of the imagination." The young Swedes were introduced to a wider set of possible lives in New York through the media, sometimes but not always lives they would want to lead themselves.

In his essay "On Multiple Realities," Alfred Schutz (1967) discusses imagination versus outer, paramount reality. Having arrived in New York bringing their media images of the city, the young Swedes had to handle these different orders of reality. On one hand, it was important to them to distinguish between imagination and real life, to show that they were not manipulated by the media. In the words of an au pair: "I want to form my own opinion about New York, not only buy everything you read or hear." But when their experiences in Manhattan did surpass what the young Swedes had imagined they would ever encounter in life, then they categorized these exceptional experiences as "it was like a movie" or "like a music video." It could be instances of professional success such as when a woman designer was offered a job at the magazine *Interview*, or when a group of friends had an extraordinary night at a party that Keith Haring, the artist, organized at a club. Then they felt that they had been a part of the action in their alluring capital of the world, fascinated by having transformed transnational media images of New York into their own reality. In this sense, it could be suggested that there was a preparation for the exceptional among the young Swedes, or at least an anticipation. Yet, my point is that they were still taken by surprise when exceptional events did happen.

"You don't have to go to the pictures here," a photographer remarked "you just go out in the street!" He continued by talking about "the mixture of colorful people," and "the clash between wealth and misery symbolized by long limousines passing by the lines of starved people waiting for a free bowl of soup." And when I asked Anna, the model, to tell me a New York story, she smiled and said:

> One of my friends, he's working as a bartender at a bar on Broadway, was on his way home late one Saturday night. He had been working all day and had his tip,

about $100, which was his salary for that day, in his wallet. Then two guys came up behind him with a knife forcing him down a back street. He gave them all his money and his cigarettes. They took off his shoes and took them with them so he wouldn't be able to run after them. Then they left. But they returned almost immediately, and gave him $6, so he could take a cab home! (Wulff 1992: 103)

This is a typical story told by the young Swedes. The stories tended to be about street violence that had happened to them, or to someone they knew. Remarkably often the stories had a comic turn that confirmed the image of New York as a "city of contrasts where everything is possible" (Wulff 1992: 103).[4]

Writing about the impact of exceptional experiences in everyday life, Moshe Shokeid (1992) describes how he went to an elegant bar on the East Side of Manhattan where he struck up a conversation with another man. Shokeid introduced himself as an Israeli tourist, and the man said he was Jewish. They had a friendly conversation, and after a while the man asked Shokeid about his occupation. Shokeid then reacted with caution and said he was a historian from Tel Aviv University. It was with mixed feelings Shokeid learned that the man was, of all things, an anthropologist! When the man started praising an ethnography on Moroccan Jews he admired, Shokeid thought it was time to confess that not only was he also an anthropologist, but in fact the author of this book. This piece of information the man did not believe was true.

At clubs and bars, the young Swedes all felt free to connect closely across class boundaries without obligation to keep in touch later on in Sweden. Some of them expressed regret over this, back in the confinement of the Swedish class system. There were some class distinctions, as well as differences when it came to regional background, among them. To let go of class in a liminoid zone (Turner 1982) such as this, was nothing unique to the young Swedes. It was a part of the setting. In the article "Reading America: Preliminary Notes on Class and Culture," Sherry Ortner (2006: 20) argues that "although class goes largely unspoken in American social life, it is not discursively absent." New York's nightlife is a special scene when it comes to classlessness, yet it is interesting to consider this quality in the American context, and to what extent it is actually more American than Swedish.

It was not only New York as a playground that attracted the young Swedes, but also New York as a workplace. Except for the au pair girls, most young Swedes went there primarily for training, qualifications, and networking. Some of the executives made a lot of money, more than they would have made in Sweden. Many of the young Swedes matured as they learned to deal with a competitive climate. Back in Sweden, an artist explained: "You discover new things about yourself. Things kept happening. You're mentally stimulated, physically and psychologically active all the time. I wanted more there! I wanted to develop myself. I discovered I was an individual."

Memories of Manhattan

Considering the cultural role of world cities in center-periphery relations, Hannerz (1996) points out how people from managerial elites to expressive specialists, as well as so called "been-tos" (returnees from Europe to West Africa) acquire social and cultural capital, and/or qualifications, in world cities that they bring back home enhancing their careers.

The young Swedes returned to Sweden, they told me, because their contract was up, or they wanted to apply their knowledge and take charge of their professional development, often by starting a company of their own. Some went back to Sweden primarily because they missed family, friends, and perhaps a partner, they were short of money, or because they missed Swedish nature and the ideology of the Swedish welfare state. They were ill at ease with the misery, especially the homeless and the violence in Manhattan. But it also seemed to me that they had burned out their Manhattan energy that they had in abundance when they indulged in the fast pulse and the pressure there. "It was a wonderful time—I would never be able to do it again!" as one of the executives, a sales manager, pointed out. He went on, "afterwards I understood that to be in New York is like sitting inside an electronic pencil sharpener: as you are being sharpened—you are eaten up!" So there was also relief in coming back to Sweden, a satisfied relief as in having passed a test.[5]

For the understanding of the central meaning of the Manhattan experience for the young Swedes, Schutz' (1964) ideas on memory and communication are also useful. Manhattan elevated them into an exhilarated state of psychological and physical alertness in which they communicate intensely with each other. United by vulnerability, they also shared what were extraordinary experiences for them. This defined their Manhattan life. "You're in a different reality," as an artist remarked when we were both back in Stockholm, thereby indicating the imbuing quality of it. This was not confined to certain prestructured bounded events, nor did it exclude setbacks or other problems. The young Swedes were quite aware that they were living in an exceptional dimension. Even though not everyone was able to verbalize this, I had many opportunities to observe this when I spent time with them late at night in clubs or in studios and offices during the day. As this exhilarated state was of an existential nature, the memory of it stays with them afterwards.

According to Schutz (1964), individual fantasies may be meaningful and reproduced within a collective connection, but as soon as we are dealing with some kind of communication between people, an event or a series of events in the outer world is required as a basis. The events that the Swedes kept coming back to in their individual and collective recollections of their Manhattan stay mostly had to do with memorable nights on the town or moments of professional breakthrough. This also relates to Csikzentmihalyi's (1975) concept of flow, an optimal experience where action and consciousness meet, often in structured forms such as during an artistic performance. The young Swedes did get this feeling of flow when as if by a stroke of magic a night on the town that seemed quite mundane from the beginning, suddenly turned into a euphoric adventure, or when a painter, or an executive working with international stock exchange, suddenly find themselves surfing on a long awaited wave of inspiration at work. Such events become a part of the state of exhilaration that kept them absorbed until they returned to Sweden and "came back to reality in a sense, which was rather difficult," as a former au pair explained it.

It thus turns out that the Manhattan experience is not completed until afterwards, when it is recreated through the young Swedes' recollections, both individually and together in groups. For the young Swedes meet, also back in Sweden, albeit in more limited networks as they are then restricted by the Swedish social structure, especially when it comes to socializing across class and age. They tend to stick to their own category in Sweden, which for the artists and the executives also entails professional exchange. But gone are the days when a young banker went out on a night on the town with a 60-year-old friend, when a woman artist from the Swedish aristocracy had a boyfriend who was homeless (even though he did not live on the street), or when executives entertained au pair girls at spectacular clubs.

It is interesting to note that the exhilaration in Manhattan did not have to have been shared by the young Swedes who later back in Sweden retrospectively celebrate it together. There were friends among the young Swedes who did not meet until afterward, when they had come back to Sweden, some through professional networks, others through personal ones. A photographer described such a friendship:

> It's this sense of community . . . it isn't just that you have been to the same coffee shop, have seen the smoke coming up from the sewer like at movies, or that you know where to find a certain hair dresser. It's that it takes a special kind of person to embark upon this kind of endeavor, adventure. To take the economic risk. To want to achieve something!

Clearly it was common that the young Swedes, virtually every one of them, kept links to people they first met in New York. A few years after having moved back to Sweden, some of them had friends almost exclusively from their stay in New York, and a number of them complained over difficulties in relating to old friends in Sweden who lacked the Manhattan experience.

Yet the past is reinterpreted time after time according to present circumstances. There was, in other words, a time lag in how some Manhattan experiences were accommodated in the Swedish context. There were events that turned out to be more memorable afterwards than they had seemed while they were happening, and there were other events fading away as not interesting or useful in the long run after all.

As time is socially and culturally constructed (Zerubavel 1981; Bender and Wellbery 1991), time in Manhattan was quite different from Swedish time, again mostly because of the fast pace. Even if the young Swedes, mainly executives and au pairs, but to a certain extent also some of the artists, had to adhere to institutional, public schedules at work, they still had a freedom to construct their own schedules of time, often working longer hours than their colleagues, and of course, partying more. One characteristic of Manhattan that figured prominently in the memories of the young Swedes, and that they missed back in Sweden, was 24-hour service. It had made it easier for them to construct their own schedules. The nightlife was a substantial part of it, but also simpler enjoyments such as buying the Sunday issue of *The New York Times* late the Saturday night before, or going shopping at the supermarket at 2 am.

Observing Little Manhattan

The circulation of the young people who moved to Manhattan did not end there. Most returned to where they came from, others moved on to other places in the US or elsewhere. Even lack of success in Manhattan might be transformed into cultural capital back home. Returning to Sweden, artists and executives kept their Manhattan network and tended to trust colleagues with New York experience—even if they did not meet there!

This experience of a state of exhilaration will not be forgotten. I met the young Swedes in Sweden when they had been at home between six months and six years, most of them for about two years. There were no indications that Manhattan meant either more or less to recent returnees than to those who had been back the longest. Instead I realized that they all more or less contributed to the creation of "Little Manhattan" in Stockholm. It was mostly nocturnal and dispersed over the city, but there were certain bars, restaurants, and clubs that had a "New York style," as they said, and where they felt at home. These clubs were located in huge warehouses, sometimes without a name, and occasionally moving to a new address in order to preserve an air of selectiveness—which was a common pattern in Manhattan. But the young Swedes did not party as much as they used to, partly because they were starting to settle down (some were having families), but the high Stockholm prices also slowed them down.

Little Manhattan was in large part constructed by way of conversation, relocations that often start with the memory of the sensory experiences of Manhattan.[6] For, as Hannerz (1996: 135) observes—you cannot really take a world city with you. It stands out by an inseparability of sense from place, you have to go there "to see, and hear, and smell it."

"All the smells! It smells differently," one of the former au pair girls exclaimed, remembering the odor of garbage and dust in the street. The noise of Manhattan was another frequent memory: traffic and raised voices, as was the taste of bagels with cream cheese, and the sight of the Empire State Building changing colors at night.

Developing the anthropology of the senses, David Howes (1991) has suggested that the patterning of sense experience is cultural, which would mean that the young Swedes' recollections of their sensory experiences of Manhattan in fact says more about Swedish patterning of senses than what it in any kind of neutral way "is like" in Manhattan, since we are dealing with a cultural contrast here. The young Swedes remembered smells, sounds, tastes, and sights that were new and different, and that they could not reclaim in Stockholm afterwards. Neither were they able to recover the contexts of their sensory experiences, such as certain atmospheres, except in Proustian ponderings. A photographer coming across a sign in a Stockholm shoe shop saying "Green Street," immediately found himself in a sea of memories of his time in Manhattan, accentuating that he was in two minds as to whether to move back or not. The most common sensory experience in Sweden that swept the young Swedes back to Manhattan, though, was the sound of some popular song that they had enjoyed listening to when they were there, and that they connect with a particular event, person or period of time.

As many as half of the young Swedes were in fact considering the possibility of moving back to New York again, keeping personal and professional links to Swedes, Americans, and others in New York by way of going there for vacations (often combined with a professional meeting or a freelance job), by letters, and by telephone (this was before the Internet). They also related to Manhattan through the media. It was mostly American films, magazines, and journals that they enjoyed, especially when they recognized places and pictures from New York life. Armed with their firsthand, bodily experience of having been immersed in New York, they took a special pleasure in "correcting" the media. When they found something they regarded as represented wrongly, they protested to anyone who wanted to listen. *They* knew what "real" Manhattan looks and sounds like, how it smells and tastes.

And in the end, the young Swedes realized that through their moratorium rite in Manhattan, they had become more confident and independent persons, also more outspoken and easygoing, but at the same time humble. They felt that they had been travelling on "a journey all around the world in one city." Theirs was a global experience not just a transnational one. The crux of the matter is that New York had taught them more about the world than about the rest of the US, providing them with a global competence and sensibility that make them take the rest of the world into account as something really there to travel, live, and work in (which a number of them soon accomplished), and relate to on an everyday basis by way of the media. All this really came about because of their momentous exhilaration in Manhattan, a state they now largely manage in their memories.

"New York is not America!" I kept being reminded by the young Swedes, "it's like a different country." Still, not only is New York one center of the world, it is also in many respects a center of the United States. This is in line with Gupta and Ferguson's (1992) idea that places such New York are produced to a great extent by movement, circulation, by migrants, sojourners, and by movement back and forth, which the young Swedes contributed to.

Finally, this chapter has brought out the point that circulation is not only geographical mobility, but also imaginary. It is important to understand how they are related, and to take both geographical and imaginary circulation seriously, not least in light of the fact that with increasing transnational connections as well as control, both types are proliferating.

Acknowledgments

I am most grateful to Virginia R. Dominguez and Jasmin Habib for their insightful comments on this chapter. I also wish to thank Jane C. Desmond and Roger Sanjek for inspiring ideas in their capacities of discussants when this chapter was an American Anthropological Association paper.

Helena Wulff is Professor of Social Anthropology at Stockholm University. Among her publications are the monographs *Ballet across Borders: Career and Culture in the World of Dancers* (1998) and *Dancing at the Crossroads: Memory and Mobility in Ireland* (2007), edited volumes *The Emotions: A Cultural Reader* (2007), *Ethnographic Practice in the Present* (with Marit Melhuus and Jon P. Mitchell, 2010), and *The Anthropologist as Writer: Genres and Contexts in the Twenty-First Century* (2016). She was editor (with Dorle Drackleé) of *Social Anthropology*.

Notes

1. See *How to Read Donald Duck: Imperialist Ideology in the Disney Comic* by Ariel Dorfman and Armand Mattelart (1975) for a Marxist analysis of the American character of Donald Duck.
2. http://sv.wikipedia.org/wiki/Kalle_Anka_och_hans_v%C3%A4nner_%C3%B6nskar_God_Jul
3. The study "Young Swedes in New York: Workplace and Playground" was funded by a Stockholm University grant.
4. See Hannerz (1996: 132–33) on stories New York sociologist Gerald Handel (1984) asked his students to collect from visitors to the city, such as this one told by a housewife from Quebec: "I seen a little old lady fighting off a mugger. It was fascinating because the old lady turned out to be a cop."
5. Since the young Swedes left Manhattan, there has, of course, been a real estate boom which has produced a displacement of artists and creative spaces from Manhattan (see Cooke, Crimp and Poor 2010; Lloyd 2010, among others).
6. The anthropology of the senses was first established in the late 1980s by Paul Stoller and Cheryl Olkes (1987), and the 1990s by David Howes (1991) and Constance Classen (1997). Howes and Classen developed anthropology of the senses by comparing sensory experience cross-culturally and hierarchies of senses and multi-sensorial contexts.

References

Appadurai, Arjun. 1996. *Modernity at Large: Cultural Dimensions of Globalization.* Minneapolis: University of Minnesota Press.
Bender, John and David E. Wellbury, eds. 1991. *Chronotypes: The Construction of Time.* Stanford, CA: Stanford University Press.

Broady, Donald. 1987. "Högskolan och det kulturella kapitalet." In *Nordisk Pedagogik* 2: 87–101.

Campbell, Joseph. 1949. *The Hero with a Thousand Faces*. New York: Pantheon.

Classen, Constance. 1997. "Foundations for an Anthropology of the Senses." *International Social Science Journal* 153: 401–12.

Clifford, James. 1988. *The Predicament of Culture: Twentieth-Century Ethnography, Literature, and Art*. Cambridge, MA: Harvard University Press.

Cooke, Lynne, and Douglas Crimp, eds. with Kristin Poor. 2010. *Mixed Use, Manhattan: Photography and Related Practices, 1970s to the Present*. Cambridge, MA: MIT Press.

Csikzentmihalyi, Mihaly (1975) *Beyond Boredom and Anxiety: Experiencing Flow in Work and Play*. San Francisco: Jossey-Bass.

Dorfman, Ariel and Armand Mattelart. 1975. *How to Read Donald Duck: Imperialist Ideology in the Disney Comic*. London: International General.

Eriksen, Erik Homburger. 1968. *Youth and Crisis*. New York: Norton.

Fava, Sylvia F. and Judith DeSena. 1984. "The Chosen Apple: Young Suburban Migrants." In *The Apple Sliced: Sociological Studies of New York City*, ed. Vernon Boggs, Gerald Handel and Sylvia F. Fava, 305–22. South Hadley, MA: Bergin & Garvey Publishers.

Gupta, Akhil and James Ferguson. 1992. "Beyond 'Culture': Space, Identity, and the Politics of Difference." *Cultural Anthropology* 7(1): 6–23.

Handel, Gerald. 1984. "Visiting New York." In *The Apple Sliced: Sociological Studies of New York*, ed. Vernon Boggs, Syliva Fleis Fava, and Gerald Handel, 291–304. South Hadley, MA: Bergin & Garvey.

Hannerz, Ulf. 1996. "The Cultural Role of World Cities." In *Transnational Connections: Culture, People, Places*, 127–39. London: Routledge.

Howes, David, ed. 1991. *The Varieties of Sensory Experience: A Sourcebook in the Anthropology of the Senses*. Toronto: University of Toronto Press.

Jacobson, Yehuda. 1987. "Secular Pilgrimage in the Israeli Context: The Journey of Young Israelis to Distant Countries." Unpublished MA thesis, Tel Aviv University.

Leed, Eric J. 1991. *The Mind of the Traveller: From Gilgamesh to Global Tourism*. New York: Basic Books.

Lloyd, Richard. 2010. *Neo-Bohemia: Art and Commerce in the Postindustrial City*. New York: Routledge.

Löfgren, Orvar. 1989. "Längtan till landet Annorlunda." In *Längtan till landet Annorlunda: Om turism i historia och nutid*, ed. Sveriges Turistråd, 9–49. Stockholm: Gidlunds.

Lowie, Robert H. 1963. *Indians of the Plains*. New York: Garden City.

Norbeck, Edward. 1961. *Religion in Primitive Society*. New York: Harpers & Brothers.

Ortner, Sherry B. 2006. "Reading America: Preliminary Notes on Class and Culture." In *Anthropology and Social Theory*, 19–41. Durham: Duke University Press.

Pfanner, Helmut F. 1983. *Exile in New York: German and Austrian Writers after 1933*. Detroit: Wayne State University Press.

Reed-Danahay, Deborah E. ed. 1997. *Auto/Ethnography: Rewriting the Self and the Social*. Oxford: Berg.

Schutz, Alfred. 1964. "Making Music Together." In *Collected Papers II: Studies in Social Theory*, 159–78. The Hague: Martinus Nijhoff.

———. 1967. "On Multiple Realities." In *Collected Papers I: The Problem of Social Reality*, 340–47. The Hague: Martinus Nijhoff.

Shokeid, Moshe. 1988. *Children of Circumstances: Israeli Emigrants in New York*. Ithaca, NY: Cornell University Press.

———. 1992. "Exceptional Experiences in Everyday Life." *Cultural Anthropology* 7(2): 232–43.

Stoller, Paul and Cheryl Olkes. 1987. *In Sorcery's Shadow: A Memoir of Apprenticeship among the Songhay of Niger*. Chicago: University of Chicago Press.

Turner, Victor. 1982. "Liminal to Liminoid, in Play, Flow, Ritual: An Essay in Comparative Symbology." In *From Ritual to Theatre: The Human Seriousness of Play*, 20–60. New York: Performing Arts Journal Publication.

Wulff, Helena. 1991. "Möjligheternas Makt: Unga svenska artister i New York." *Antropologiska Studier* 48: 59–63.

———. 1992. "Young Swedes in New York: Workplace and Playground." In *Networks of Americanization: Aspects of the American Influence in Sweden*, ed. Rolf Lundén and Erik Åsard, 94–105. Stockholm: Almqvist & Wiksell International.

———. 1994. "Moratorium på Manhattan: Unga svenskar och globalisering." In *Ungdomskultur i Sverige*, Johan Fornäs, Ulf Boëthius, Michael Forsman, Hillevi, Ganetz and Bo Reimer, eds., 127–41. FUS-rapport nr. 6. Stockholm: Symposion.

Zerubavel, Eviatar. 1981. *Hidden Rhythms: Schedules and Calendars in Social Life*. Chicago: University of Chicago Press.

Chapter Two

Is It Un-American to Be Critical of Israel?
Criticism and Fear in the US Context

Jasmin Habib

> Whatever happened to two Jews, three opinions?
> —Placard

> What the history of American Jews and Judaism has
> communicated . . . is that Jews become Americans by becoming
> both certain types of Jews and certain types of Americans
> —Riv Ellen Prell, "Response to Jonathan Sarna's Marshall Sklare Award Lecture"

> The notion of the homeland draws on comforting images of a
> deeply rooted past to legitimate modern forms of imperial power
> —Amy Kaplan, *Homeland Insecurities*

In his piece entitled "Free Speech, Israel, and Jewish Illiberalism," Alan Wolfe (2006) writes:

It is difficult to know why honest discussions about Israel have become so difficult to conduct. Is it, perhaps, because the rise of the Christian right, no matter how ostensibly supportive of Israel it claims to be, reminds Jews that they live in a Christian country and thereby makes them more likely to circle the wagons? Or does the reason perhaps lie in the fact that Jews have become part of America's multicultural mosaic, one more group proclaiming its identity and difference? Or perhaps it has to do with the charge made by many pro-Israel Jews that Israel is held to a different standard when it comes to judging the morality of a country's foreign policy than other states, including Israel's enemies in the Middle East? Whatever the reason, discussions of Israel in the United States resemble a shouting match filled with insult and invective more than a reasoned debate over the proper relationship between that country and this one.

Notes for this chapter begin on page 76.

The question Wolfe never asks: Is it un-American to be critical of Israel? It is the question that I was compelled to think about after several periods of living in the US where I met, interacted, and interviewed Jewish community members as well as several of the peace and human rights activists among them.

The core of this chapter takes up activist perspectives on Israel/Palestine but is not limited to those concerns. What I believe makes this study unique is that it considers activist perspectives in the context of wider US Jewish community concerns. I will discuss who these activists are while also considering the perspectives of their compatriots—those I met in the wider circles that formed their community. I think it worth noting that in some of the US communities in which I conducted my research, Jews were a small minority. What I also found interesting (though it does not form the core of my argument) was that while the language non-activists used to describe a sense of fear that Jews do not fully belong to the US was framed in less politically charged language, there was a high degree of convergence between those who were activists and those who were not.

How Did I Get Here and Why "Diaspora Dissidents"?

In my doctoral project, begun in the early 1990s, fortuitously perhaps, in the month that the Oslo Accords were signed (1993), I examined North American Jewish affiliations with and attachments to Israel. I did so by living in two large Canadian cities and visiting US cities with significant Jewish populations and institutions. Over the course of close to five years, I also traveled on organized tours of Israel, arranged by Canadian, US, and international Jewish organizations. I chose to travel to Israel because I had learned—from the literature on Jewish identification with Israel—that such a trek was a mark of one's commitment to Zionism and the state. I then also conducted interviews with travelers and sometimes also their friends, both in the US and Canada.

As the daughter of a Jewish mother and a Palestinian father, I found it difficult to understand or, better, to appreciate the type and range of attachments of those who had never lived in the state and/or who did not have any family living there. My own visits to Israel were to see family and friends. For these other travelers, organized visits to Israel were to "sites" that held religious, communal, or national significance, and only rarely did these include visits to family or friends. I had not been exposed to this form of identification with the state: not by my Ashkenazi grandparents, whose move to Israel in 1932 and 1933 saved their lives and, in the case of my grandfather, his entire family's life; and not by my father, whose family was forcibly displaced from Beisan to Nazareth, with the founding of the state. Zionism was never a point of discussion. Although there were always Israeli politicos (Israeli Jewish and Palestinian) who would come to Canada for visits, most of them associated with the Israeli Communist Party (a party that spawned many "mixed marriages," I might add), rarely were the discussions focused on Zionism as such. Rather, there were discussions about the Israeli Communist Party's failure to fully support Palestinian self-determination; the role of the Soviet Union in the Cold War; the role of Marxism, Trotskyism, and the future of revolutionary thought. Zionism was not ever *the* issue so I never really knew any of its contours, or its cultural meaningfulness. It was not until I was into my undergraduate years that my identity would be transformed from "the commie" or "socialist" I had been labeled in high school, to "the Palestinian" at university. The transformation did not take long. Most of my professors were Marxists and, it seemed, so were many of my peers. Socialism, then, was not a problem; it was debated much the same way as it had been at home. What my peers did not, or perhaps better still, did not *want* to think much about was Israel or Palestine. So, when I organized a panel on the 1982 invasion of Lebanon, I was threatened with hate mail. When a group of students interested in international affairs and development issues was formed on campus, I was asked to "represent" Palestine. Even so, Zionism was not a part of any of our discussions. It was not until I had had a long and convoluted conversation with my roommate's father, a Toronto-based secular Jew who said he could not wait to meet me *because* I was an Israeli, that I sensed just how strange it was to speak to someone who believed Israel was entirely Jewish, especially as I had experienced it, not only in my travels but at home, as a mix of European and Arab cultures. I too, had idealized "home" though in ways obviously different from those of my roommate's father. So, when I finally made the circuitous route into the PhD, my project was ready to go.

What I learned over the course of my doctoral research was not only of North American travelers' limited access to the diversity and complexity of Israel, they were on tour after all, but that the strength of their commitment could actually be measured by the extent to which they could live with and appreciate that very complexity. In the end it was the leftists in the groups that I traveled with who happened to be Israel's most critical yet ardent supporters. They were its most frequent visitors, and they had donated their time as well as large sums of money to organizations they believed would help Israel to develop into a more equitable, just, and peaceful society. They were also among the most vocal in their disapproval of "Diaspora politics" as one called it, or "the Jewish establishment" as many others described North American community leaders and major organizations. Some said that they "could barely stand to be on the bus" with their fellow Diaspora travelers, but that they would regularly take organized trips to Israel to see how their donations were being expended. Once my book based on this research was published (2004), several Jewish scholars wrote and approached me to say that I should have taken more seriously Israel's critics in the community. But, I responded at the time, that positioning would not have been representative of those who I met in the many years that I was conducting my research, whether in the community or on tour.

I thought I had left it all behind when in the late 1990s and early 2000s, I moved on to do research on North American Palestinian diaspora and refugee histories, memories, and advocacy, which led me to a wide range of cyberactivist sites many of which, I was surprised to learn, were linked directly to Israeli human rights and peace organizations, most of them located in Israel. In the course of that research, I often heard diaspora Palestinians lament: "Israeli Jews know so much more about our plight than North American Jews; look at their organizations, their media, their newspapers. Why can't Jews here learn about being open to these ideas from Jews there?" While I had promised myself that after the research with and among Palestinians I would set aside research about the Israel-Palestine conflict for a time (I was honestly sick of the misrecognition, of either being "too Jewish" or "too Palestinian" to be taken seriously), these questions and assumptions about Jews in the Diaspora led me to the present project. It was important to learn more about those who had made the commitment to challenge "the establishment" and in a sense to give voice to those conventions in Israeli politics, a politics with which I felt greater affinity perhaps because it was part of my own family's experience and tradition. I thought I might even find some joy conducting research on what I described as a project on "what's left of the Jewish left" in US and Canadian traditions. I also believed, naively perhaps, that I would be entering a much "safer" activist, and thus more familiar, political terrain where my identity would not be the source of curiosity or suspicion.

In this chapter, which follows the work of Desmond and Dominguez (1996), as well as Amy Kaplan's work in American Studies, my aim is "both to decenter the United States and analyze its centralized [and I would add, its internalized] imperial power" (Kaplan 2004: 10). I do not mean to idealize or to romanticize the efforts of Jewish activists living and "acting out" in the US, though it has to be said that I do admire their work. The point is to understand and to appreciate the extent to which their lives are marked by difference because they live in the center of an empire. That is, while there are similarities with how Jewish community members respond to Jewish activists in Canada, there is one important feature that strikes me as equally important to think about and through: the fear of speaking out and being castigated by non-Jews. This never came up in my discussions with Jewish activists in Canada.

Apart from post-Zionist debates, which are mostly oriented to academic audiences, we have only recently seen the emergence of a few book-length studies that offer Jewish dissident perspectives on Israel (see, for example, Landy 2011; Kushner 2003; Katz 2004; Chomsky 2014, among others). These often supplement and reprint articles that have been available on alternative and indie-media sites. Missing from all of this are ethnographies of Jewish dissident organizations, of groups that aim their criticisms of Israel to North American as well as Israeli audiences. However, I do not believe that any of these books or articles point to the kinds of challenges or forces that people experience in their everyday lives, in activist as well among non-activist circles.

This chapter presents one strand of my thinking about the relationship of Jewish identity and Diaspora activism in the US. It suggests that dissident identities are rooted in a particular recognition of Jewishness, a recognition that is shaped in the context of US and Israeli relationships. As Pnina Werbner noted: "Diasporas . . . are both ethnic-parochial and cosmopolitan" (2005: 130) (see also Boyarin and Boyarin 1993). I argue that by foregrounding their Jewish identity, dissidents both challenge and compel the legitimation of Zionism; and that the presence of the dissident invites the opportunity for negotiating their Diaspora identities and relationships. With the pervasive charge that criticism of Israel is tantamount to a new form of anti-Semitism, I think it is also important to examine the context and role of Jewish Diaspora dissidents: those who identify a strong attachment to Israel but who are resolutely critical of the state's practices.

I want to argue that dissidents in the US have an additional burden, one that I do not believe has been fully articulated from within a critical post-Zionist or what I will call a post-diasporicist perspective (e.g., Butler). While it is important for readers to understand the history of US anti-Semitism, it is equally important to appreciate the extent to which several periods of US history have been marked by Jewish activism in progressive movements including labor, civil rights, and antiwar movements (e.g., Brodkin). Many in these communities claimed that Jews were disproportionately and negatively affected by the backlash—for example, McCarthyism. This point becomes important in the analysis I provide below. I argue that, for many dissidents, engaging in these activist organizations is part of a long history of Jewish engagements rather than a break. But, in the conjuncture since the attacks on the US in 2001, it seems (based on interviews, discussions on blogs, newsletters, and media) as well as the literature on the US "homeland" (see esp. Kaplan 2003, 2004), some have come to experience a certain vulnerability, not only from within their own institutions (e.g., from synagogue leaders) for their criticism of Israeli policy, but also for what may be identified as their intertwined criticism of US foreign policy. This exposes Jews to anti-Semitism, from both left and right, and continues to affect Jewish life in the US.[1] For the right, these activists endanger all Jews by producing a counter-narrative that can be interpreted as exposing a certain crisis of belonging—for they do not simply contradict the US's self-aggrandizing narrative of support for human rights and democracy but they openly criticize US foreign policy and its support for Israel. This is a many-layered argument, one that relies to a great extent on my access to and examination of relevant blogs, newsletters, and listservs since 2007, and on a number of informal discussions as well as open-ended interviews conducted in the US.[2]

Diaspora dissident activism leads to questions about the nature and meaning of exclusion and has implications for understanding the diverse forms and meanings of belonging, especially for those who self-identify as diasporic. Rather than looking at the role of the Israeli state—that is, officially-sanctioned effects on Diaspora organizing in the US and Canada, I became more interested in the relationships and alliances that grassroots Israeli civil society organizations had built and the extent to which they were affecting US and Canadian Jewish organizations and community activism with respect to the Israel/Palestine crisis. I was not interested in assessing whether Jewish dissent is justified, but rather in understanding the discourse of dissent—at once cultural and political—and what hopes and longings were expressed and deferred. Several more interviews were conducted in earnest between 2008 and 2010, some in Canada (which I do not refer to here) and the rest in the US Midwest (which I do).

Spending time with activists, I learned that they seek to redefine the US public's interpretation of the Israel/Palestine conflict and the toll it has taken on Israeli and Palestinian lives. Their actions constitute a refusal to allow the Jewish institutional establishment, the Israeli government, or the US government to obscure the political and experiential realities of the conflict. In their public performances, they set about to disturb the official discourse about Jews and their relationship to Israel—with placards like: "I am Jewish and I oppose the Occupation"—while also undermining the legitimacy of the US's role in supporting Israeli policies. Activists rely on a politics of visibility and performance, existing in imagined, discursive, and physical domains of the public sphere. Their stated goals include encouraging discussions across the political spectrum. While often paying tribute to Israeli and Palestinian activists, they mobilize the rhetoric of shame against those who uphold the status quo. Witness the "Young Jewish and Proud" organization, which emerged after the November 2010 Annual General Meeting of the Jewish Federation held in New Orleans. Since I first presented this study at the American Anthropology Association meetings, which happened to also be held in New Orleans that year, I think it appropriate I share a few lines from "The Young Jewish Declaration," which is framed by four headings, as follows: "We exist"; "We remember"; "We refuse"; and "We commit." In the final stanza, they write: "We are young Jews, and we get to decide what that means." I think it important to note that those of us interested in Diaspora politics and the Israel/Palestine conflict may well have focused too much of our attention on the role that Israel and, in particular, Zionist narratives play in imagining Diaspora and Diaspora imaginings. I include myself in this (forthcoming [2004], 2007, but see also Beinart 2012; Boyarin and Boyarin 1993; Boyarin 1994, 1996). In doing so, we have neglected to focus our attention on the attachment of Jews to the United States and what it means for them to be "Americans." I argue, as well, that this has implications for how they might perceive their roles—as well as their vulnerabilities—when taking a critical stance, with respect to US-Israel and US-Palestine relations as well as, more broadly, US foreign policy.

My interest here, and the contribution that I think US-based ethnographic research can make, is in understanding what difference it makes that these activists are establishing and engaging in US Jewish organizations; what pressures they endure; and how they overcome such challenges. What I want to share is how I learned to examine Jewish identity and experiences from the perspective of Empire.

I would suggest that by reorienting ourselves from the uncritical perspectives on Israel we can better explain how Jewish vulnerabilities circulate: not so much because it is dangerous to come out Jewish and American as it is to come out Jewish and un-American. On more than one occasion, I was told that Jews in the US are not willing to take any chances, surrounded as they are by Christian communities or in environments, like the one where I conducted some of my interviews, where "Palin 2012" signs were abundant. US Jews may have established their own institutions and gained access to formal, elite, and state institutions, corporations, and the academy, but they still feared being singled out.

A crucial empirical and ethnographic pivot in this project is the issue of why Jews would choose to campaign against support for Israel, why they choose to mobilize specifically as Jews, instead of joining more broad-based peace and human rights organizations, for example. It seems that their self-conscious desire to perform their activist identities as Jews, compels their audiences—Israelis, US citizens, Jews, and non-Jews—to recognize the performance itself as a transgression of essentialist expectations associated with that identity. It seems, as well, that the presence of the dissident within the Jewish community invites the opportunity for negotiating Diaspora identity for, on the one hand, it compels a critique of Zionism's dismissal of the possibility for the full expression of Jewishness outside of the State of Israel (i.e., in the Diaspora) and, on the other hand, it re-inscribes the importance of Zionism—with Israel at the center of Zionist thought and practices—for Jewish expressions of identity.[3]

I think it is important to note that the definition of Diaspora that I use here limits the discussion to one that is about Jews who feel and enact some attachment to Israel as their homeland. Zionist definitions would have it that all Jews living outside of Israel are "Diaspora" Jews. But I think this wrong, not only because it assumes a Zionist framing of the issue (wherein Jews belong in Israel), but it is also too broad a stroke as it undermines or under-appreciates the extent to which some Jews have very little or no attachment to the Israeli state (see also my discussion in Habib 2004). What may be more controversial about my definition, or the way I use the word here, is that I would argue that any Jew who is active—whether as a Zionist, anti-Zionist, post-Zionist, or diasporicist (which I will explain below)—the very fact that they are actively engaged places them in a diasporic relationship to Israel. If one looks at the way that even those critical of Israel speak of their positioning—as Jews engaged in primarily Jewish organizations—their engagement is primarily on the basis that Israel claims to be a Jewish state and as such they believe they have a "responsibility" to speak out (the name of one organization, Not in My Name, epitomizes this). So, whether as liberal Zionists (who support the idea of a Jewish state and a two-state solution—organizations like American Friends of Peace Now,[4] the New Israel Fund, or J Street); anti-Zionist or post-Zionist (as, for example, Jewish Voice for Peace, Not in My Name, or Independent Jewish Voices) whose members believe Israel should become a state that would define itself as representative of all its citizens rather than primarily as a Jewish state; are supporters of a secular one-state idea; and/or support the Boycott Divestment Sanctions campaign—all have a deep attachment to and resolve for a different Israel.

My definition allows for Diaspora dissidents to be included in discussions about Israel and Diaspora politics. In the main, and until very recently, only those who were uncritical of Israeli politics were taken seriously in such discussions. Witness, for example, the degree to which representatives from AIPAC (America Israel Political Action Committee) make it into the news; or examine the tenor of the discussions that followed the publication of Mearsheimer and Walt's *The Israel Lobby* or Peter Beinart's *The Crisis of Zionism*. The assumption is that all US Jews support the actions of the state; that they would only support a politician who does the same, and as such, politicians are beholden to a certain type of support for the state; and that, as such, if there is a real problem for contemporary Jewish identity, it is the extent to which such attachments have declined.

Dissidence and the Israel-Palestine Conflict

What dissident Jews do in a range of organizations is to simultaneously publicize their outrage and concern as well as to educate the US public on the Israel-Palestine crisis, from a perspective that is generally allied with left-of-center political parties as well as Israeli Jewish peace and human rights organizations. As I noted earlier, they do so as Jews and from within Jewish organizations and as individuals. Some (like Alan and Alf, below) live in smaller communities that cannot support a larger organization so they find themselves affiliated with those—such as Not in My Name—in larger, urban centers, sharing the expenses of speakers, educational materials, and the like. They often find themselves working in self-styled ecumenical peace groups, Christian-based pacifist circles (for example, Mennonite or Quaker organizations); or in organizations that emerge in response to a crisis (for example, antiwar organizing around the invasion of Iraq). These activists also shared how difficult it has been to be singled out in such organizations; often forced to explain Israeli actions or US policy vis-à-vis Israel and/or the Palestinians, as well as Iran and the Arab world. This is one of the reasons they preferred to work in Jewish organizations. As they tell it, Jewish activists living in larger urban areas and active within Jewish organizations can find greater comfort because they are working alongside other Jews. To have such communal support, especially in times of crisis when there is more criticism from family, friends, and community members, is invaluable and the toll of isolation also underestimated.[5]

Among the things that Jewish dissent organizations have in common is their support of nonviolence; their criticism of Israel's military occupation of the West Bank and settlement practices; their opposition to militarism and Israeli human rights abuses; and criticism of US inaction on the peace process. Some organizations have also, in times of war, criticized the US's seemingly unconditional support of Israeli actions (e.g., the 2006 war in Lebanon; the 2008 and 2014 wars in Gaza). All support some form of Palestinian autonomy or state sovereignty and self-determination.

In the course of my preparation for conducting fieldwork in 2007, I began to follow and to keep a log of some of the activities of organizations that had informed the work of Diaspora dissidents, including the US-based Jewish Voice for Peace, Jewish Witnesses for Peace, Not in My Name, UK and Canadian Independent Jewish Voices, Friends of Peace

Now, Settlement Watch, as well as Israeli human rights organizations like B'Tselem, Rabbis for Human Rights, Checkpoint Watch, and the Israeli Committee Against Housing Demolitions. Several organizations have been established since 2007, the most prominent of which are the US-based J Street, which is more center than left, and the Boycott, Divestment and Sanctions movement, which is more radical than center.

Some of the most prominent organizations in the mid to late 2000s in the US included Friends of Peace Now, Settlement Watch, Jewish Witnesses for Peace, The Jewish Voice for Peace, Jews Against the Occupation, and Independent Jewish Voices. J Street emerged after I had begun my initial research so I did not meet US activists involved in this organization but I have been following their work and their prominence has certainly risen in the last few years.

Except for Americans for Peace Now, which was founded in the early 1980s in response to Israel's war in Lebanon, many of these organizations emerged in the years following the signing of the Oslo Peace Accords between the Palestine Authority and the State of Israel in 1993. Some of these groups are considered more radical than others, because of their recognition of the Palestinian right of return but, in the main, their policies support Oslo-like proposals for what is commonly referred to as the "two-state solution" or "land for peace" solution, which broadly speaking, would place Israel's official border along the "Green Line" (the armistice line or border between Jordan and Israel as well as between Israel and Egypt before the 1967 War) and lead to the evacuation of Israeli settlements built beyond that line. It is commonly referred to as an exchange of land for peace, the end result of which would be to establish a Palestinian state alongside a Jewish one.

During times of extreme violence and crises, these organizations often called for an immediate ceasefire and the resumption of negotiations between the combatants, often carefully calling on "both sides" to take responsibility for the upsurge in violence. Interestingly enough, most of the policies and principles taken up by these organizations are not especially radical—if one were to take seriously that official Israeli policy is also for a negotiated settlement with the Palestinians. However, these activist organizations do not rely on official statements so much as on reports by Israeli journalists, academics, and Israeli, Palestinian, and international NGOs that often give the lie to Israel's official position on progress and peace.

Here we take a closer look at some of these groups. The Brit Tzedek v'Shalom/Jewish Alliance for Justice and Peace was founded on 30 April 2002 in Washington, DC. Its Founding Principles included, and I quote from their platform at that time:

The evacuation of Israeli settlements in the Occupied Territories. These settlements are a major obstacle to peace, a tremendous financial burden to Israel and do little, if anything, to enhance Israel's security . . . and they bring grave harm to the Palestinians living under Occupation . . .

The termination of terrorism and state-initiated violence against all individuals with special care being taken to avoid harming civilians. We seek to build a future in which both peoples use non-violent means to resolve social and political inequities . . .

A complete end to the Israeli military occupation of the territories occupied since 1967 in the West Bank, the Gaza Strip and East Jerusalem with border adjustments agreeable to both parties.

The establishment of a viable Palestinian state based on the pre-1967 borders alongside Israel . . .

The establishment and recognition of Jerusalem as the capital of both states . . .

A just resolution of the Palestinian refugee problem that takes into account the needs and aspirations of both peoples. Such a resolution is crucial to achieving a just peace, and therefore must acknowledge Israel's share of responsibility for the plight of Palestinian refugees while also respecting the special relationship between the State of Israel and the Jewish people.

Furthermore, they note: ". . . as Jews and US citizens, we have a special responsibility to urge our government to pursue policies consistent with the requirements of a just peace for Israel and the Palestinian people."[6]

Probably the most well-known and most-cited organization among activists is Jewish Voice for Peace (JVP). It was formed as early as 1996 in response to, as they write, "the provocative opening by the Netanyahu government of an archaeological tunnel under Jerusalem's Temple Mount that led to confrontations in which 65 Palestinians and 14 Israelis were killed." They held their first demonstration outside San Francisco's Federal Building and they write, "The original message was intended for the Clinton Administration: American Jewry is not a monolithic movement which categorically supports all of the policies of the government of Israel, and thousands of American Jews, in partnership with the interfaith community, demand justice and equality for Israelis and Palestinians."

They describe themselves as "a diverse and democratic community of activists inspired by Jewish tradition to work together for peace, social justice, and human rights." They seek: "A US foreign policy based on promoting peace, democracy, human rights, and respect for international law"; "[a]n end to the Israeli occupation of the West Bank, the Gaza Strip, and East Jerusalem;" "[a] resolution of the Palestinian refugee problem consistent with international law and equity"; and "[a]n end to all violence against civilians." Furthermore, they state: "We are among the many American Jews who say to the US and Israeli governments: 'Not in our

names!'" It is important to note the language used to describe Israeli practices. For example, JVP's position is as follows:

> The United States must stop supporting repressive policies in Israel and
> elsewhere. US military aid to countries in the Middle East must be based on
> rigorous enforcement of the Arms Export Control and Foreign Assistance Acts,
> which mandate that military aid may be used for only defensive purposes
> within the recipient country's borders, and that aid may not be delivered to
> countries that abuse human rights. Under these guidelines, US military aid to
> Israel must be suspended until the occupation ends, since the occupation itself
> is in violation of these guidelines. Military aid allows Israel to avoid making
> serious efforts to resolve the Israeli-Palestinian conflict, as well as conflicts with
> its other neighbors. It enables the occupation, contributes to the devastation of
> Palestinian society and fosters the increasing militarization of Israeli society.

JVP also calls for:

> the suspension of military aid to other human rights abusers and occupiers in
> the Middle East. This aid helps prop up autocratic and repressive regimes, pro-
> motes violations of human rights and international law, obstructs democratic
> movements, prolongs the Israeli-Palestinian conflict, and fosters militarism
> and violence at home and abroad.

One of the most radical of the organizations is Jews Against the Occupation
based in New York. One of their "points of unity" is as follows: "We as
American Jews reject the Israeli government assertion that it is 'necessary'
to subjugate Palestinians for the sake of keeping Jews safe. We assert that
security can only come from mutual respect, and that the occupation of
Palestine is only worsening the position of Jews in the Middle East and
around the world."

On aid to Israel, they point to the following: "The US government provides more aid to Israel than to any other country—the vast majority of
this is for military purposes. . . . This aid must end."

Their position on the return of Palestinians is fairly straightforward
in its simplicity, though not in its implications. They write, as follows:
"Thousands of Palestinians were driven out of their houses and off of their
farms during and after the creation of Israel. They must be allowed to
return to their homeland."

On anti-Semitism versus critiques of Israel, they are as defensive as the
other organizations seem to be:

> Jews Against the Occupation stands firmly against anti-Semitism and racism
> in all its forms. We see our historical struggle against anti-Semitism—a
> cornerstone of European white supremacist ideology—as inherently linked

to all struggles against oppression. We therefore stand in solidarity with the Palestinian people in their struggle for freedom.

But they go further than other organizations by rejecting the national basis for Jewish identity. For example, they note: "Judaism is a cultural and religious identity, which must not be equated with Zionism, a political movement. Criticism of the State of Israel, its policies, or the idea of a Jewish state does not by itself constitute anti-Semitism. Dismissing critics of Israel or of Zionism as 'anti-Semitic' is a means of stifling debate and masking the impact of the occupation."

Diasporic Relationships to Israeli Activists and Activism

Jewish peace organizations located in the US rely heavily for information and inspiration on Israeli activist organizations. The Israeli organizations include: Bat Shalom (a coalition of women's organizations, including Women in Black), B'Tselem, Checkpoint Watch, Physicians for Human Rights, Rabbis for Human Rights, Association for Civil Rights in Israel (ACRI), Bimkom (planning rights), and the Israeli Committee against Housing Demolitions (ICAHD). B'Tselem is probably one of the best known. It is an organization that explicitly calls upon Israelis to reflect on the image that they project to other Israelis, to the Palestinians, and to the world. According to their own documents, the name of the organization means "in the image of, which is derived from a biblical reference in Genesis 1:27: 'And God created humans in his image, in the image of God did He create him.'" In the context of their advocacy on behalf of those who are the victims of human rights abuses, B'Tselem wishes to reflect a more humane and humanitarian image.

In accordance with United Nations rulings and with the position of the majority of the world's governments, these organizations identify the West Bank and Gaza as militarily occupied territories whose populations must be governed in conformity with humanitarian law. At the broader political level, their positions are that Israeli settlements in the territories occupied in the 1967 war are illegal and that they must be evacuated. Moreover, they claim that the courts have been manipulated by policy-makers who, while claiming that land expropriations are necessary for the security of the state, are in actual fact aiming to change the demographic character of these areas in order to thwart any serious efforts for Palestinian self-determination, and to make more viable territorial annexation to the State of Israel.

Checkpoint Watch, in existence since 2001, is an organization of Israeli women who are opposed to the Israeli occupation in the territories and what they call "the systematic repression of the Palestinian nation." They "call for Palestinian freedom of movement within their own territory and for an end to the Occupation that destroys Palestinian society and inflicts grievous harm on Israeli society."

Empire, Jewish Activism, and Belonging

What I did not consider before I did this research was the extent to which being an American Jew also means being aware or fearful of US anti-Semitism; in part, this seems to be generated by historical practices wherein activist Jews were on the wrong side of power. This is historical memory and experience that needs to be understood not only from the right but also from the left.

I turn to Amy Kaplan's work on empire as it alerts us to the kind of work that has garnered an enormous amount of attention in American Studies and that might prompt anthropologists to consider this element when conducting their own field research in the US. In her work—a work that extends Said's work in *Culture and Imperialism* (1993)—we learn that empire (writ large) frames not only the terms for engagement with "the foreign" but also the domestic. Kaplan does not focus her attention on the domestic "front" in the way I use her work, but her piece was closest to articulating the position or positionality of activists who felt fearful about not only sharing their criticisms of Israeli politics but also making the connections between US foreign policy in relation to the Middle East (and Israel in particular) and their own criticisms of that policy. This led to the question: is it un-American to be critical of Israel?

In her article, "Homeland Insecurities" (2003: 87–88), Amy Kaplan, writes about the establishment of the department of Homeland Security, which followed the 2001 Al-Qaeda attacks on the US and with unpopular wars raging in Iraq and Afghanistan. Kaplan focuses her attention on the word "homeland" and I think it worth attending to what she writes:

> Although supporting the homeland, according to [Tom] Ridge [first Secretary of Homeland Security], calls for a unified nation, the meaning of homeland has an exclusionary effect that underwrites a resurgent nativism and anti-immigrant sentiment and policy. Where is there room for immigrants in the space of the homeland as a site of native origins, ethnic homogeneity, and rootedness in common place and past? How could immigrants possibly find inclusion in the homeland? How many immigrants and their descendants may identify with America as their nation but locate their homelands elsewhere,

as a spiritual, ethnic, or historical point of origin? Or how many go back and forth between two homes, let's say New York and the Dominican Republic? How many American citizens see Africa or Ireland, Israel or Palestine, each in very different ways, as their homeland, as a place to which they feel a spiritual or political allegiance and belonging, whether it literally constitutes a place of birth or not? Does the idea of America as the homeland make such dual identifications suspect and threatening, something akin to terrorism? *Are you either a member of the homeland or with the terrorists, to paraphrase Bush?* As Tom Ridge put it in his homey way, "the only turf is the turf we stand on," which precludes an urban vision of America as multiple turfs with contested points of view and conflicting grounds on which to stand. [my emphasis]

Most notably, she writes (p. 90):

. . . I am suggesting that the choice of the word puts into play a history of multiple meanings, connotations, and associations that work, on the one hand, to convey a sense of unity, security, and stability, but more profoundly, on the other hand, work to *generate forms of radical insecurity by proliferating threats of the foreign lurking within and without national borders.* [my emphasis]

The fear of criticizing the US takes on a much greater weight when the lens—in the search for "enemies"—has turned inward, to the domestic front. As such, criticizing US policy toward Israel, which is a policy of Empire, is tantamount to being critical of the US and as such could be considered "un-American" (in the same way that criticism of the US war in Vietnam and Iraq were also considered "un-American").

Profiles of the Activists

In this section, I draw extensively on interviews that I conducted in the late 1990s and later in the spring of 2009 in mid-sized cities, one on the East Coast and the other in the Midwest. I choose to profile these particular activists because I think they offer us a good deal to think about and they give us historical perspectives. Both are very articulate and committed activists. One—I call him Alan—has been entirely isolated from (and he would argue by) "the Jewish establishment," while the other—I call him Alf—continues to maintain strong ties to that community. In Alan's case, I was also able to learn quite a bit about how his fellow Jewish community members felt about him and his activism. Neither is "representative" of all of the activists I met or spoke with, but it is through both of them that I came to appreciate the role of "empire," the histories (and tradition) of Jewish social justice activism, of emplacement, as well as the continued sense of vulnerabilities among Jews living in the US. Before shifting to a deeper analysis of two activists, I would like to provide a glimpse into some of the issues and concerns that others, activist and non-activist, raised with respect to anti-Semitism.

One of the older activists that I spoke to, she was in her sixties at the time, I call her Beth, began as a feminist activist working in association with the Democratic Party. She had shifted her attention to Jewish causes and especially the Israel-Palestine conflict during the Oslo period. Making that shift, she tells me, was very difficult on her marriage. Her family, as well as her spouse's family, "was practically wiped out" in the Holocaust. She told me that "[f]amily is pretty much what my husband and I created. I have one sister and he has no siblings so our family is very small . . . and it's a very close family." For her spouse, any association with Israel is "complicated." As she explained, it is:

> about a deliberate strategy to try not to be persecuted again by assimilating. He feels that way even more than I do. I mean, for example, he worked for [a major transportation manufacturer] and became pretty high up and in a very large corporation and he felt rightly or wrongly that . . . if it was well-known that he was Jewish, he would not have risen to that point that he did. Now I could say that's ludicrous but he felt that way and so he totally assimilated and it will be problematic for me on Friday nights, for example, when I am going to want to go to this little group that's formed . . . it's a group of people that get together who are Jewish . . . it is a new progressive [organization that has formed] around the country . . .

For reasons I cannot fully explain, Beth's concerns—and those of her spouse—did not even strike me as interesting when she first shared them with me, perhaps because the focus of my attention was on activist practices rather than her experiences of them in relation to her community. It was only after my interview with Alan that I returned to look over my research transcripts and notes, and I found to my surprise that she and her spouse's attitudes were not entirely unique. By 2012, and on more than one occasion, I was repeatedly being told by non-activist Jews that the US is an anti-Semitic society; but that most anti-Semites knew how to be "polite" and "politically correct," especially in the company of other Jews.

In May and June 2012, I had several conversations with US Jews, some but not all of whom were involved in the Republican Party who went so far as to tell me that they feared the re-election of Obama would lead to the destruction of Israel. They believed that Obama had "hidden" his more "radical views" in the 2008 election so that he could "get the Jewish vote" but that he would "rightfully lose all those votes" in 2012. In October 2012, several life-long Democrats expressed a similar sentiment, telling me that while their position was driven mostly by emotion, they did not believe they were alone. Many felt as much or more threatened by a left than a right anti-Semitism, more frightened by, as one person put it, Jews who are "openly and avidly . . . even madly pro-Palestinian . . . always critical of Israeli and US foreign policies in the region." Their fear was that activist Jews gave legitimacy to left anti-Semitism (where Israel is blamed for all that ails the Middle East) as well as right anti-Semitism (where Jews are represented as "controlling" the US's foreign policy culture in the interest of Israel).

Let me now turn to more in-depth overviews, with activists who are very articulate as well as very much engaged. I will begin with a profile of Alf, since his interview occurred in the time before the September 11 attack and the rise of "homeland security" but during what has often been referred to as the "Oslo Period" (between 1993 and 2000) following the signing of the Oslo Accords between the State of Israel and the Palestine Authority. The period signaled a time for changing perspectives and heated debates not only within Israel but also in Jewish communities across the US.

Alf

I interviewed Alf in a small café. He was a recently retired academic at the time. As a young boy, Alf had lived in Germany. His father had been "one of these archetypal German Jews who were very patriotic. [He had] been in the First World War and so on." Alf lived out World War II, from 1939 to 1948, with his mother in England. His father had been incarcerated in a concentration camp during the same period. All survived. After the war, Alf came to the United States.

When I asked Alf what relationship he had had to Israel as a young man, he initially said, "none," but then he went on to tell me that he had arranged to have his grandfather, who had been a rabbi in a large German city before the war, honored by a Zionist organization, and that his uncle, who had "fled [to Israel] from Hitler a month after he got to power" later "committed suicide there . . . [R]eally . . . it should be in my bones to be a Zionist in the sense of . . . wanting the Jewish State . . . as a refuge . . . [T]here were an awful lot of Jews from . . . my home town . . . who . . . went to Palestine as it . . . was . . . a refuge." For Alf, Israel was a site of refuge but not for himself, and while he said he did not have "any particular attachment to the state," explaining that he felt he had always identified as a Jew without any relationship to either communal or religious institutions in the Jewish community.

Since the mid-1980s, Alf had made his connections to Israel through activist organizations. It was his strong "sense of duty" that led him to his activism, which included writing many memoranda to the community about his position on Israel's military occupation of the Palestinian territories and its settlement policies in those regions. He had traveled to Israel as well as the Palestinian territories on many activist-organized and community-based organization trips, some organizations were more radical than others, he told me. As he reflected on his activist practices, and the criticisms that he endured, he noted that he had the ability to speak to Germans as well as to Palestinians and, he practically whispered: "I told you, I get along well with 'the enemy'."

While in many ways Alf reflected Peace Now's pragmatism, an organization that was committed to a land-for-peace resolution to the Israel-Palestine conflict, Alf went further. For Alf, Israel would become the Jewish state while the majority of the West Bank and Gaza would eventually become a Palestinian state. At the time Alf held this position, through the 1980s and into the late 1990s, the US administration had not yet made any commitment to support a Palestinian State.[7]

In all of his accounts, Alf expressed both a sentimental attachment and activist devotion to the cause for peace in the region. When I asked him why he was so engaged in Israeli-based politics, he said: ". . . I see myself as literally contributing to the solution of these problems. I mean I regard myself as an activist in that sense. Now the only way I can be an activist is with a financial contribution plus talking it out. And I think that is really all one can do from the outside."

Alf felt that the kind of engagement he participated in was all he could do as someone who had chosen not to live in the state. He told me that through activism he hoped to achieve: "[o]ne thing: to see the kind of Israel that one dreamed about . . . but also I think I'm really committed to the Palestinians, I mean as a liberal person and thirdly, I guess that as a social scientist, I'm interested [in Israel because] . . . it's an intriguing situation . . . [T]here's no doubt that sort of intellectual curiosity also plays a part."

The Israel that Alf dreamed of is democratic and just. His hope is that one day Palestinians would have a democratic state alongside Israel's. Alf had been "pleased" with the signing of the Oslo Agreement saying he had "read [it] very carefully" and had been "struck" by, as he put it, "the repeated use of the phrase 'legitimate national aspirations of Palestinians.' It struck me as just about coming as close to promising that there would be a state as any document would."

Despite the fact that what circulated in the community as well as within US foreign policy circles at that time was an emphasis on Palestinians as "terrorists" who posed a "security" threat to all Israelis, Alf never used this language. In fact his only concern with the then-Palestinian leader, Yasser Arafat, was that he was "not the world's greatest administrator." He felt that Arafat's corruption was "understandable, in a way" and would not be so troubling except for the fact that "the need for efficient people" was "great" at this point and time. But Alf also saw Israel as a kind of living lab.

What most intrigued me about Alf's interest was that he was a man who professed to be "in love with statistics" but who was engaged in a scenario where the numbers did not add up, so to speak. He continually distanced his emotional tie to Israel and yet it was clear that there was an attachment that was not at all objective. It seemed that Alf was driven by a general liberal orientation but it was one that was also informed by his own experiences as a child survivor. For example, Alf told me he was more afraid of the unreasonable, ambitious, and ideologically driven agenda of some of Israel's leaders than the role that Orthodox religious leaders played in Israeli society; and it was not that the Palestinians or any outsiders that endangered Israel's existence, it was an incompetent leadership and a confused public.

When speaking to friends and family about Israel Alf tended to discuss the problems there. He would not be afraid to tell people what he saw while traveling through the Palestinian areas, though he recognized that this would mean he was not very popular when he did so. He was especially worried that Jews in the US were not active enough about Israeli issues. He said:

> . . . [I]t is time to take offense [at the things that Israel does] and here again I will have to be extraordinarily careful in the way I put it, but the American Jews continue to blame the Germans of 1933 for not speaking up when after 1933 speaking up meant you were in physical danger . . . of going to concentration camps and so on. They can't even speak up within their own communities when there is absolutely no danger whatsoever . . . They get nasty and people don't like having nastiness thrown at them and I think all it takes . . . is a firm counter and saying, 'Look this is unacceptable behavior, you cannot do this.'

For Alf it was important to stand up and to declare one's opposition to Israel and the US's position on the Israel-Palestine conflict, and especially vis-à-vis the Palestinians. He said that he had few emotional ties to the state but he was highly committed to helping Israel become a place he could be proud of. His reference to Germany was telling:

> I think this is a very complicated situation in which Israel is supposed to represent something for Jews as a whole and, after all I don't vote [in Israel] . . . not being a resident, but I think otherwise, as I say, it is an unusual relationship. It isn't even an unusual relationship. The Irish in America support . . . the IRA and I'm sure some don't think that the IRA is a bloodthirsty organization and disapprove of it. So it's fairly typical I think of people who are bound to a certain other country to do this.

Note how Alf assumes he has a special responsibility as a Jew to Israel, to Israelis, and to Palestinians while then also comparing Jews' ties to Israel to that of Irish-Americans to the Irish Republican Army (IRA). Perhaps because he is a secular Jew, he believes that the Jews' relationship to Israel is normal in a historical rather than sacred sense.

Alan

Alan, who was once an insider, now offers an outsider's or dissident's perspective. His contention—made in the context of the ongoing wars in Iraq and Afghanistan and just months after Obama had been inaugurated in 2009—is that speaking out against Israel puts Jews in the uncomfortable position of speaking out against US foreign policy as well.

Alan grew up in upper middle class Los Angeles in the late 1950s and early 1960s. "[T]here were lots of Jews and in my high school . . . I never felt distant from being Jewish [growing up there]." His ex-wife who had been born in a Displaced Persons camp in Germany had grown up in Brooklyn. In 1974, he spent five months on a kibbutz in Israel. He told me, with some sarcasm, that theirs was a "mixed marriage": he had a bourgeois Jewish upbringing, and she had an orthodox and socialist one. He had always been politically involved but it was not until the mid-1990s, when he was living in Delaware, that he became more aware of "what was really going on." By the time he had moved from the northeast to the Midwest in the late 1990s, he had become outspoken and engaged. He recounted how enthusiastic he had been about a Jewish history series at his new Temple, until the professor began the contemporary history lecture with "if you want to be critical of Israel, you should move there and vote." Alan had not been in town for long so he did not speak up. He said: "I'd been . . . volunteering . . . [M]y wife . . . was a very good synagogue member, and our kid was a model synagogue student . . . I wasn't gonna [mess that up] . . ."

By 2000, the second Palestinian *intifada* (uprising) had erupted in the West Bank and he had begun writing letters to the editor. In response, he told me: "There were several very nasty letters . . . 'We've had enough of this guy.' 'We're going to call him a self-hating Jew.' 'We're going to compare him to 'capos' in the concentration camps.'" He explained:

> There is this sort of spectrum within a Jewish community like this . . . [where "Palin for 2012" signs abound]. There are people who identify as moderate . . . [I]t's not that they're really critical of Israel. They just think of themselves as . . . people who . . . tone down the rhetoric a little bit and . . . and maybe reach out to the local Muslims a little bit . . . [W]hether they're identified as moderate, or . . . they . . . understand that the *Nakba* [Arabic for "the catastrophe"] was a *Nakba* . . . that there really was . . . ethnic cleansing . . . they really don't follow

up on the implications of that . . . There's very little dissonance between being a good liberal, and a civil libertarian even . . . and supporting Israel . . .

Alan describes his experience with his local rabbi this way:

> I always felt like I was dealing with this big pillow, this . . . large cushy thing in which I couldn't penetrate. I couldn't get through to him what was really upsetting me. And his attitude was sort of like, "Well, you have to support Israel." There's just an awful lot of incentive . . . not to . . . question the authorities. That relates to the fact that . . . [y]ou're a privileged white person [in this society]. You want to identify with US foreign policy. . . . I really think that . . . being radically critical of US foreign policy and radically critical of Israel, I mean, that's the same thing, and they don't want to go either place. I mean, if you went one place, you'd be in the same place. . . .

The fact that Jews in the US were once "radicals" was something he held dear, but he noted that:

> people would look back and say that they were proud of Jewish involvement in the labor movement in the 1930s and . . . everybody loves to identify with the . . . anti-sweatshop movement . . . but this doesn't connect to radicalism. . . . Everybody has this lineage, but now it's just history, because to get through the [McCarthyism of the] '50s . . . I mean, it really left its mark, it really scared people.

But it was Alan's next point that caught me off guard, and which led me to thinking further about the place of US Jewish activists both within their own communities as well as in the US more generally. He said:

> But then I think the '67 war gave us a win . . . We were floundering in Vietnam and people . . . could look at Israel and say, "you know what? Israel—they know how to fight a war. They do it; they get it over with. It's done!" And there's all this mystique about . . . Israel, Israelis, and their fighting capabilities. . . . Israel really came to the fore and people really started to love Jews . . . It was in that militaristic context. . . . [I]t kind of counteracted what was going on in Vietnam.

Since the war in Iraq, he told me:

> There just wasn't any Jewish person who wanted to be seen as Jewish and . . . who would show their face [at an anti-war demonstration]? Out of all these liberal[s], many of whom . . . were opposed or had a lot of doubts about the Iraq war . . . couldn't express their opposition in that context. . . . show any solidarity whatsoever with that cause. I . . . believe . . . that for elites . . . let's say one of the benefits for the identification of the US with Israel is the fact that it serves to silence what might be more vocal Jewish criticism of US foreign policy. It sort of de-radicalize[s] . . . Jewish culture . . .

Later, he says: "[E]ven if it weren't for Israel, you'd have a bourgeois Jewish culture that supports basic US foreign policy."

Alan told me that he believes the communal narrative supporting Israel is one that community leaders—many of them Jewish men—feel they must aggressively protect from an anti-Semitic world that once cruelly rejected them. He added:

> And Jewish men, older Jewish men—[have] what I call the "big shot" factor . . . Once the Israel thing kicked in [in the 1960s], that was the hook they hung their hat on, and they've been doing it . . . ever since. And it's the last thing . . . they're going to give up. . . . [T]hat's what makes them feel important. And I may be a little cynical, but . . . these were business people. They were hardware store owners and stuff . . . and they don't see it in any kind of intellectual or political terms. . . . [T]hey may not even be interested in the politics of it in any sophisticated sense . . . [N]ot only are they identified with these institutions, . . . these people have grown these institutions, they've funded these institutions . . . It's their money. . . .

Moreover, Alan suggested, a rigid or fixed communal narrative is what silences others and it is what the leadership uses against activists, especially those considered by outsiders (non-Jews) to be "insiders" (Jews). In other words, any criticism of the US must be managed but especially if it might expose the community to criticism from a hostile environment. More often than not, when addressing these activists or their performances, leaders are entirely dismissive. The statement heard most often: "They're not one of us."

Alan was also scathing in his criticism of the popular book *The Israel Lobby* by Mearsheimer and Walt. On the one hand, he explained, it gives the "big shots" in the community a sense of their own power. On the other hand, and this worries Alan, it assumes you accept "the basic goodness of US foreign policy. Like, *we would be doing the right thing if it weren't for these Jews*. I think it's a very dangerous argument . . . I don't want the Palestinian rights movement and the general antiwar movement to be about Jews . . . I think that [our Jewish] identification with Israel makes all these things more difficult, not less difficult . . ." (my emphasis).

After nineteen years, Alan's marriage breaks down in no small part due to his activism. Reflecting on how he antagonized others and asking himself if there was another way, he explained:

> Maybe if I really got to know people . . . so that they knew that I was a good guy and a serious person and a good Jew and they could see how wonderful my son is and how wonderful my wife is, and my god, she's a Holocaust survivor! . . . Maybe if I had gone through this whole thing and been very conscious and cautious and pragmatic and diplomatic about it, I could have

been someone who worked from within, you know? But, in the final analysis, I would say, probably not. . . . [There are] . . . these institutional forces . . . [and] once you go there, then people will . . . step back . . . and say . . . "What are you saying here—are you really one of us?" . . . [I]t's not just where you're going in relationship with Israel and Palestine, it's where you're going in relationship with US foreign policy, Iraq, militarism, the whole thing. Who wants to hang out with those peaceniks? They're not us . . . I've always called it "thick propaganda."

"Thick propaganda" was a term I thought a good deal about after meeting with Alan and learning how others in his community felt about Jewish activists and their "anti-Israel" or "pro-Palestinian" activities (mostly negative). In light of what I was learning in 2009 from activists like Alan, I felt I needed to think about the US as a culture of imperialism that engenders a vulnerability for Jews who as Biale et al. (1998) make clear are "insider/outsiders."

In a way that I think may be unique, these activists alert us to an imperial presence. Their perspective leads us to see important political and cultural processes and institutions shaped by and within the context of empire. They reveal how empire is alive in institutional life, how heroic narratives are developed and incorporated into US history, as well as how militaristic and masculinist patriotism/patriotic citizenship may be embodied. As far as I know, these questions have not been taken up in the context of US Jewish identity or rather, Jewish American identifications in the context of the Israel/Palestine conflict.

I want to make one proviso: what dissident activists identify as "American" is not necessarily very different in form from non-Jewish identifications. However, in the context where there is the ever-present fear of the emergence of a repressed anti-Semitism, we can better appreciate how any dis-identification with the US Empire would be perceived to be dangerous or put the community in peril, especially with all the discourses, institutions, policies and practices that make the contemporary US look imperial.

In "Not Really White—Again," as well as in his article on the Beastie Boys, Jon Stratton (2001) argues that Jews are not-quite-white. I am not as concerned with "race" politics as I am with the extent to which activists who organize as Jews might feel the pressures of "coming out Jewish" in an environment where their Jewish identities are considered ambiguous at best. Consider what Stratton writes in another of his discussions on US Jewish identity, this time in his book on *Jews, Race and Popular Music*: "Jews were also considered to have qualities—perhaps it would be better to say they continued to be considered to have qualities—which marked them as different from other whites and, indeed, might *place them outside* of whiteness" (my emphasis, 2009: 110; see also Stratton 2000). As such, they remain vulnerable.

Alan's and Alf's responses to my questions compelled me to understand their "isolation" from the perspective of a global analysis of empire. They describe their own activism in response to imperial projects and elucidate why they cannot identify with or relate to Israel except from within a framework that interrogates the late twentieth century's global landscape, which has been largely shaped by nationalism as well as US imperialism. By situating Jewish activism as anti-imperial, and their own work as against nationalism and its consequences, they bring to this discussion a consideration of US settler identification that might be (or has) otherwise been ignored if one were to focus exclusively on the activists' national— that is Jewish/Diaspora—context. By asking me to turn to explore the place of Jews in the imperial politics of the US's late-twentieth-century storyline, Alan and other activists compelled me to understand Jewish "American" identity in the context of the US's history of anticommunism, anti-Semitism, and Empire, and the very pressures that Jews—as well as other US citizens—have placed upon them to conform.

In their dissent, the activists literally demonstrate Israel's centrality in their lives, allowing it to become an important source of their Jewish identification. Their activism reveals their attachment to a Jewish social and political imaginary that does NOT require a re-articulation to the state through *aliyah* (immigration to Israel), rather expressing an affirmation of a legitimate Jewish and diasporic relationship to it. It is, after all, a struggle to claim a share and a voice in the Jewish, Israeli, and North American public and political spheres. The claim is that those who refuse that engagement because they believe it endangers Israel, reflect only an obedience to the state/establishment; they are accused of forming responses to what they perceive to be forbidden rather than a response to the criteria of what is just or unjust. In the range of their activities, including public demonstrations, action alerts, vigils, and information gathering and distribution, activists claim a democratic sensibility centered not on fear but confidence, even pride, and yet they endure the fear of and pressure from compatriots who fear their outspoken positioning.

Two things are happening simultaneously and may even appear contradictory in these excerpts. On the one hand, the strong relationship to Israel is expressed and its importance to Jewry is realized, reinforced, and performed. There is real investment in its future, its role in the international community, and its citizens. On the other hand, the relationship to Israel is not one of inferiority or deference; it is from a position of security and strength that the dissidents speak and act. Jewish investment in the social justice of others—Jews and Palestinians—constitutes a heroic value and commitment that affirms their identification with other activists but especially Israeli activists. Their practices of dissent strengthen and perform this commitment.

The activists appear to be saying, "We have a right to speak about Israel *because* we are Jews. We do not need to be Israelis to have that right." Thus, recognizing the agency afforded by the normalization of Diaspora identities is key for understanding the challenges that the dissidents have taken on.

In this chapter, I hoped to add a new dimension to the work on Diaspora Jews by suggesting that dissenters' relationships to Israel, while not guided by the same framing of Zionism that might be found among those who, for example, travel to Israel on organized tours or support the United Israel Appeal, is based on an awareness of a particular framing of or identification with Jewishness and Israeliness, and equally importantly, the responsibility that such a relationship entails (Habib 2004, 2007, 2013). These activists show not only the ability to listen to their Israeli compatriots but to act in their name.

Acknowledgments

For my mom, Amit Habib, whose faith in social justice activism is undaunted.

I would like to thank all of the activists and community members in the US who took part in this research from the mid-1990s through the mid-2000s. My thanks to the anonymous reviewers as well as Jane C. Desmond, Roger Sanjek, Geoffrey White, Virginia R. Dominguez, Ed Bruner, Melinda Bernardo, Matti Bunzl, Andrew and Harriet Lyons, Jim Novak, and the IFUSS seminar group for sharing their thoughts (many of them critical) on the first drafts of this paper. Research for this study was supported by the International Forum for US Studies at the University of Illinois, Urbana-Champaign, as well as the Robert Harding Fund/SSHRC, University of Waterloo.

Jasmin Habib is Associate Professor teaching political science at the University of Waterloo and the Global Governance Program at the Balsillie School of International Affairs. She is the editor-in-chief of *Anthropologica* (the journal of the Canadian Anthropology Society) and series editor of *Cultural Spaces*, University of Toronto Press. Among her honors is an Outstanding Teaching and Research Award from the University of Waterloo. A second edition of her book *Israel, Diaspora and the Routes of National Belonging* is forthcoming (University of Toronto Press, [2004] 2016).

Notes

1. Note, for example, authors like Foxman and Chesler on the right, and Dershowitz, Beinart, Walzer, Mersheimer and Walt on the liberal/left.
2. I was first alerted to these experiences in interviews I conducted in the late 1990s (though they were about Jewish travel to Israel and not peace and human rights activism) with people who lived in or around major urban centers (Washington, DC, San Francisco, New York, Boston).
3. There is a third way that I would call "post-diasporicist," celebration of diasporcist positionings and identities (e.g., Butler 2012) as against the nationalist/identitarian politics of Zionism/Israel—and though it is beginning to have some momentum in academic circles, at least, it does not yet resonate at the community level. I believe that Jonathan Boyarin (1994, 1996) is among the first to have written from this perspective in the US.
4. At the time of my early research in the 1990s in Canada and the US, Peace Now was considered "radical," engendering raucous responses to speakers' appearances at synagogues and community centers, mostly because the organization supported the "exchange" of land for peace and a two-state model and, as such, the right of Palestinians to a state of their own (see especially Habib 2004).
5. In one mid-sized Midwestern city, several people spoke to me about this, noting the fact that their children did not have access to the quality of Jewish education one would find in larger US cities, such as New York. In their "town," as they put it, Jewish education was provided on a weekly basis as "Sunday School."
6. Found at http://btvshalom.org//btvshalom.org/pressrelease/press040202.shtml.
7. In fact, this support would only come during George W. Bush's administration.

References

Beinart, Peter. 2012. *The Crisis of Zionism*. New York: Times Books. Kindle Edition.

Biale, David, Michael Galchinsky, and Susannah Herschel. 1998. *Insider/outsider: American Jews and Multiculturalism*. Berkeley: University of California Press.

Bodnar, John. 1992. *Remaking America: Public Memory, Commemoration, and Patriotism in the Twentieth Century*. Princeton, NJ: Princeton University Press.

Boyarin, Daniel and Jonathan Boyarin. 1993. "Diaspora: Generation and the Ground of Jewish Identity." *Critical Inquiry* 19(4): 693–725.

Boyarin, Jonathan. 1994. *Storm from Paradise: The Politics of Jewish Memory*. Minneapolis: University of Minnesota Press.

——. 1996. *Palestine and Jewish History: Criticism at the Border of Ethnography*. Minneapolis: University of Minnesota Press.

Brodkin, Karen. 1998. *How Jews Became White Folks and What That Says about Race in America*. New Brunswick, NJ: Rutgers University Press.

Burke, Carol. 2004. *Camp All-American, Hanoi Jane, and the High-And-Tight: Gender, Folklore, and Changing Military Culture*. Boston, MA: Beacon Press.

Butler, Judith. 2012. *Parting Ways: Jewishness and the Critique of Zionism*. New York: Columbia University Press.

Desmond, Jane C. and Virginia R. Dominguez. 1996. "Resituating American Studies in a Critical Internationalism." *American Quarterly* 48 (September): 475–90.

Glenn, Susan A. "The Vogue of Jewish Self-Hatred in Post World War II America," *Jewish Social Studies* 12(3): 95–136.

Habib, Jasmin. Forthcoming [2004]. *Israel, Diaspora and the Routes of National Belonging*. Second Edition. Toronto: University of Toronto Press.

———. 2007. "Memorialising the Holocaust: Diasporic Encounters." *Anthropologica* 49: 245–56.

———. 2013. "On the Matter of Return: Autoethnographic Reflections." *Ethnographic Reflections*. Fran Markowitz (ed) University of Indiana Press. Pp. 156–170

Kaplan, Amy. 2003. "Homeland Insecurities: Some Reflections on Language and Space." *Radical History Review* 85(Winter): 82–93.

———. 2004."Violent Belongings and the Question of Empire Today Presidential Address to the American Studies Association, Hartford, Connecticut, October 17, 2003." *American Quarterly* 56(1).

Katz, Adam, ed. 2004. *Prophets Outcast: A Century of Dissident Jewish Writing about Zionism and Israel*. New York: Nation Books. Kindle Edition.

Kushner, Tony and Alisa Solomon, eds. 2003. *Wrestling with Zion: Progressive Jewish-American Responses to the Israeli-Palestinian Conflict*. New York: Grove Books.

Landy, David. 2011. *Jewish Identity and Palestinian Rights: Diaspora Jewish Opposition to Israel*. London: Zed Books.

MacLeish, Ken. 2005. "The Tense Present History of the Second Gulf War: Revelation and Repression in Memorialization." *Text, Practice, Performance* 6: 69–84.

Manning, E. 2006. *The Politics of Touch: Sense, Movement, Sovereignty*. Minneapolis: University of Minnesota Press.

Mearsheimer, John J. and Stephen M. Walt. 2007. *The Israel Lobby and US Foreign Policy*. New York: Farrar, Straus and Giroux.

Morris, Benny. 1988. *The Birth of the Palestinian Refugee Problem*. Cambridge: Cambridge University Press.

Pershing, Linda. 2007. "Review of *Camp All-American, Hanoi Jane, and the High-And-Tight: Gender, Folklore, and Changing Military Culture*, by Carol Burke." *Journal of American Folklore* 120(477): 368–9.

Prell, Riv Ellen. 2003. "Response to Jonathan Sarna's Marshall Sklare Award Lecture" *Contemporary Jewry* 24(1): 170–73.

Said, Edward. 1993. Culture and Imperialism. New York: Vintage Books.

Stratton, Jon. 2000. *Coming Out Jewish: Constructing Ambivalent Identities*. London: Routledge.

———. 2001. "'Not Really White' Again: Performing Jewish Difference in Hollywood Films Since the 1980's." *Screen* 42: 142–66.

———. 2009. *Jews, Race and Popular Music*. Surrey, UK: Ashgate Publishing.

Werbner, Pnina. 2005, The predicament of diaspora and millennial Islam: reflections on September 11, 2001, in Sigrid Nokel and Levent Tezcan (eds), *Islam and the New Europe: Continuities, Changes, Confrontations*, Bielefeld: Verlag, pp. 127–51.

Wolfe, Alan. 2006. "Free Speech, Israel, and Jewish Illiberalism." *Chronicle of Higher Education* November 17.

Wolosky, Shira. 2003. "Israel and America: Revisioning History." *Michigan Quarterly Review* 42(1): 39–50.

Chapter Three

Biosecurity in the US
"The Scientific" and "the American" in Critical
Perspective

Limor Samimian-Darash

From a Small Ethnography to a Global Phenomenon

During the American Anthropological Association's annual meeting
in 2008, I participated in a panel on "uncertain futures" and presented
aspects of my research on preparedness for biological threats (including
infectious diseases and bioterrorism) in Israel. I suggested a conceptual-
ization of uncertainty in light of findings from a case study of that
country's preparedness for pandemic flu. The presentation that followed
mine involved a similar case study, focused on an analysis of preparedness for pandemic flu in the US that was carried out during the same years
I conducted my research in Israel.

   After all the participants had presented the papers, a discussant, a US
anthropologist, summarized the panel and the presentations. He referred
first to my paper, which he called "a beautiful ethnography of a small
country," and to the paper that followed mine, which he characterized as
presenting "the global aspects of the phenomenon [of preparedness]." My
paper's theoretical aspects and its examination of the concept of "uncertainty" went unmentioned; the discussant understood my study as an
ethnography of an exotic, small country—that is, as "cultural," detached,
as it were, from theories and concepts. Meanwhile, the US study was
viewed as reflecting a global phenomenon, not grounded in a specific field
and seemingly free of any local cultural prism.

What was interesting in that encounter was not just the discussant's cultural reading of my study and non-cultural reading of the US study but my subsequent realization that I myself had regarded my study as focused on the phenomenon of preparedness and, in a sense, as beyond culture. By framing it with theories of science and society, I had thought that my study did, indeed, investigate "the phenomenon" detached from local context. The discussant's external reading made me take another look at the cultural aspects of my case study.

Similarly, I had not considered the US case to be a study of a specific, local field. Much like the discussant, I had read the ideas in that presentation as part of an analysis of the broad phenomenon of preparedness and had paid no attention to its local cultural and social nuances. For me, both the US context and the scientific literature were disconnected from culture. That is to say, my theoretical analysis had provided me with a tool for reading my field non-culturally, as beyond the local. My own use of scientific professional discourse seemingly did not allow me to attribute local and cultural characteristics to it.

After I completed my research on Israeli preparedness for biothreats, I moved to the US where I conducted research on science and security in 2010–12. The research addressed the problem of biosecurity and types of solutions developed at the national level and in local scientific practices (i.e., committees of experts, regulation, and oversight). In particular, I studied the work of the National Science Advisory Board for Biosecurity (NSABB), which was established to advise the US government on the problem. My research combined perspectives of the anthropology of science and the anthropology of security, and examined security risks stemming from scientific developments and what was called the "dual-use problem." This unique arena (and despite my previous critique) might have led me to perceive both the US research field and the scientific discourse as non-cultural and global (as I had conveyed in my conference presentation).

In this chapter, I analyze the problem of biosecurity in the US to highlight the double binds that emerge when one sees science and the US as both *global* and *non-cultural*. In analyzing biosecurity in the US, and in focusing especially on research into the H5N1 ("bird flu") virus, I reconstruct this perceptual framing. My aim, in short, is to disconnect two double binds: the one that sees science as beyond local culture and society, and the other that accepts the US as "the global case." By presenting an empirical US study, then, I offer a concrete observation of what is usually taken as an abstraction and generality. Moreover, I locate the case in its particular historical context: how biosecurity became a problem in the US and how it was handled accordingly constitute the core of the discussion. My analysis is enabled by my particular positioning as a non-US researcher and by a particular anthropological mode of inquiry. Put another way, it addresses Virginia Dominquez and Jasmin Habib's questions in this volume, i.e., why *non-US-based* anthropology of the US might be necessary, and why *anthropology* as a discipline can contribute to that lacuna.

Biosecurity and the US

Biosecurity and the Life Sciences

The discourse on biosecurity that has emerged in the past two decades has included a concern with threats in four interconnected domains: emerging infectious diseases, bioterrorism, cutting-edge life sciences, and food safety (Lakoff and Collier 2008: 8). In the US, and especially since the anthrax attacks that closely followed 9/11, there has been a growing concern about bioterrorism and about how particular developments in the life sciences might contribute to that threat.

Originally, the concept of "biosecurity" referred to animal and agricultural safety: protecting livestock and crops (and, by extension, human consumers) from diseases. The formal discourse on the matter first came to prominence in the context of ranching operations in New Zealand (Masco 2014: 202). After the Bush Administration's declaration of a war on terror, the US biosecurity discourse gained in importance to the point of becoming a form of governance (Masco 2014), and part of a preparedness apparatus (Lakoff and Collier 2008).

The preparedness rationale caused a proliferation of laboratories devoted to research on dangerous pathogens. The number of laboratories devoted to BSL-4 pathogens (e.g., smallpox, Lassa fever, Ebola) in the US has grown from five, before 2001, to fifteen today. BSL-3 laboratories (researching pathogens such as SARS, West Nile virus, tuberculosis, and anthrax) have also multiplied; there are now 1,356 registered BSL-3 laboratories across the US. A different study found hundreds of such laboratories, including 219 laboratories registered with the Centers for Disease Control and Prevention to work on anthrax alone (Masco 2014).

Thus, although the anthrax attacks were not a result of new capacities of biology, they were perceived as such and opened "strategic spaces" of a "biosecurity" problem and possible interventions (Rabinow and Bennett 2012: 126). In particular, "the total US government spending on civilian biodefense research between 2001 and 2005 [increased] from $294.8 million to $7.6 billion" (Lakoff and Collier 2008: 10). Most of this funding was directed to life sciences research to improve defense against biothreats. Ironically, the proliferation of defense research also increased the concern about possible misuse of the same biological material and information that was produced in the name of preparedness and defense. In 2004 the National Academy of Sciences, which was set to investigate the problem of biosecurity in life sciences in the US, issued a report titled "Biotechnology Research in an Age of Terrorism," also known as the Fink Report. The report included a listing of select, dangerous agents identified as early as 2001 as requiring control to prevent their use in bioterrorism.

The report reframed the problem of biosecurity in the life sciences, moving away from the discussion of biosecurity, broadly defined, to what was named the "dual use dilemma." The term was borrowed from the language of arms control and disarmament—"Dual Use refers to technologies intended for civilian application that can also be used for military purposes" (Fink Report 2004: 18)—and applied to a case in which "the same technologies can be used legitimately for human betterment and misused for bioterrorism" (Fink Report: 1). In light of this definition, the Fink Report presented the following recommendations:

- To educate scientists regarding the dual use dilemma;
- To expand the existing biosafety oversight system before research is conducted;
- To review research plans according to seven criteria for review of experiments "involving microbial agents that raise concerns about their potential for misuse" (Fink Report: 130);
- To conduct a self-review of scientists and scientific journals before publication; and
- To establish the National Science Advisory Board for Biosecurity (NSABB).

Dual Use and Dual Use Research of Concern

In 2004, Health and Human Services (HSS) Secretary Tommy G. Thompson announced the establishment of the NSABB: "The new board will advise all Federal departments and agencies that conduct or support Life Sciences research that could fall into the 'Dual Use' category. The NSABB will be managed by the National Institutes of Health (NIH)" (HHS Press Office 2004).

As Dr Simon Natcher, an NIH policy consultant, who assists in the work of the NSABB, clarified:

> [The NSABB] wasn't meant to be a biosecurity board, even though it's in the name, but rather its goal was to deal with dual use research. It was set up to

establish some mechanism to deal with information that could be misused, the results of scientific research or the technologies, information technologies, products of the research that could be misused. It was only in the life sciences.

Thus, with the establishment of the NSABB, the problem of biosecurity was reframed as the problem of dual use, that is, how to prevent misuse of the results of scientific research and technologies. As Christian Venicci, another staff member of the NSABB member, put it, "[The board was established] to define and articulate the concept of dual use and develop [a] sort of a framework for oversight." Moreover, as an NSABB member colleague Daniel Reynolds recounts, the goal was to deal with misuse that arises from negligent actions of scientists and not with intentional malfeasance, which usually remains out of this framework because it emanates from a nonscientific source.

Dealing with biosecurity in general, and specifically with dual use, raised another problem: how to identify potentially dangerous studies or agents requiring oversight. As Dr Simon Natcher put it: "One of the big issues in dual-use research is, how do you promote it [the awareness of the problem], when people aren't really clear what it is?" Christian Venicci explained, "Any piece of information in the life sciences can be misused."

In March 2006, the NSABB held a meeting in which the term "Dual Use Research of Concern" (DURC) was presented. This term derived specifically from the assertion that, "*most* if not *all* Life Sciences research *could* be considered Dual Use"; therefore, "the Working Group wanted to focus [the criteria of dual use research] to identify *specific* Life Sciences research that could be of greatest concern for misuse" (Dual use criteria working group 2006, my emphasis). Christian Venicci explained the "of concern" part of the term to me:

> It's useful, but I do sometimes wonder about the whole concept of dual use, calling it dual use, as opposed to yesterday when we heard a lot of people saying that we should just call it life science research of concern. From my perspective, it's a little hard because I've been engaged with dual use for a few years now so it's not a strange concept to me. But, if I did bring it up to my scientific colleagues, I'm not sure what they would think of it. They might respond better to something like "life science research of concern" [that] distinguishes all the rest of research [from] that very small subset, which really is a very small subset, which has the high probability of being misused.

Thus, only certain kinds of life sciences research are considered "of concern" and should be subjected to oversight. Daniel Reynolds elaborated: "The difference between 'Dual Use' and 'Dual Use Research of Concern' is somewhat semantics . . . [The NSABB] wanted to acknowledge that everything has potential for misuse, but only a very little of it deserves real attention."

In June 2007 the NSABB published its proposed framework for the "Oversight of Dual-Use Life Sciences Research: Strategies for Minimizing the Potential Misuse of Research Information," and it defined dual use research of concern as "a subset of Dual Use Research that has the highest potential for generating information that could be misused" (NSABB 2006).

The problematic framing of DU (dual use) and DURC (dual research of concern) "turns on a core distinction—that there are *good* and *bad* uses of science and technology" (Rabinow and Bennett 2012: 124). However, the "danger of nefarious use of contemporary scientific capacities can be cantoned off into the 'bad guys' and the 'good guys' . . . It by now goes without saying, [that the latter] only want to do the right things" (Rabinow and Bennett 2012: 127).

The scientists in my research adhered to a view similar to that of the synthetic biologists described by Paul Rabinow. As Daniel Reynolds put it:

> I think there's a surprising number of life scientists who would never even think about that. If they had an early thought about that, they'd think "it's none of my business." You hope that people, once they had this first thought would stop and say, "maybe as a good citizen I do have some responsibility," enough to ask at least one question of someone else, or say something to someone else and let them take over. But until you get one person to say one thing . . . there's no chance.

Separating "good science" and the danger of its external misuse generated a perception that vesting responsibility for monitoring and improving science in the "good guys" was sufficient. The definition of DURC narrowed the broader problem of dual use to only a few studies that could be marked in their early stages as being "of concern." It was the NSABB's role to initiate measurements and practices of oversight to better apply to the DU and DURC problem.

Self-Regulation: From Security to Awareness

Good science was not only differentiated from the intended security problem, but it was also protected from the external intervention of security, which should target only nonscientific actors. Thus, protecting the freedom of science and self-regulation becomes a central goal. As Stanley Lane, a member of the NSABB noted: "[it was a committee of] scientists protecting their own discipline." The NSABB was composed of about twenty-five voting members who were mostly life sciences experts—microbiologists and virologists—and about twenty additional ex-officials from various government departments, who were nonvoting members.

In October 2010, I attended an NSABB meeting at the NIH, in Bethesda, Maryland. I had read online that the meetings were open to the public. I had thought that, like security discussions in Israel, the meetings would be closed to the public. But this case was different—I could even register online. Attending the meeting marked my entry into the field and observation of the way the problem of life sciences biosecurity was framed in the US. The acting NSABB chair at the time opened the meeting, saying: "We are all scientists and we are here to protect the 'freedom of science' and to avoid regulation . . . [we prefer] volunteered oversight."

Whereas I had expected to observe a security committee dealing specifically with biosecurity, I found a scientific committee verifying the importance of "freedom of science" in light of security concerns. These scientists were concerned less with biosecurity than with avoiding state/government regulation of their research in relation to biosecurity. The scientists ardently supported keeping security mechanisms externally focused and promoted internal voluntary oversight based on a "code of conduct," "culture of responsibility," and more generally increasing "awareness" of the problem among scientists.

The last session of the first NSABB meeting in 2005 dealt entirely with "Codes of Conduct in the Life Sciences . . . [to] provide guidelines, raise awareness and debate; [and to] foster moral agents." The Code of Conduct addressed the "lack of awareness of Biological Weapons Dual Use concerns or prohibitions." Additionally, a Code of Ethics was set to "Alert; Set realistic or idealistic standards" (NSABB 2005). The NSABB subsequently issued a report titled "Strategic Plan for Outreach and Education on Dual Use Research Issues" (NSABB 2008) and one titled "Enhancing Personnel Reliability among Individuals with Access to Select Agents" (NSABB 2009). Thus, it understood that a good way to convey the problem of biosecurity to the scientific community was, first, to externalize security and relate it to governance and society and, second, to translate the problem of DU into a professional ethical concern that could be handled by self-awareness and self-regulation.

Thus, instead of regulation, NSABB meetings were centered on developing mechanisms to increase awareness and responsibility among scientists of the problem of dual use research. In this regard, the idea was to "approach scientists on their terms and embed some of these concepts in the idea of responsible conduct of research," as Christian Venicci from the NIH, explained. The rationale was that if scientists could demonstrate that they produced responsible science and were aware of the risk of its misuse, then there would be no need for security regulation. In other words, ensuring that security mechanisms and regulation remained external to the scientific vocation rendered the problem of dual use an internal ethical issue, with scientists acting as responsible moral subjects who had no reason to deal with externals such as security governance. And as Dr Simon Natcher summarized during our conversation: "Biosecurity is more of an emerging area and you're looking at such things as personnel reliability, you're looking at the culture of what goes on in laboratories . . . how you should act, how you should conduct yourself in terms of care . . . and codes of conduct."

In summary, although biosecurity had emerged as a new problem, especially in relation to life sciences research, in action, security regulation was constructed as something the scientific community should avoid. At first, the problem was framed as a dual use problem that distinguished between good and bad users. Accordingly, the scientific community could not be held responsible for the intentional misuse of science by nonscientists. The emphasis on self-regulation of "good science" enabled scientists to promote the idea of self-oversight and non-state regulation with regard to possible dangers caused by science or scientists, as I discuss below.

At the end of 2011, its failure to propose any concrete biosecurity measures raised the question of whether the NSABB is necessary at all. Not surprisingly, some scientists challenged the continuing need for the NSABB. In September 2011, in a critical meeting, the future of the committee was discussed. A second meeting of all relevant sides was scheduled for the end of October, during which the future of the committee was to be determined. Should the committee continue its work? And if it should, what should its role be? That meeting never took place. In October 2012, the NSABB was engaged with a major biosecurity event, and the DURC problem had taken a concrete form.

The Dynamic between Science and Society

The problematic framing of biosecurity in the US and scientists' approach to it can be broadly located in the literature discussing the relations between science and society.

Society and Scientific Knowledge Production

In *The New Production of Knowledge*, Gibbons et al. (1994) coined the fundamental terms *Mode 1* and *Mode 2* in relation to forms of knowledge production in society and to characterize the radical shift in such production in contemporary societies:

> The old paradigm of scientific discovery ("Mode 1")—characterized by the hegemony of theoretical or, at any rate, experimental science; by an internally-driven taxonomy of disciplines; and by the autonomy of scientists and their host institutions, the universities—was being superseded by a new paradigm of knowledge production ("Mode 2"), which was socially distributed, application-oriented, trans-disciplinary, and subject to multiple accountabilities. (Nowotny et al. 2003: 179)

Mode 2 knowledge production represents the move from hegemonic disciplinary knowledge to the involvement of a multiplicity of actors with a heterogeneity of skills in problem solving. In particular, scientific knowledge is perceived to be integral to society and to have become more socially accountable; there exists "a societal value that needs to be integrated into the definition of good science" (Nowotny et al. 2001: 2). In this new era, the openness of scientific boundaries for reverse communication with society gives rise to the process of "contextualization," which brings society into knowledge production. Hence, society becomes what Helga Nowotny et al. (2001: 20) referred to as "the context (can and does) speak back." This dynamic refigures forms of science and scientific knowledge and their relations with society as well as the definition of what is social and societal. Thus, the literature emphasizes the openness of the boundaries between science and society and how attention to social factors becomes a good value for scientific practice.

Combining the concepts of mode 2 knowledge production, and audit, Strathern argues:

> Science that was once robust through its own validation procedures [mode 1] must now acquire an [other] efficacy from beyond itself [mode 2] . . . Scientific knowledge makes itself robust in being seen to be "socially robust". In effect, science incorporates society into its aims and objectives in order to anticipate or pre-empt society's verdict . . . that will require among other things, keeping stable what counts as "society". And society will need to be kept visible. (Strathern 2005: 467)

Put differently, science has become robust by society's verdict, and the social has become internal to scientific knowledge production through the operation of a mode 2 paradigm.

An extreme case, when a situation involves a nonmeasurable overflow, is termed a "hot situation." In a hot situation, there is no stable knowledge, and the overflows are not numerically calculable:

In "hot" situations, everything becomes controversial: the identification of intermediaries and overflows, the distribution of source and target agents, and the way effects are measured. These controversies, which indicate the absence of a stabilized knowledge base, usually involve a wide variety of actors. The actual list of actors, as well as their identities, will fluctuate in the course of the controversy itself and they will put forward mutually incompatible descriptions of future world states. (Callon 1998: 260)

Applying some of these concepts to the analysis of the current case study, we see that although biosecurity is recognized as a problem in the US, in terms of the scientific approach to it, and the relationship between life sciences and society, security remains external. Thus the US case expresses a particular dynamic between science and society that does not necessarily reflect the general mode 2 theoretical explanation/paradigm of scientific knowledge production.

The case of the H5N1 flu virus discussed in the following pages represents a hot situation, challenging the framing of science and society in this regard. Moreover, this event challenges the allegedly transparent US scientific and security approach on the matter, the problem of the issue in terms of biosecurity in the US, and the understanding of the US as the global case.

A Biosecurity Event or a Public Health Preparedness Event?

An Engineered Doomsday

In late 2011, this ongoing discussion of biosecurity in the US was triggered by two studies, conducted at Erasmus Medical Centre in Rotterdam in the Netherlands by researcher Ron Fouchier and at the University of Wisconsin-Madison in the US by Yoshihiro Kawaoka (who is also affiliated with Tokyo University). In these studies, researchers created strains of H5N1 viruses that spread easily among ferrets. Since ferrets are generally considered to provide the best model for predicting how a flu virus might behave in humans, it was assumed that these strains exemplified human pandemic strains as well. The studies were funded by the NIH and were conducted to understand the molecular characteristics underlying transmissibility.

On 13 September 2011, Fouchier presented his study at a meeting in Malta and announced that his lab had "discovered that only 1–3 substitutions are sufficient to cause large changes in antigenic drift . . . [and that] large antigenic differences between and within H5N1 clades could affect vaccine efficiency and even result in vaccine failure" (Influenza

Conference Newspaper 2011). The Influenza Conference Newspaper reported that Fouchier and his team "introduced mutations, by reverse genetics into laboratory ferrets. They then collected a nasal wash from each infected ferret and inoculated another ferret after a few days. They repeated this process ten times. The result? H5N1 had been transmitted to three out of four ferrets." Fouchier asserted that the virus he created "is airborne and as efficiently transmitted as the seasonal virus . . . this is very bad news, indeed" (Influenza Conference Newspaper 2011).

Fouchier's study caused turmoil in the US scientific community: on 19 September *Scientific American* published an article titled "What Will the Next Influenza Pandemic Look Like," describing an H5N1 pandemic as "topping the worst-case scenario list for most flu experts" and raising the question of whether "the dreaded H5N1" would become transmissible in humans. The answer was presented in the study of Fouchier and his team, who "mutated the hell out of H5N1" and found that with "as few as five single mutations it gained the ability to latch onto cells in the nasal and tracheal passageways" (Harmon 2011). On 26 September, in an article titled "Five Easy Mutations to Make Bird Flu a Lethal Pandemic," *New Scientist* reported on Fouchier's work:

> H5N1 bird flu can kill humans, but has not gone pandemic because it cannot spread easily among us. That might change: five mutations in just two genes have allowed the virus to spread between mammals in the lab. What's more, the virus is just as lethal despite the mutations. (MacKenzie 2011a)

Because of these concerns, in October 2011, the NSABB was called to review the two studies, which had been submitted to *Science* and *Nature* for publication. The committee was to examine their publication in relation to the risk of DURC with regard to the potential misuse of the information they presented. As Daniel Reynolds explained:

> The work provides information about [properties of infectious agents] . . . it's the information that allows someone else to create these things with these properties. Two of the most serious properties to give an infectious agent are *high virulence* and . . . *aerosol transmission between people*, and this was the case with new H5N1 strain. (Emphasis added)

According to the editor of *Science*, Bruce Albert, when Fouchier's paper arrived at the magazine, "it was obvious" that it needed special review. The journal "quickly recruited outside specialists, including biosecurity experts who serve on NSABB. NSABB itself was first alerted to the studies by NIAID (National Institute of Allergy and Infectious Diseases) [in late summer 2011] and received copies of the papers in mid-October" (Enserink and Malakoff 2012). It is interesting that the editors called on the special US board review, given that Fouchier's article was based on research conducted in the Netherlands and Kawaoka held an appointment with Tokyo University as well as UW-Madison.

This event was presented by all actors as a dual use biosecurity event: a new lethal virus had been introduced into the world and scientists were responsible for creating it. Many spoke of it as "a man-made flu virus that could change world history if it were ever set free" (Enserink 2011); Paul Keim, NSABB chair at the time, said he "can't think of another pathogenic organism that is as scary as this one . . . anthrax is [not] scary at all compared to this" (Enserink 2011); and Laurie Garrett, a US Pulitzer Prize-winning science journalist, wrote a piece titled "The Bioterrorist Next Door" (Garrett 2011). The perception that science had created the next global pandemic or the next bioterror event shocked the scientific world and raised major objections to publication of the studies. Once the papers arrived at the NSABB for review, the question was whether preventing their publication would remove the threat. Thomas Ingelsby of the Center for Biosecurity at the University of Pittsburgh in Pennsylvania objected to publication:

> The benefits of publishing this work do not outweigh the dangers of showing others how to replicate it, . . . Someone might try to make it into a weapon . . . but a more likely threat is that more scientists will work with the modified virus, increasing the likelihood of it escaping the lab. Small mistakes in biosafety could have terrible global consequences. (MacKenzie 2011)

At the heart of the debate, the critical question was raised of whether it was right to conduct the study in the first place. Thomas Inglesby and colleagues criticized the H5N1 research and asked, "Should we purposely engineer avian flu strains to become highly transmissible in humans? In our view, no." He cited three reasons: first, because the deadly strain could "escape accidentally from the laboratory"; second, the idea that the engineered strain could help scientists identify similar characteristics in currently circulating strains of H5N1 "is a speculative hope but not worth the potential risk"; and, third, the assertion that the creation of the strain would motivate scientists to search for H5N1 vaccines was also speculative. Moreover, "it is unclear that vaccine protection against this engineered strain would correlate with vaccine protection against an H5N1 pandemic strain that evolves naturally in the world" (Inglesby et al. 2011).

The *New York Times*'s position on the matter was definite, as expressed in an editorial titled "An Engineered Doomsday."

... it is highly uncertain, even improbable, that the virus would mutate in nature along the pathways prodded in a laboratory environment, so the benefit of looking for these five mutations seems marginal. We cannot say there would be no benefits at all from studying the virus. We respect the researchers' desire to protect public health. But the consequences, should the virus escape, are too devastating to risk. (*New York Times* 2012)

In other words, without any evidence that such a strain could naturally develop, and without a proven ability to develop a vaccine following the research, what good could this research do?

However, it is important to note that even those who rejected publication due to security concerns still opposed governmental intervention, preferring self-regulation instead. Anthrax expert and retired Harvard University professor Matt Meselson, for example, expressed: "If I were a journal editor and I received an article that said how to make a bioweapon, I'd never publish it, but that would be based on self-regulation, not any government restriction" (Garret 2011).

Authorized Scientists vs a Global Sharing System

At the height of the discussion, in December 2011, the NSABB published its recommendations following its review of the article. It said:

While the public health benefits of such research can be important, certain information obtained through such studies has the potential to be misused for harmful purposes ... Due to the importance of the findings to the public health and research communities, the NSABB recommends that the general conclusions highlighting the novel outcome be published, but that the manuscripts not include the methodological and other details that could enable replication of the experiments by those who would seek to do harm. (NSABB Press Statement 2011)

The NSABB recognized the potential benefit of the studies but recommended that, to minimize the risk of the experiments being repeated, the articles should not be published in full. Additionally, emphasizing the importance of the studies as contributions to public health research, the NSABB recommended designating a group of scientists to receive the complete study information. This group would consist of a closed network of "authorized" scientists (flu experts) who could use the information to continue to conduct "responsible" research on the topic. What remained unsaid was that "authorized scientists" was another name for US and European scientists whose laboratories could be trusted in terms of keeping biosafety and biosecurity procedures. On the one hand, these recommendations acknowledged the security problem related to science and, on the other hand, they imposed US management of the problem as well as a hidden assumption that the US represented the world's perspective on the issue. This triggered an international debate.

On 30 December 2011, the WHO (World Health Organization) released a statement of concern about limiting dissemination of information from the work of Fouchier and Kawaoka as undermining the international Pandemic Influenza Preparedness (PIP) framework. Limiting the information raises the concern that such studies would be limited: "studies conducted under appropriate conditions must continue to take place so that critical scientific knowledge needed to reduce the risks posed by the H5N1 virus continues to increase" (WHO Statement 2011).

Additionally, the WHO was concerned about the decision to confine the information to a limited group of scientists located in countries that received the viruses and not in countries where flu occurs. The PIP program was an international effort to connect between infected countries (with local endemic Avian Flu), and other countries in which most research on the virus (and on the way to confront it) was conducted.

> In order to enable . . . public health gains, countries where these viruses occur should share their influenza viruses for public health purposes while countries and organizations receiving these viruses should share benefits resulting from the virus sharing. Both types of sharing are on equal footing and equally important parts of the collective global actions needed to protect public health. (WHO Statement 2011)

Moreover, it appears that the WHO's international lab provided Fouchier and Kawaoka with the viruses they used in their research. Fouchier, one of the researchers at the center of the controversy, noted that in the US biosecurity experts dominated the discussion and that flu experts had little input. Defending the research, he asserted,

> I think we have done that very well in the Netherlands. We were very proactive; before we submitted the paper for publication we informed all the relevant authorities, so they knew what was happening and had the time to prepare, and when the story started making the rounds in the US media, we spent 3 days talking to newspapers, TV, and radio. And that nipped the debate in the bud. In the US, this hasn't happened. And the people who are the most vocal in the press are the biosecurity experts. It's a pity that so few people from the flu field have jumped in front of the cameras, especially in the US. (Enserink 2012)

Whereas the US discussion was initially concerned with the issue of security, the international discussion that ensued was mainly concerned with public health preparedness and the development of treatment for endemic H5N1 disease in non-Euro-American counties. Claims regarding international efforts and reciprocal relations between different countries were also raised. At once, the entire US biosecurity concern was reframed internationally by the WHO as "one country's concern":

> WHO's [Feiji] Fukuda, however, notes that "we are not a regulatory agency. We know we are not going to put out any regulatory framework." Instead, he says a first step will be simply getting the facts. NSABB members haven't briefed WHO on their reasoning, he notes, and "my overall sense is that most people are pretty confused about what are all the issues. Most people are standing back to see if they should feel one way or another. . . . *One country or research group doesn't reflect the concerns of others.* (Malakoff 2012a: 389, emphasis added)

Reflecting this line of thought, Ed Rybicki, a virologist at the University of Cape Town, published a blog post in *Nature* in which he criticized the US for monopolizing the decision about who could get the information about the studies, when multiple countries are in danger:
Consider the following:

- H5N1 HPAI [highly pathogenic avian influenza] is endemic in countries such as Indonesia, Vietnam, Thailand, possibly Cambodia and Turkey, and almost certainly in China—and NOT in western Europe, or the US;
- While a US agency may have funded the research, the viruses used certainly came from outside of the US—and at least half of the research was done outside the US;
- Results of the research would be of immediate use to countries where the virus is endemic, in informing surveillance efforts, as opposed to being of only academic interest in countries where the virus does not occur.

Yet, authorities in one country—the US—are presuming to dictate to everyone just what can be disseminated, on the grounds that the information *may* be useful to terrorists who could "weaponise" H5N1 (Rybicki 2012).

On 16 and 17 February 2012, the WHO held a meeting of members from around the globe. Participants reached a consensus that redaction was not a viable option with regard to the two studies because of urgent public health needs and that a mechanism to limit access was not practical at that moment and might cause problems:

> On the question of limiting access to the results through publication of redacted versions, some participants observed that there was no current practical mechanism to limit access . . . Limiting access to those with a need for the information would pose insurmountable practical problems. Chief among

these problems are the development and implementation of a mechanism to disseminate the information to diverse and geographically distributed groups while maintaining the confidentiality of the detail. Therefore, such a mechanism would not realistically resolve concerns about Dual Use research. (WHO Report 2012)

Concurrent with this debate, the internal US position continued to reject publication on the basis of biosecurity concerns. This view was reflected in the mainstream US press. For example, the *New York Times* opinion piece cited above categorically opposed the two H5N1 studies and supported the NSABB recommendations:

We nearly always champion unfettered scientific research and open publication of the results. In this case it looks like the research should never have been undertaken because the potential harm is so catastrophic and the potential benefits from studying the virus are so speculative . . . We doubt that anything at all should be published, but it seems clear that something will be . . . We cannot say there would be no benefits at all from studying the virus. We respect the researchers' desire to protect public health. But the consequences, should the virus escape, are too devastating to risk. (*New York Times* 2012)

Similarly, Michael Osterholm from the NSABB and Donald Henderson explained in *Science Express* why the security concerns raised by the two H5N1 papers outweighed the proposed benefits of their publication and provided arguments against the rationales offered in defense of the work:

Although H5N1 candidate vaccines using the isolates from these studies should be developed and tested, this does not require sharing all of the mutational data outside of a very small group of established researchers already working within the WHO network . . . The current circulating strains of influenza A/H5N1, with their human case fatality rate of 30 to 80%, place this pathogen in the category of causing one of the most virulent known human infectious diseases . . . We can't unring a bell; should a highly transmissible and virulent H5N1 influenza virus that is of human making cause a catastrophic pandemic, whether as the result of intentional or unintentional release, the world will hold Life Sciences accountable for what it did or did not do to minimize that risk. (Osterholm and Henderson 2012)

As the above statements demonstrate, the positions of the international scientific community and of US scientists vis-à-vis the dissemination of Fouchier's and Kawaoka's research diverged at a fundamental level. Outside the US, the paramount concern appeared to acquire data useful in battling endemic influenza, whereas in the US, biosecurity seemed the overriding concern, and, with it, an interest in avoiding increased governmental oversight of scientific work.

Merging the Global and the Scientific

At a certain point, the leading US discourse started to change. In January 2012, *Nature* published an interview with Amy Patterson, director of the NIH, in which she mentioned that the construction of a dissemination mechanism would be led by HHS (US Department of Health and Human Services) with the collaboration of international organizations (the "international flu community"—both research and flu pandemic preparedness communities). She emphasized the importance of strong international participation in crafting the mechanism as well as the importance of sharing information with countries in which the virus was endemic (Ledford 2012).

In February 2012, the American Society of Microbiology (ASM) hosted a meeting on "Biodefense and Emerging Diseases," during which an ad hoc session on the H5N1 work took place. In this session, Fouchier defended his work and provided a fuller explanation of the question of pathogenicity.

At that meeting, Tony Fauci (the NIAID director at the NIH) announced that he had asked the two researchers to revise their papers and that the NSABB would review the revised manuscripts. Eventually, that same month, a gathering of NSABB members and more than a dozen observers, including NIH head Francis Collins and WHO member Keiji Fukuda, took place at the NIH campus. At the gathering, the participants read the original and the revised reports. Afterwards, they voted (though not unanimously) to allow publication of the revised studies.

> The Board was asked to consider the revised manuscripts from Dr Ron Fouchier of Erasmus Medical Center and Dr Yoshihiro Kawaoka of the University of Wisconsin and to recommend whether the information they contain should be communicated and, if so, to what extent . . . After careful deliberation, the NSABB unanimously recommended that this revised Kawaoka manuscript should be communicated in full. The NSABB also recommended, in a 12 to 6 decision, the communication of the data, methods, and conclusions presented in this revised Fouchier manuscript. (Malakoff, 2012b)

Commenting on this outcome, NSABB member Susan Ehrlich said:

> We have not, not, not reversed ourselves, because these were revised manuscripts that we reviewed, not a reconsideration of the original ones. (Cohen and Malakoff 2012)

The NSABB decision reassured critics concerned about improving international surveillance and public health preparedness. Consequently, the two articles were published, the Kawaoka study in *Nature* in May 2012 and the Fouchier study in *Science* in June 2012 (Imai et al. 2012; Herfst et al. 2012).

Following the event, a new US federal policy titled "Policy on the Oversight of Life Sciences Dual Use Research of Concern" was published (29 March 2012). The new policy reflects the US dual approach: on the one hand, it acknowledges the problem of biosecurity, and, on the other hand, it reflects the scientific establishment's opposition to external regulation. The policy repeated what had already been presented in the Fink Report, with specific attention to the H5N1 virus. First, according to the new policy, the H5N1 pathogen was added to the Select Agents list and, thus, subjected to oversight. Second, proposed studies involving both a Select Agent and DURC were to undergo further review before national funding was approved (United States Government Policy, OSTP 2012).

Discussion: What is the US in the Anthropology of the US?

The foregoing discussion focuses on the problem of biosecurity in the US and analyzes an intervention related to dangerous flu (H5N1) viruses and the dynamics between the scientific perception of, and security claims about, their study. In it, I challenge both the internal discourse of US presumption and American scientific discourse on the matter. I argue that these discourses construct the US field and the scientific profession as global, thus disconnecting biosecurity issues, here the risks of studying highly pathogenic avian flu, from their particular context.

The US discourse on biosecurity, on the highly pathogenic H5N1 case in particular, decontextualizes the problem, stripping it of any national-local emphasis and framing it in global terms. This approach is read by external actors as US domination of the issue, and they offer rationales that challenge that preeminence, such as the need for unfettered research to respond to "natural" endemic flu in non-Euro-American countries (which is also termed preparedness rather than security).

In that sense, this case challenges both the global, non-cultural perspective of science and scientists, and the US perception of biosecurity as representing a unified global concern. Moreover, not only is scientists' discourse presented beyond culture, but the anthropological literature of science is as well. Put differently, the literature and the theory of science, which discusses the dynamics between science and society, unifies the topic under a general discussion on the relationships between the two spheres (science and society) external to any particular culture or state. That is, in a way, how the literature of the anthropology of science takes science as a homogenized form, ontologically and epistemologically, beyond "culture."

In this chapter I present the case from a different perspective; I move from broad observation of science and the US to the analysis of local discourses and practices, and challenge the generality of this approach both in understanding the case of biosecurity and the "field" of the US. In adopting this analytical mode, I paraphrase Steve Woolgar's question "what is 'anthropological' in the anthropology of science?" (Woolgar 1991) and ask both "what is science in the anthropology of science?" (Rabinow 1992) and "what is 'US' in the anthropology of the US"?

First, my discussion is consistent with Rabinow's argument about early studies of scientific practices which have sought to "lower-case the abstraction" of science (Rabinow 1992: 7). The current study thus approaches biosecurity in the US through analysis of practices and discourses expressed in concrete cases. Moreover, rather than merely addressing the form level, that is, the level of abstraction at which US science should be studied and represented, my positioning as a non-US scholar enables me to see the case of biosecurity in light of a particular US problematization, to trace how the problem emerged, and to identify the various local reactions and attempts to solve it. In particular, it also allows me to see the disconnect between science and security and the emphasis on freedom of science as US characteristics, and to pay attention to scientists' avoidance of regulation in the name of so-called liberal values.

Second, I follow Eyal Ben-Ari (2011) in looking at the unique meaning/content of the multiple objects that together constitute what is usually perceived as the "US" or the "American." In his view, there are "American" aspects expressed both in the US fields of study and in US anthropological inquiry, that is, the work of American anthropologists. As Virginia R. Dominguez and Jane Desmond (1996) do, Ben-Ari (2011) refutes the level of abstraction of the broad US imaginary to focus on recurring US attitudes and behavioral patterns, such as the commitment to liberal values, the incorporation of political issues into moral and ethical discussions "involving impulsion toward activism" and the perception of the US as the global case.

In that sense, I follow Virginia Dominguez and Jasmin Habib's call (in this volume) for examining the multiple and conflicting ways in which "America" is imagined and experienced and how this imaginary is created and reproduced in various ways. Hence, rather than inquire into the US as a unitary figure, I ask how anthropological analysis of biosecurity contributes to a better understanding of the multiple elements that compose it.

This anthropological position does not necessarily entail the "anti-American streak found among some scholars outside the United States (and within it) by criticizing [it]" (Ben-Ari 2011: 168). Opening the "black box" does not mean immediate denunciation of the US but, rather, as Rabinow puts it, "an ethnographic and anthropological call to be attentive to existing minor practices that escape the dominant discursive trends of theories . . ." (1996: 7). More broadly, as Rabinow claims, this approach moves from the politics of the objects studied to the ethics of anthropological inquiry. As he explains, "I was not expected to play an expert role of analyzing them sociologically, nor a therapeutic role of helping them 'work through' problems, nor a denunciatory role of identifying malevolent forces and actors, but a problematizing role, one in which having an observer status allowed a certain overview of the situation, including its fluidity" (Rabinow: 21–22).

Thus, to answer the question "what is the US in the anthropology of the US?" I would suggest that one should consider the multiple objects subsumed by this complex imaginary, as well as its uniquely "American" aspects. But, in addition—and crucially—one must consider "what is 'anthropology' in the 'anthropology of the US'?" That is, how do particular scientific ethics enable scholars to view those "American" aspects without considering them global and at the same time without denouncing them and, thus, avoid theoretically reproducing their imaginary power?

Limor Samimian-Darash is Assistant Professor at the Federmann School of Public Policy and Government at the Hebrew University of Jerusalem. Her research interests include: anthropology of the state and policy, anthropology of security, and theory of risk and uncertainty. She was chosen as one of five promising early-career social scientists in Israel, for the Alon Fellowship (2013–16). Recent publications include: *Modes of Uncertainty: Anthropological Cases* (University of Chicago Press, co-edited with Paul Rabinow); "Practicing Uncertainty: Scenario-Based Preparedness Exercises in Israel" in *Cultural Anthropology,* and "Preparedness for Potential Future Biothreats: Toward an Anthropology of Uncertainty" in *Current Anthropology*.

References

Ben-Ari, Eyal. 2011. "Anthropology, Research, and State Violence." In *Dangerous Liaisons*, ed. Laura A. McNamara and Robert A. Rubinstein, 167–83. Santa Fe, NM: SAR Press.

Berg, Paul. 2008. "Asilomar 1975: DNA Modification Secured." *Nature* 445: 290–91.

Callon, Michel. 1998. "An Essay on Framing and Overflowing: Economic Externalities Revisited by Sociology." *The Sociological Review* 46(S1): 244–69.

Cohen, Jon and David Malakoff. 2012. "On Second Thought, Flu Papers Get Go-Ahead." *Science* 336: 19–20.

Dominguez, Virginia R. and Jane Desmond. 1996. "Resituating American Studies in a Critical Internationalism." *American Quarterly* 48(3): 475–90.

Enserink, Martin. 2011. "Scientists Brace for Media Storm Around Controversial Flu Studies." *Science Insider*. Retrieved on 20 Feb. 2013, from http://news. sciencemag.org/scienceinsider/2011/11/scientists-brace-for-media-storm.html.

Enserink, Martin. 2012. "Flu Researcher Ron Fouchier: 'It's a Pity That It Has to Come to This'" *Science Insider*. Retrieved on 20 Feb. 2013, from http://www. sciencemag.org/news/2012/01/flu-researcher-ron-fouchier-its-pity-it-has-come.

Enserink, Martin and David Malakoff. 2012. "Will Flu Papers Lead to New Research Oversight?" *Science* 335: 20–22.

Fink Report. National Research Council. 2004. *Biotechnology Research in an Age of Terrorism*. Washington, DC: National Academies Press. Available at http:// books.nap.edu/openbook.php?record_id=10827&page=1

Fouchier, Ron. "Flu Researcher Ron Fouchier: 'It's a Pity That It Has to Come to This'." By Martin Enserink. *Science Insider*. Retrieved on 27 April 2013, from http://news.sciencemag.org/scienceinsider/2012/01/flu-researcher-ron-fouchier-its.html?ref=hp.

Garrett, Laurie. 2011. "The Bioterrorist Next Door." *Foreign Policy*. Retrieved 20 Feb. 2013 from http://www.foreignpolicy.com/articles/2011/12/14/ the_bioterrorist_next_door.

Gibbons et al. 1994. *The New Production of Knowledge*. London: Sage.

Gusterson, Hugh. 2007. "Anthropology and Militarism." *Annual Review of Anthropology* 36: 155–75.

Harmon, Katherine. 2011. "What Will the Next Pandemic Look Like?" *Scientific American*. Retrieved on 19 Feb. 2013 from http://www.scientificamerican.com/ article.cfm?id=next-influenza-pandemic.

HHS Press office. 2004. *HHS will Lead Government-Wide Effort to Enhance Biosecurity in 'Dual Use' Research*. National Institutes of Health. Retrieved 16 Feb. 2013 from http://www.nih.gov/news/pr/mar2004/hhs-04.htm.

Herfst, S., E.J.A. Schrauwen, M. Linster, S. Chutinimitkul, E. de Wit, V.J. Munster, . . . R.A.M Fouchier. 2012. "Airborne Transmission of Influenza A/H5N1 Virus Between Ferrets." *Science* 226(6088): 1534–41.

Imai, M., T. Watanabe, M. Hatta, S.C. Das, M. Ozawa, K.Shinya, and Y.Kawaoka. 2012. "Experimental Adaptation of an Influenza H5 HA Confers Respiratory Droplet Transmission to a Reassortant H5 HA/H1N1 Virus in Ferrets." *Nature* 486: 420–28.

Inglesby, Thomas, Anita Cicero, and D.A. Henderson. 2011. *The Risk of Engineering a Highly Transmissible H5N1 Virus.* Center for Biosecurity of UPMC. Retrieved on 20 Feb. 2013 from http://www.upmc-biosecurity.org/website/resources/publications/2011/2011-12-15-editorial-engineering-H5N1.

Influenza Conference Newspaper. 2011. "Scientists Provide Strong Evidence for Pandemic Threat." *The Influenza Times—Conference Newspaper,* The Fourth ESWI Influenza Conference. Retrieved on 26 Feb. 2013 from http://www.eswiconference.org/Downloads/FEIC_news_1.aspx.

Lakoff, Andrew and Stephen J. Collier. 2008. "The Problem of Securing Health." In *Biosecurity Interventions,* 1–32. New York: SSRC.

Ledford, Heidi. 2012. "Bird Flu and the Future of Biosecurity." *Nature.* Retrieved on 11 Feb. 2013 from http://www.nature.com/news/bird-flu-and-the-future-of-biosecurity-1.9784.

Lutz, Catherine. 2001. *Homefront: A Military City and the American Twentieth Century.* Boston: Beacon Press.

MacKenzie, Debora. 2011a. "Five Easy Mutations to Make Bird Flu a Lethal Pandemic." *New Scientist.* Retrieved on 19 Feb. 2013 from http://www.newscientist.com/article/mg21128314.600-five-easy-mutations-to-make-bird-flu-a-lethal-pandemic.html.

———. 2011b. "Bioterror Fears Could Block Crucial Flu Research." *New Scientist.* Retrieved on 20 Feb. 2013 from http://www.newscientist.com/article/dn21195-bioterror-fears-could-block-crucial-flu-research.html.

Malakoff, David. 2012a. "Flu Controversy Spurs Research Moratorium." *Science* 335(6067): 387–89.

———. 2012b. "Breaking News: NSABB Reverses Position on Flu Papers." *Science Insider.* Retrieved on 20 Feb. 2013, from http://www.sciencemag.org/news/2012/03/breaking-news-nsabb-reverses-position-flu-papers.

Masco, Joseph. 2006. *The Nuclear Borderlands: The Manhattan Project in Post-Cold War New Mexico.* Princeton, NJ: Princeton University Press.

———. 2014. *Biosecurity Noir: 'WMDs' in a World Without Borders. The Theater of Operations: National Security Affect from the Cold War on Terror.* Durham, NC: Duke University Press.

Nader, Laura. 1996. "Introduction: Anthropological inquiry into boundaries, power and knowledge." In *Naked Science: Anthropological Inquiry into Boundaries, Power and Knowledge,* ed. Laura Nader, 1–28. London: Routledge.

New York Times. 2012. An Engineered Doomsday. *The New York Times—Sunday Review.* Retrieved on Feb. 20, 2013, from http://www.nytimes.com/2012/01/08/opinion/sunday/an-engineered-doomsday.html?_r=0

NSABB (National Science Advisory Board for Biosecurity). 2005. "First meeting of the National Science Advisory Board for Biosecurity, June 30–July 1, 2005: Agenda. Office of Biotechnology Activities, NSABB—Past Meetings." Retrieved 16 Feb. 2013 from http://oba.od.nih.gov/biosecurity/meetings/200506/Rappert%20and%20Dando.pdf.

———. 2006. "Oversight of Dual-Use Life Sciences Research: Strategies for Minimizing the Potential Misuse of Research Information." Office of Biotechnology Activities—Dual Use Research. Retrieved on 16 Feb. 2013, from http://oba.od.nih.gov/biosecurity/biosecurity_documents.html.

———. 2008. "Strategic Plan for Outreach and Education on Dual Use Research Issues." Office of Biotechnology Activities—Dual Use Research. Retrieved on 16 Feb. 2013 from http://oba.od.nih.gov/biosecurity/biosecurity_documents. html.

———. 2009. "Enhancing Personnel Reliability among Individuals with Access to Select Agents." Office of Biotechnology Activities—Dual Use Research. Retrieved on 16 Feb. 2013 from http://oba.od.nih.gov/biosecurity/biosecurity_documents.html.

———. 2011. "Press Statement on the NSABB Review of H5N1 Research." NIH NEWS—National Institutes of Health. Retrieved on 20 Feb. 2013 from http://www.nih.gov/news/health/dec2011/od-20.htm.

———. 2012. "March 29–30, 2012 Meeting of the National Science Advisory Board for Biosecurity to Review Revised Manuscripts on Transmissibility of A/H5N1 Influenza Virus," NSABB. Retrieved on 27 April 2013 from http://oba.od.nih.gov/oba/biosecurity/PDF/NSABB_Statement_March_2012_Meeting.pdf.

NSABB. "Office of Biotechnology Activities." Retrieved on 16 Feb. 2013 from http://oba.od.nih.gov/biosecurity/biosecurity_documents.html.

Nowotny, Helga, Peter Scott, and Michael Gibbons. 2001. *Re-thinking Science: Knowledge and the Public in an Age of Uncertainty*. Oxford: Polity Press.

———. 2003. "'Mode 2' Revisited: The New Production of Knowledge." *Minerva* 41: 179–94.

Osterholm, Michael and Donald Henderson. 2012. "Life Sciences at a Crossroads: Respiratory Transmissible H5N1." *Science* 335(6070): 801–2.

Price, David. 2002. "Lessons from the Second World War Anthropology: Peripheral, Persuasive and Ignored Contributions." *Anthropology Today* 18(3):14–20.

Rabinow, Paul. 1992. "Studies in the Anthropology of Reason." *Anthropology Today* 8(5): 7–10.

———. 1996. *Essays on the Anthropology of Reason*. Princeton, NJ: Princeton University Press.

Rabinow, Paul and Gaymon Bennett. 2012. *Designing Human Practices: An Experiment with Synthetic Biology*. Chicago: Chicago University Press.

Racaniello, Vincent. 2012. "Science Should Be in the Public Domain. mBio—American Society for Microbiology." Retrieved on 20 Feb. 2013 from http://mbio.asm.org/content/3/1/e00004-12.full.

Rybicki, Ed. 2012. "We Will Speak for You: Nature—TradeSecrets." Retrieved on 11 February 2013 from http://blogs.nature.com/tradesecrets/2012/01/23/we-will-speak-for-you.

Strathern, Marilyn. 2002. "Externalities in comparative guise." *Economy and Society* 31(2): 250–67.

———. 2003. "Re-describing Society." *Minerva* 41: 263–76.

Strathern, Marilyn. 2005. "Robust Knowledge and Fragile Futures." In *Global Assemblages: Technology, Politics, and Ethics as Anthropological Problems*, ed. Ong, A. and S. J. Collier, 464–81. Malden, MA: Blackwell.

———, ed. 2000. *Audit Cultures: Anthropological Studies in Accountability, Ethics, and the Academy*. London: Routledge.

United States Government Policy for Oversight of Life Sciences Dual Use
   Research of Concern (OSTP). 2012. Office of Biotechnology Activities.
   Retrieved on 20 Feb. 2013 from http://oba.od.nih.gov/oba/biosecurity/PDF/
   United_States_Government_Policy_for_Oversight_of_DURC_FINAL_
   version_032812.pdf.
Woolgar, Steve. 1991. "What is 'Anthropological' about the Anthropology of
   Science?" *Current Anthropology* 32(1): 79.
WHO (World Health Organization). 2011. "Statement—WHO Concerned
   that New H5N1 Influenza Research Could Undermine the 2011 Pandemic
   Influenza Preparedness Framework." World Health Organization—Media
   centre. Retrieved on 20 Feb. 2013 from http://www.who.int/mediacentre/news/
   statements/2011/pip_framework_20111229/en/.
———. 2012. "Report on Technical Consultation on H5N1 Research Issues." World
   Health Organization. Retrieved on 10 February 2013 from http://www.who.
   int/influenza/human_animal_interface/mtg_report_h5n1.

Chapter Four

American Theater State
Reflections on Political Culture
Ulf Hannerz

> Fred D. Thompson, a former United States senator, actor,
> and Republican presidential candidate, died on Sunday in
> Nashville. He was 73. . . . Mr. Thompson had an unusual
> career, moving back and forth between national politics and
> mass-market entertainment. He left a regular role on the hit
> NBC drama "Law & Order" to run for president in 2008.
> —*New York Times* obituary, 3 November 2015

Twice I shook hands with American presidents, although neither of them was in office at the time: Governor Bill Clinton at a campaign rally in front of Faneuil Hall, Boston, in 1992; and twenty years later, ex-President Jimmy Carter, on a Delta Airlines flight from Amsterdam to Atlanta, when he walked through the aisles to greet everybody on the plane. (It was 3 November, election day was three days later, so perhaps President No. 39 was coming home to vote for No. 44.) For them, of course, these were moments of fleeting contact with people anonymously co-present—in one case seeking their votes, in the other most likely hoping for some peace and quiet thereafter in his part of the cabin. As an alien, I could never vote for any one of them.

Before either of those encounters, my first anthropological field study in the 1960s was in an African-American neighborhood in Washington, DC.

Notes for this chapter begin on page 116.

My most recent field study, transnational and multi-sited, on news-media foreign correspondents, began some thirty years later with pilot interviews in New York. And then it ended a few years later on one of the first days of the year 2000 with an interview with a Washington correspondent for Radio Sweden—her studio was more or less within walking distance of my old 1960s neighborhood. Even before any of that, I was an exchange student at a US university, and in between, I have held some variety of visiting teaching and research positions in the US. So at one time or another, I have lived on the East Coast, in the Midwest, in the Rustbelt, and in California. Moreover, my sister, who was born and grew up in Sweden like me, has spent much of her adult life in the American South. Visiting her regularly, I am in close touch with that region as well.

Mirrors and Binoculars: The Uses of Outsiders

What it comes down to is that I have engaged in a kind of relaxed America-watch for most of my life, as a sort of ethnographer at large. This is not the way anthropologists are usually understood to work. Most typically, field research may be high-intensity, fairly short-term: perhaps a year on site (such as for a dissertation project), busily and intently gathering data every day, then back to the desk to write it up. My involvement with the United States, in contrast, has in large part been low-intensity but long-term, not field work by a strict definition, but extended over a period of some fifty years. Furthermore, in these times, not everything that may be defined as field research need be local and face-to-face. Even when I am not in the United States, I can follow rather closely what goes on there on the Internet, through cable television, by way of newsmagazines and journals of commentary, and in other ways. (It has happened that I have my alarm clock ring at 3am, Central European time, so I can get up and watch debates between American presidential candidates.)

But for whom could a point of view toward America such as mine really be of some interest or value? Drawing on the classic imperial heritage of their discipline, where most field workers were expatriates, anthropologists have sometimes made statements about the superiority of outsider insight that could seem rather arrogant and counterintuitive.[1] I think we should recognize, however, that there are in principle two ways in which the traveling observer can perform a useful service.

On the one hand, the claim might be that there actually could be an intellectual niche for perceptive outsidership: instances of consciousness-raising in relation to what is usually taken for granted, some way of making fresh connections between what locals habitually keep apart, perhaps occasionally a daring overview. At times, too, the possibility of impartiality with regard to some conflict between insiders.

Americans have tended to be quite generously inclined toward outsider commentary of this kind. This intellectual hospitality obviously goes back in history at least to Alexis de Tocqueville, and includes the invitation, three quarters of a century or so ago, to my compatriot Gunnar Myrdal to lead a comprehensive research effort on "the American race question"; resulting in the massive work *An American Dilemma* (1944). Yet in the United States as elsewhere, I suspect, such acceptance is most likely when the visitor's point of view is not too far from what is more or less the inside consensus, or at least in substantial agreement with one well-represented local line of thought. In the American instance, moreover, I believe the generosity has gone readily with the fact that national self-images have mostly been fairly clear, stable, satisfying, not easily challenged: "the city on a hill," "the indispensable nation," "American exceptionalism." Under such circumstances, outside opinions are affordable.

On the other hand, the argument about the value of an outsider's point of view can be that the outsider serves as a cultural broker. Let me point here to a book by Amin Maalouf, a Lebanese writer and cultural critic, long in the Paris diaspora, now a member of the Academie Francaise. His *Disordered World* (2011) is an essay on various troubles at present facing humanity—and here Maalouf sees coping with cultural differences as perhaps *the* major challenge, globally and locally. What is to be done? Maalouf proposes that if everyone were to become enduringly passionate about one culture other than his or her own, the result would be "a closely woven cultural web covering the whole planet" (2011: 161).

That is obviously a utopian idea (and no doubt it can provoke some rather complex critical scrutiny), yet it strikes me that anthropologists with their personal commitments to widespread fields could be seen as a kind of avant-garde here. But those passionate outsiders and their special insights may really be most important, most valuable, when they have returned home. This is where the outsider observers become insider reporters, insider storytellers; people who can interpret the foreign place to their compatriots, against the background of what they share (which they may of course do in a language other than English).

Here, then, whether the outside observers see anything of interest to their hosts may not be the most important question. (Moreover, they certainly do not need to argue that they understand the hosts better than these do themselves.) To Maalouf's web of global understandings, anthropologists contribute not so much by holding up mirrors as by offering their binoculars. Yet they may of course do both.[2]

Having inserted that reminder, I should note that in what follows, I assume that (although there may be others looking over their shoulders) my readers are mostly at home in America—people familiar with its national scene, and its prominent personae, at present and in that more or less recent past when I have been coming and going, entering and leaving.

Spectacle and Politics

On a Sunday afternoon some years ago, at the end of an American Anthropological Association annual meeting in Washington, DC, walking away from it through streets long familiar to me, I came upon the image that I thought fits my long-term engagement with the United States: it has been the theme park of my life.

Now that may sound facetious, but I do not really intend it that way. A theme park, as I understand it here, is a place one visits in large part for sheer enjoyment, a bit separated from the grind of everyday life. Many Americans have probably had that kind of stance toward the pleasures of "old Europe." If this is not quite "a native's point of view," perhaps it still involves some experiences that many Americans also recognize as they look at their society. The metaphor of the theme park, of course, has connotations of spectacle and entertainment. The United States has the world's most successful entertainment industry, and its forms penetrate much of other parts of American life as well. I have too much respect for the diversity of that life to believe that it can ever be reduced to some single formula. Nonetheless, the relationships between the media, performance, commentary, humor, satire, and dramatic moral outrage, on the one hand, and politics on the other, seem to me to involve a remarkable richness of cultural form in American life. So let me sketch one point of view toward contemporary American political culture.[3]

Early in the 1960s, I could hear Paul Harvey's folksy, nationally syndicated commentary in the slot just after the farm news, on the local radio station in the small town to which my exchange scholarship had taken me.[4] That was just before the actor Ronald Reagan took the step from hosting a television theater series to joining the supporting cast of Barry Goldwater's presidential campaign. A few years later, in the field in Washington, I was at the public birthday celebration for Nighthawk, one of most popular disc jockeys at one of the local black radio stations—and I could join Stokely Carmichael, the Black Power advocate, and others likewise present, in singing "Happy Birthday" to Nighthawk. Carmichael was much in the news at the time, and there were those among his radical comrades who mockingly referred to him as "Teevee Starmichael." As for me, I was actually more interested in the way black radio hosts, and their stations, had a major part in creating black Washington as an imagined community.

And the years went by. Paul Harvey was constantly present, if I cared to tune in. He only went off the air in 2008, at the age of 90, a year before his death. In 2005 he had been awarded the Presidential Medal of Freedom. At later points he was joined, on radio or television, by commentators and hosts like Oprah Winfrey and Rush Limbaugh. I could hardly fail to notice that former vice president Al Gore became the first person to win both an Oscar award and a Nobel Peace Prize; in the same year, for the same achievement. Ronald Reagan, for that matter, was not alone in making it from Hollywood to the governorship of California. Later in that office there was Arnold Schwarzenegger, who had arrived as a young Austrian immigrant, and as a remarkably successful body builder, to become The Terminator, and to marry the niece of a president (herself a TV personality).[5] For a while, some years ago, it seemed that the favorite president of many Americans was Martin Sheen, appearing in *The West Wing* television series. It was also reported around the same time that they often preferred to get their political news and commentary not from regular news programs, but from satirical comedy programs such as *Saturday Night Live* or Jon Stewart's *The Daily Show*. Then one *Saturday Night Live* star, Al Franken, did indeed move on to become a US senator from Minnesota. There had also been the late senator and somewhat drowsy presidential candidate Fred Thompson, of Tennessee and *Law & Order*.

As politics had become so intertwined with performance, it was perhaps not surprising that in 2010, when the major oil spill disaster in the Mexican Gulf occurred, the story for a while became a debate about whether President Obama was "emoting" enough, displaying his feelings—or perhaps a little unexpected, after all, as it had already been noted that this president's name rhymed with "no drama."[6] As the Obama presidency drew toward an end, and the campaign to succeed him began, Donald Trump launched his candidacy. It was a complicated spectacle, dramatically divisive in ethnic and religious terms, provoking even members of his own party to warn of fascist overtones. Yet one could hardly disregard that this figure out of the real estate business had its show business linkages as well. He had owned *Miss Universe* and other beauty pageants, participated in wrestling entertainment events, and most conspicuously he had hosted the TV reality show *The Apprentice*, where his key response to contestants was "You're fired."

Over the years other foreign observers have certainly also dwelt on the power of popular culture in American life—someone like Theodore Adorno of the exiled Frankfurt School more critically, Jean Baudrillard out of French postmodernism less so, in his celebration of hyper-reality and simulacrum. It has also continued to draw the concerned attention of American commentators. Robert Kaplan (2000: 95), a noted world watcher of conservative persuasion, has worried about "the gladiator culture of the masses" that in these times he finds characteristic of his home country. And Fareed Zakaria, one foreign student who did stay on to become a citizen, and recently himself a TV star of sorts with his own weekly CNN talk show, concludes rather harshly in his bestselling book *The Post-American World* that:

> An antiquated and overly rigid political system to begin with—about 225 years old—has been captured by money, special interests, a sensationalist media, and ideological attack groups. The result is ceaseless, virulent debate about trivia—politics as theater—and very little substance, compromise, and action. (Zakaria 2008: 211–12)

Theater States Compared

So here is politics as theater. Zakaria may never have read Clifford Geertz, but let me, as an ethnographer at large, turn Geertz' (1980) notion of the theater state into a traveling concept, and play with the idea of America as one of its varieties. What I want to do is not so much to criticize the conduct of American politics, nor just make fun of it or oversimplify it, but to try to point to some aspects of its theatricality. Here again, obviously, my point of view is likely not to be quite that of the native. Again, as I am not a citizen, I do not vote, and am not directly involved in the voting process; neither am I so immediately affected by the consequences of elections and the political process. But then we may be reminded that in some people's occasionally expressed opinion, here and there in the world, since the United States is a global power influencing everybody's lives, everybody in the world should be allowed to vote in American elections. Moreover, the actual proportion of the American electorate who exercises its voting rights is rather low by some standards.[7] So there may be Americans as well who take national politics to be a spectator sport, for some of them possibly even of rather mild interest.

Now certainly America is not the same kind of theater state as Geertz portrayed when, thirty years ago, with his interpretation of precolonial Bali, he brought the concept into anthropology. This, however, is not a notion on which the Balinese can claim any intellectual monopoly; it was not a story that the Balinese told themselves about themselves. Geertz' own wording in characterizing the theater state was itself a reflection in an American mirror. The early Balinese type of state, he writes, was always pointed not toward tyranny, whose systematic concentration of power it was incompetent to effect, and not even very methodically toward government, which it pursued indifferently and hesitantly, but rather toward spectacle, toward ceremony, toward the public dramatization of the ruling obsessions of Balinese culture—social inequality and status pride. It was a theater state in which the kings and the princes were the impresarios, the priests the directors, and the peasants the supporting cast, stage crew, and audience (Geertz 1980: 13).

The impresarios, the directors, the supporting cast, the stage crew, and the audience seem rather more out of Hollywood, or Broadway—tools for the translation of Balinese political culture to mostly American readers. If Geertz argued that the Balinese state did not amass power very competently, and governed only hesitantly, that judgment of Fareed Zakaria's quoted above may suggest that this is true in the contemporary United States as well. But in other ways, comparing Balinese and American theater states serves precisely the purpose of bringing out their differences. In America, the state does not produce all performances itself. Much of the activity is outsourced, in large part to the market. As behooves a democracy, rather than performing order and consensus, this theater state tends to dramatize its differences—in my period of observation, from Woodstock to costumed Tea Parties, perhaps Occupy Wall Street as well. Social inequality and status pride may have been big in Bali, but they are hardly the main motifs on the American stage. If there is a "ruling obsession," it may rather be the opposite, one of a performance of equality. And even as a growing inequality has recently seemed to be a social, economic and political fact, the display of egalitarianism may have been no less central as a symbolic principle.

It has been shown recently, for instance, when despite security concerns and when the weather permits, it has been good form for a newly inaugurated president to get out of his limousine and walk for a stretch in his own parade. If you are George W. Bush, flying Air Force One across the world to lend a hand in serving your troops in Baghdad their turkey at Thanksgiving shows you are regular guy (although apparently this was a decoration turkey, not to be eaten). Acting on this stage, too, you may want to show a well-rounded character, with interests outside politics, and other talents that people can sympathize with. If you are Bill Clinton, Arkansas governor who wishes to become the leader of the world's one indispensable nation, it can still help establish your public persona if you put on aviator glasses and play the saxophone on a late night TV show.[8] There is a strong tendency here to go beyond the official role, and to personalize. But at the same time, to show your leadership qualities, you must communicate a capacity to be in control. Certain remembered one-liners—"make my day" (Ronald Reagan), "read my lips" (George H.W. Bush)—may be recognized as quotes from entertainment heroes.

But there are risks in this as well, not only opportunities. As an important part of the arena is in advertising, negative campaign ads portray adversaries as villains. With the arrival of the super-PACs in financing, this appears to have set new records. Also, in a society now strongly oriented toward the visual, there are those moments frozen in public memory when justly or unjustly, leaders become fixed as fools—President Carter in his rowboat, attacked by the Killer Rabbit coming out of the pond, the younger President Bush having shoes thrown at him by an Iraqi journalist. The Republican primary campaign leading up to the 2012 election was also noteworthy in this regard: the take-out pizza entrepreneur with a vague sense of the world map, the major-state governor who had three important points to make but could only remember two of them, the pro-ignorance candidate who thought college education was for snobs. And then the supporting cast, too, may subvert the show. In 2008, the audience may have felt that it was a short leap from the Addams Family to the Palin Family.

Theatricality and Its Limits

Moreover, and most importantly for comparative purposes, Geertz claimed that theater was what the Balinese state was really about. It would be more difficult to claim the primacy of the dramatic in the American case—someone will quickly be there to point out that "it's the economy, stupid" (originating as a key idea, of course, in Governor Clinton's 1992 campaign), or make some other more or less credible counterclaim. It may be remarkable that some prominent American politicians have been drawn from the entertainment world, but certainly many more of them have law degrees. (I remember one newspaper columnist noting that the final candidates in the Democratic presidential primaries in 2008 were three lawyers, married to three other lawyers.) Backstage, American politics also has its policy wonks, pollsters, and precinct workers, and much of it lends itself to being televised only on C-SPAN. The lobbyists may prefer to stay off the screen altogether.[9] I would not want to disregard the impact of the wide range of voluntary groupings, in large part at the local grassroots level, although again, as a non-resident, non-citizen, I have less continuous experience of them. (But my sister, whom I mentioned, has long been active in the League of Women Voters, so I have some vicarious insight.) Nonetheless, it seems to me that there is in American culture—even in many of its diverse subcultures—a remarkable interpenetration between politics and show.

(Again, my own recollection is that of Stokely Carmichael singing "Happy Birthday" to Nighthawk.) Entertainment becomes a kind of fifth estate, at a time when the fourth estate, conventionally understood as the serious print media, is in a difficult period. In the end it will certainly be the interface of the theatrical with other politics that requires close scrutiny. Meanwhile, I claim an anthropological license to comment on the context of politics as show, and some possible consequences, to some degree from a comparative perspective.

The first thing to say should perhaps be that this theater state belongs to a media-saturated society—from the latter half of the twentieth century onward, particularly that of television everywhere, anytime. Even before that, radio and film had their quite considerable impact. Theatrical politics is a long-term fact, enduring through the swings of political conjunctures, and does not belong entirely on either side of the political spectrum. It does belong in a society prosperous enough to set considerable resources aside for consciousness industries. Even the least well-off can have some bread and circus, too.

More specifically, however, there is a characteristic of this society that has often been referred to as a main fact of "American exceptionalism." More than a century ago another outside observer, the German economist-sociologist Werner Sombart (1906), famously tried to explain why there is no socialism in America. By now, in the early twenty-first century, that is hardly so uniquely American any longer. It remains a fact that however we may want to describe the American class structure, it has not generated the kind of political parties clearly based on the material interests of groups that for a century or so have been much more typical of Europe. The appearance of Senator Bernie Sanders as an advocate of "democratic socialism" in the 2016 presidential campaign still had to find a place within the frame of Democratic Party primaries, and on the whole, the two-party system in the United States has been quite stable. The dominant parties only seem to have to reinvent themselves every so often, putting together new coalitions of voter blocs nationally, based on class, region, race, ethnicity, religion, gender, and age in varying mixes. As they face these hotly contested primaries even before getting to the real elections, however, candidates must create their own brands, and their own temporary assemblages of available and willing campaign professionals, and more or less amateur enthusiasts. As one of the regular political commentators at the *New York Times* pointed out some years ago, local and state party machines, once famous for their ability to deliver the vote, are no longer what they used to be (Bai 2010). Machines are place-bound, voters increasingly mobile. There is a large proportion of "independent voters" and (to repeat) often a low voter turnout.

Possibly, I should note, the situation is now changing somewhat in this regard—the social media may have played a part in changing the rules of the game, in the United States and elsewhere in the world. Opinion polls are clearly as important as ever, although they are volatile and really of uncertain value.[10] In America, the bring-out-the-vote exercise of one party has lately appeared more successful than the (selective) keep-out-the-vote attempts of its adversary. Perhaps the watchword now must be "It's the demography, stupid!!"

Sources of Stardom

Even so, this remains to a degree a setting for a theatrical politics, capable of commanding mass attention. Every major candidacy has to put on its own show. Once candidates enter that arena, it seems, they will also be mingling with other people in show business, blurring genre boundaries. I wonder if once the politicians are there, allowing themselves to be judged by the standards of dramatic performance, they do not place themselves at some disadvantage. While in the end they have to deal with the tedious detail of statecraft, continuously juggling matters large and small, inevitably compromising and being compromised, in shades of gray, their interlocutors, and to some extent, competitors on the dramatic arena can concentrate more effectively on making pronouncements on values and reality claims in their starkest form; on ideas that unite and ideas that divide. Or at least can be made to seem to do so. Thus the stars emerge as the nation's moral guides: Walter Cronkite long ago, then from later TV and radio talk shows Oprah Winfrey, Bruce Springsteen, Michael Moore, Rush Limbaugh, Bill O'Reilly, Glenn Beck, Rachel Maddow. And from that position, they may or may not interfere in other kinds of politics.

Are there other possible sources of stars from outside the political scene itself? One might think that sports would have some potential—especially the major team sports are also a part of the national entertainment complex, with major spectator events. But there seem to be no major American examples of sports-to-politics careers, probably because sports require a cultivation of quite different kinds of skills, and because their stars are usually too young to go straight into upper-level electoral politics.[11]

Yet there is one other notable path into politics. As a country born in a revolutionary war, engaged in many armed conflicts since then, and with "the frontier" as a dominant historical motif, it may not be so surprising that the United States has a certain inclination toward a military imagination. It is in the nature of things that soldiers can be heroes. One recurrent expression is that of the president as "the commander in chief." George Washington was a general before he became the first president, and about a century later there was Ulysses Grant. Theodore Roosevelt, with his background as a lieutenant-colonel with the "Rough Riders" (in the Spanish-American War in Cuba, and as popularized in road shows by Buffalo Bill), also drew on military symbolic capital. The first American presidential election I personally remember brought Dwight Eisenhower to the White House, and just before that it had seemed possible that General Douglas MacArthur, coming home from Asian postings, might become a presidential candidate. The most recent ex-soldier to go far in electoral politics was Senator John McCain, prisoner-hero of the Vietnam War, and presidential candidate in 2008. In between, and after, I believe there have been speculations about the political prospects of Generals Alexander Haig, "Stormin' Norman" Schwarzkopf, Colin Powell, and David Petraeus. Air Force General Curtis LeMay was George C. Wallace's vice-presidential candidate in 1968; basically a disaster for this third-party campaign. (This was after Wallace, ex-Governor of Alabama, had tried to recruit John Wayne from Hollywood for the slot—Wayne was just then on screen in *Green Berets*, the Vietnam War epic.[12]) One might reflect, too, on the media attention to General Petraeus' resignation from the directorship of the CIA, just after the 2012 election, focusing on two socialite twins in Tampa and their odd involvements with the nation's military elite. One veteran commentator on American politics, the journalist Barton Gellman (2012: 37), described the general as a "four-star rock star," and quoted one outspoken high-ranking officer as arguing that Petraeus was "a remarkable piece of fiction created and promoted by neo-cons in government, the media and academia."[13] So if President Eisenhower, leaving office, warned of the growth of a military-industrial complex, perhaps there is a military-entertainment complex as well.

Conspiracy Theories, Postmodern Monarchies, and Soft Power

I conclude with a few final speculations. I wonder what the relationship may be between the sense of politics as entertainment and a certain weakness for conspiracy theory. Almost a half-century ago, Richard Hofstadter (1965), the historian, described a "paranoid style" in American politics; I think the suspicion that things are not what they seem to be, or are made out to be, continues to find new expressions. It is true that "conspiracy theory" is a broad term that can cover many things. For those who prefer to practice conspiracy denial, it may sometimes become merely a convenient label for certain inconvenient views. In times of erratic security apparatuses and concealed surveillance practices, some conspiracy theorizing may be in order.

Some common varieties of it are more dubious. To a degree, conspiracy theories may be a simple outcome of scale. The United States is a large and complex country, naturally less transparent than a smaller place. If people perhaps have a sense that all this theatrical politics could not be quite everything there is to it—that behind the show there must also be a back stage—then the theater state and somewhat routinized conspiracy thinking could become symbiotic in yet a different way. It is also true that conspiracy is itself a significant genre in popular media fiction, and this can then offer an interpretive model for real life as well. Personally, I am more inclined to think that the more complex a society gets, the more difficult it becomes to achieve an overview of its structures, to manage them, and to predict how they will behave. There will be lots of room for variably deliberate actions with unintended consequences. I am inclined to offer more room for what has been called "confusion theory." Of course it might also be that this is just the view of a naïve visitor from a smaller and seemingly more transparent society.[14]

Now you may also feel that it involves some audacity for somebody from a small European monarchy to speak of America as a theater state. What about these countries with all their kings and queens and princes and princesses? Well, indeed. I have been told that Geertz had some inspiration for his notion of the theater state from his understandings of early twentieth-century central Europe, the Habsburg Empire and beyond. But then consider the possibility that this kind of ancient political arrangement, in its current fairly postmodern version, just might make some sense. In its late twentieth-century, early twenty-first-century variant, largely powerless kings and queens and their offspring play their specialized roles as super-celebrities, performing for the nation, while the state in a stricter sense is not so theatrical. The American combination of the divisive potential of governance, of statecraft, with the need for unity in hailing the chief, the personification of the nation, may well be trickier. Admittedly I offer this as a sort of tongue-in-cheek interpretation; but I could add that two *New York Times* columnists, Nicholas Kristof (2010) and Gail Collins (2013), have at different times, seemingly independently of one another, taken rather similar views.[15] Then I must also note that the theatrical element has lately tended to spread in European politics as well—again with a decline of party organizations, again under expanding media influence. Italy's on-again, off-again prime minister, Silvio Berlusconi, media tycoon, soccer team owner, occasional comedian and crooner, and host of scandalous parties, was to a degree a case in point, although that may be yet another kind of theater state. The breed of neo-nationalist politicians—such as the late Jörg Haider in Austria, and Pim Fortuyn as well as Geert Wilders in the Netherlands—perhaps offers closer comparisons.[16]

Finally, a few words about the American theater state in the global ecumene. Now all the world's a stage, and to a degree a single stage. The American blend of entertainment and politics becomes available, hardly in full but in bits and pieces, across borders. I last heard Paul Harvey rather regularly in 2004 when I was in Tokyo, his daily commentary featured on an Armed Forces Network radio station that happened to be the most readily available English-language news source. So how is American political culture received, and perceived, abroad?

There are international relations scholars who argue that American influence in the world should be anchored as much as possible in what they like to term "soft power." Harvard professor Joseph Nye (e.g., 2002, 2004), who coined the concept, is the most prominent spokesman for this view. Perhaps a somewhat paradoxical notion, soft power rests on the ability to set the political agenda in a way that shapes the preferences of others. It co-opts rather than coerces people; "if I can get you to *want* to do what I want, then I do not have to force you to do what you do *not* want to do" (Nye 2002: 9). This may resemble a certain older concept: Nye is aware that Antonio Gramsci, classic Italian Marxist, used the term hegemony to describe something like this. In any case, soft power in large part involves culture. Nye cites values of democracy, personal freedom, openness and upward mobility as characteristic of American soft power, projected in a multiplicity of ways, through higher education or through foreign policy, but not least through popular culture. With the latter in mind, he quotes with approval a leading German publicist (Josef Joffe, editor of *Die Zeit*) who concludes that what America has at present is a soft power that "rules over an empire on which the sun never sets."

I think that is an interesting suggestion, but I suspect that reality is a little more complicated. As people elsewhere catch fragments of the stories Americans tell themselves about themselves and their politics, they, too, may often be entertained, sometimes charmed, but also at times alarmed. My own view would be that American soft power is really more multifaceted than that.[17] It can draw effectively on the global, but differentiated, outreach of the country's internal diversity, so that people elsewhere in the world often find their own niches of more intense personal engagement in particular, more or less subcultural American contexts—whether these are professional, regional, or recreational, or involve lifestyles or kinship networks. These connections, in turn, may place them in different corners with regard to the wider American political culture and its internal disputes. But that is another matter that I think about as I continue my visits to the theme park of my life.

Ulf Hannerz is Professor Emeritus of Social Anthropology, Stockholm University, Sweden, and a member of the Royal Swedish Academy of Sciences, the Austrian Academy of Sciences, and the American Academy of Arts and Sciences. He is a former Chair of the European Association of Social Anthropologists. He has carried out field studies in West Africa, the Caribbean, and the United States, as well as a multisite study of the work of news-media foreign correspondents. Among his books are *Soulside* (1969), *Transnational Connections* (1996), and *Foreign News* (2004). He was awarded an honorary doctorate by the University of Oslo in 2005.

Acknowledgments

The first version of this chapter was presented as a paper in the Executive Session "America Observed: Ethnographic Perspectives from the Outside World" at the annual meeting of the American Anthropological Association, New Orleans, 17–21 November 2010. I thank the organizers, Jasmin Habib and Virginia R. Dominguez, for inviting me to the session; Roger Sanjek and Jane C. Desmond, who served very constructively as discussants; and also those others who contributed to the discussion in that session. Sophia Balakian commented very usefully on a later version, and I am grateful for that as well.

Notes

1. I have gone over some of this in my book *Anthropology's World* (2010: 98–102).
2. Gunnar Myrdal (not an anthropologist) did indeed write about the American dilemma in race relations mostly for Americans, and also about the United States for a Swedish audience; after returning to his native country, he wrote a short book, *Amerika mitt i världen* (America in the middle of the world), which in large part dwelt on what Sweden could learn from the United States (Myrdal 1943).
3. Since this chapter was written in its first version, a leading US cultural sociologist, Jeffrey Alexander (2011), has published a book-length study of the role of performance in politics; largely a theoretical treatise, although with a focus on the 2008 election and President Obama. As he does not dwell much on the particular features of US politics from a comparative point of view, however, I have not endeavored to relate my presentation to his interpretation here.
4. Perhaps Paul Harvey's name is not now familiar to everybody. His broadcasts were carried on 1,200 radio stations and 400 Armed Forces Network stations, with a listening audience peaking at an estimated 24 million per week. His broadcasts and newspaper articles "have been reprinted in the Congressional Record more than those

of any other commentator." At various times, a number of American politicians substituted for him in his programs: Mitt Romney, Mike Huckabee, Fred Thompson. "The most noticeable features of Harvey's folksy delivery were his dramatic pauses and quirky intonations." This is from *Wikipedia*, accessed on 30 October 2010.

5. Before that, Hollywood had also provided a US Senator for California, the song-and-dance man George Murphy, who served between 1965 and 1971.

6. The popular comparison of President Obama with Spock, the figure in the *Star Trek* television series, obviously fits very well with the line of interpretation followed in this essay. A couple of years later, as it was widely held that Obama had not done so well in his first televised campaign debate with his Republican adversary Mitt Romney, he commented in an interview, after having been re-elected, "that particular format has never been a strength of mine. I don't approach most interactions with people trying to insult them or show how stupid they are. And that's how you score points in those things. It's a very artificial construct. It's theater" (Stengel, Jones, and Scherer, 2012/13: 67). At the end of the 2012 campaign, too, it drew much attention and was widely and repeatedly televised that the president twice shed tears.

7. In recent presidential elections, more than 60 percent of US voters have participated, but in earlier elections the vote may have been closer to 50 percent, and in congressional elections in the years between presidential elections, it can be lower still. In Scandinavian parliamentary elections, the voter turnout is normally between 80 and 90 percent.

8. A less memorable instance of displaying presumably unexpected talent was that of Tom DeLay, former Republican Congressman and ex-Majority Leader, appearing in the television show *Dancing With the Stars*. But this was after his time in Congress had ended, after charges of money laundering, although he was still politically active.

9. The journalist Mark Leibovich's book *This Town* (2013) is a vivid account of local political life in Washington, but it also shows the close connections between politicians, lobbyists, and the media. The opening scene, the funeral of a political talk show host, is certainly from an event of the theater state.

10. I note here the critical account by Jill Lepore in *The New Yorker* (2015) of the past and present of polling, and of commentary on it over time. (Indeed I often find the long-form journalism in this and other American weeklies and monthlies particularly illuminating as I try to stay informed of the workings of US politics.)

11. The Republican vice-presidential candidate in 1996, former Congressman Jack Kemp, had been a professional football player, and President Gerald Ford had been on the University of Michigan football team. This may have mattered early in their political careers, but probably not much in later stages. President Obama's preference for basketball may have endeared him to some, and broadened his public persona, but does not precisely involve stardom.

12. Wallace had apparently also attempted to get Colonel Harland Sanders, founder of Kentucky Fried Chicken (KFC) to take on the vice presidential candidacy.

13. I interviewed Gellman for my study of foreign correspondents in Jerusalem in 1997, when he was the Middle East correspondent for *The Washington Post*; he had already been his paper's Pentagon reporter before that (Hannerz 2004: 80–81).

14. While I cannot go into this here, the understanding of conspiracy theories has certainly by now developed beyond the point where Hofstadter left it. It has become more comparative—the belief in conspiracies is certainly not a uniquely American phenomenon. There is now also less inclination to see it in terms of pathological delusion, and more interest in considering the variety of collective understandings and their social bases. See on this West and Sanders (2003), and with regard to recent American circumstances, especially Harding and Stewart (2003), Hellinger (2003), and deHaven-Smith (2013). A non-academic but serious study of conspiracy theory in modern history,

focusing on American and British materials and stretching into the very recent past, is by Aaronovitch (2009).

15. I could also note, on the other hand, that after spending an extended period as foreign correspondent in the United States, one prominent British journalist, Jonathan Freedland, wrote a book named *Bring Home the Revolution: The Case for a British Republic* (1998).

16. See Gingrich and Banks (2006) on neo-nationalism in Europe and beyond.

17. I first sketched this view quite some time ago (Hannerz 1992) and then related it more directly to the notion of soft power, which had developed in the intervening years, in a book chapter in Swedish more recently (Hannerz 2011).

References

Aaronovitch, David. 2009. *Voodoo Histories*. London: Jonathan Cape.

Adorno, Theodor W. 1991. *The Culture Industry*, ed. J.M. Bernstein. London: Routledge.

Alexander, Jeffrey C. 2011. *Performance and Power*. Cambridge: Polity Press.

Bai, Matt. 2010. "Illinois Keeps Obama at Arm's Length." *New York Times*, August 5.

Baudrillard, Jean. 1988. *America*. London: Verso.

Collins, Gail. 2013. "Windsors Versus Weiner." *New York Times*, July 24.

deHaven-Smith, Lance. 2013. *Conspiracy Theory in America*. Austin: University of Texas Press.

Freedland, Jonathan. 1998. *Bring Home the Revolution*. London: Fourth Estate.

Geertz, Clifford. 1980. *Negara*. Princeton, NJ: Princeton University Press.

Gellman, Barton. 2012. Spyfall. *Time* November 26: 32–38.

Gingrich, Andre, and Marcus Banks, eds. 2006. *Neo-nationalism in Europe and Beyond*. Oxford: Berghahn.

Hannerz, Ulf. 1992. "Networks of Americanization." In *Networks of Americanization*, ed. Rolf Lundén and Erik Åsard. Uppsala: Studia Anglistica Upsaliensia/Acta Universitatis Upsaliensis.

———. 2004. *Foreign News*. Chicago: University of Chicago Press.

———. 2010. *Anthropology's World*. London: Pluto Press.

———. 2011. *Café du Monde*. Stockholm: Carlssons.

Harding, Susan, and Kathleen Stewart. 2003. "Anxieties of Influence: Conspiracy Theory and Therapeutic Culture in Millennial America." In *Transparency and Conspiracy*, ed. Harry G. West and Todd Sanders. Durham, NC: Duke University Press.

Hellinger, Daniel. 2003. "Paranoia, Conspiracy, and Hegemony in American Politics." In *Transparency and Conspiracy*, ed. Harry G. West and Todd Sanders. Durham, NC: Duke University Press.

Hofstadter, Richard. 1965. *The Paranoid Style in American Politics*. Cambridge, MA: Harvard University Press.

Kaplan, Robert. 2000. *The Coming Anarchy: Shattering the Dreams of the Post Cold War.* New York: Random House.

Kristof, Nicholas D. 2010. "A Modest Proposal: A King and Queen for America." *New York Times,* June 9.

Leibovich, Mark. 2013. *This Town.* New York: Blue Rider Press.

Lepore, Jill. 2015. "Politics and the New Machine." *New Yorker,* November 16.

Maalouf, Amin. 2011. *Disordered World.* New York: Bloomsbury USA.

Myrdal, Gunnar. 1943. *Amerika mitt i världen.* Stockholm: Kooperativa Förbundet.

———. 1944. *An American Dilemma.* New York: Harper & Row.

Nye, Joseph. 2002. *The Paradox of American Power.* New York: Oxford University Press.

———. 2004. *Soft Power.* New York: Public Affairs.

Sombart, Werner. 1906. *Warum gibt es in den Vereinigten Staaten keinen Sozialismus?* Tübingen: Mohr.

Stengel, Rick, Radhika Jones, and Michael Scherer. 2012/13. "Setting the Stage for a Second Term (Interview with Barack Obama.)" *Time* December 31/January 7: 64–67.

West, Harry G., and Todd Sanders, eds. 2003. *Transparency and Conspiracy.* Durham, NC: Duke University Press.

Zakaria, Fareed. 2008. *The Post-American World.* New York: Norton.

Chapter Five

Observing US Gay Organizations and Voluntary Associations
An Outsider's Exposition

Moshe Shokeid

I intend to present my long-term observation of a subject that has fascinated me for the last few decades, since I was first introduced to the field of gay life in New York. As later portrayed in detail, I was attracted to the variety and the continuing emergence of new voluntary associations among gay people. My observations expose another reality of gay life neglected in most ethnographic studies among gay men in particular, removed from the field of anonymous sexual relationships in commercial sites and public spaces. I compare these observations with the circumstances of gay voluntary associations in my Israeli home society. However, I start with a few biographical notes about my academic background and research engagements prior to my work in New York.

I completed undergraduate and MA studies in sociology at the Hebrew University in Jerusalem. I also worked for some years as an applied sociologist with the Jewish Agency Land Settlement Department, advising on the absorption of the massive post-1948 wave of Jewish immigrants in new urban and rural communities. "Discovering" the benefits of research in close proximity to the observed people, I decided to change my professional venue and methodology and pursue anthropological studies. I graduated with a degree in anthropology from the University of Manchester in 1968 having written my PhD dissertation on how Jewish immigrants from the Atlas Mountains experienced social change and handled modern farming in an Israeli cooperative village. I made my first trip to the US a few years later, in 1971. But it took another ten

Notes for this chapter begin on page 137.

years, till 1982, to start my fieldwork project among Israeli emigrants in Queens (Shokeid 1988). That study, though relevant to my Israeli citizenship, evoked in me the intriguing idea of researching "up" at the center of Western metropolitan society rather than pursuing anthropologists' more common ethnographic projects of colonial, post-colonial, ethnic urban enclaves or disadvantaged marginal groups in Europe and the US. This proved to be the start of a chain of ethnographic studies that led me to the field of gay life; from the gay synagogue in Greenwich Village (Shokeid 1995/2003) to the various voluntary organizations operating in the Gay and Lesbian Community Services Center, also in the Village.

However, my choice of New York seemed at the time an unusual departure from the mainstream research field sites in Third World societies remote from Western cultures, or from the new trend of research projects "at home." The US seemed the least suitable for an ordinary ethnographic project. The leading world economy and the most powerful nation on the planet had not been included in the map of ethnographic fieldwork sites envisioned by the founders and later generations in the evolution of anthropology. Whatever the social problems observed in US society, such as the issues of race, ethnicity and social stratification, it seemed far from the current interests and the practical expertise of an outsider anthropologist. No doubt, it was the urge to study the Israeli emigrants nicknamed *Yordim* (those who go down) with whom I shared a national history, culture, and language that made me feel suited to conduct a research project in the US.

Since then, however, New York remained my mecca, reminding me of my teachers in Manchester who dedicated their lifelong careers to the research of individuals and tribal groups in African villages and towns. Their informants' habits and customs seemed to them to represent some basic universal elements of social behavior, particularly in the domains of family life, economics, religion, and politics. Thus, my mentor, the late Max Gluckman, developed a theory of social conflict based on his observations as well as on ethnographic works of others conducted in African societies (e.g., *Custom and Conflict in Africa* 1963). I also share with my Manchester teachers and colleagues a commitment to "thick description," demonstrated in particular through a fieldwork strategy they promoted: "the extended case method."[1]

However, my ongoing dedication to fieldwork sites in New York and my fascination with Americans' habits of association arise no less from my comprehension of the United States' exceptionality, as compared with my Israeli home society and culture in particular. At the same time, however, it raised my awareness about the unique role of voluntary associations in US culture, revealed long ago by de Tocqueville (1956 [1835]) and other early visitors, among them the Dutchman Johan Huizinga (1972 [1927]). But local and later observers also commented on this cultural habit of their compatriots (e.g., Bellah et al. 1996 [1985]; Ginsberg 1989). This type of civil organization has over time expanded tremendously in its range of themes and field of action, engaging its participants in a far more therapeutic model than that linked with their traditional tasks and style of sociability (e.g., Wuthnow 1994). Thus, early and more recent observers have commented as follows:

> de Tocqueville: "Americans of all ages, all conditions, and all dispositions, constantly form associations." (1956: 198)

> Huizinga was impressed by the "frequency of groups," which he perceived as *illusiongemeinschaft*. (1972 [1927]: 275–80)

> Bellah et al.: "For all their doubts about the public sphere, Americans are more engaged in voluntary associations and civic organizations than the citizens of most other industrial nations." (1985: 167)

> Ginsberg: ". . . the means available [in the American social system] for achieving identity are through voluntary affiliation with others in a group . . ." (1989: 220–21)

> Wuthnow: ". . . the small-group movement . . . reflects the most fundamental dilemmas of our society. It stands in the tradition of voluntary associations and it emulates the work of churches and synagogues." (1994: 4)

My claim, based in particular on my later observations at the Greenwich Village Center, calls attention to the ever-changing characteristics of voluntary associations in contemporary American urban life. These are no longer confined to reputable and worthy agendas in terms of mainstream society. These new groups do not necessarily intend to contribute to commendable goals of communal or national improvement and reform, nor are they an authentic extension of religious congregational life. Indeed, recent observations identified signs of the decline of associational involvement—"the crisis of civic engagement," in contrast to the growth of support groups such as twelve-step groups (e.g., Bellah et al. 1996: xvii). As indicated earlier, my enchantment with the phenomenon of associations in New York was sparked by observations in my Israeli home society—comparisons that remained potent in my thoughts all through my research engagements in New York. I will return to this perception of social duality below.

Conducting Research at Gay Venues

When I was starting to sum up my observations at the gay synagogue, the bulk of ethnographic studies available on gay life in the US had been conducted mostly by US observers who concentrated in particular on gay men's interactions at venues of anonymous sex. Not surprisingly, following the eruption of gay liberation, the gay male scene offered an ever-widening choice of commercial sites and public spaces providing numerous opportunities for sexual encounters at safe and inexpensive premises (bathhouses, bars and back rooms, video parlors, porno stores, parks and rest areas, and so on). These places were no less attractive for ethnographic fieldwork and sociological analysis. However, these studies were mostly based on Goffman's methodology and theoretical premises of symbolic interaction (e.g., Humphreys 1970; Delph 1978; Levine 1979; Style 1979; Altman 1986; Bersani 1988; Brodsky 1993; Bolton 1995; Leap 1999). Both the participants and the ethnographers in these sites maintained a silent presence with very little verbal communication, disguising their identities and other personal and social interests. Thus, these studies repeatedly set forth anonymous relationships among the participants as well as between the observed subjects and their observers.

In contrast, my observations in the 1990s and 2000s among the various groups meeting at the Village Center exposed another reality of gay life, removed from the field of anonymous relationships. Moreover, I had begun circulating a few years earlier among a different type of gay social venue: the gay and lesbian synagogue in New York. This engagement led me in later years to extend my observations also to the major gay Christian congregations in New York: Metropolitan Community Church (MCC)—Protestant; Dignity—Catholic; and Unity—Afro-American (Shokeid 2015).

The SAGE Circle

I will begin by quoting from the first summary of my six months of observations at the weekly gatherings of the SAGE Circle, a group of senior gay men who met at the Gay and Lesbian Community Services Center in Greenwich Village:

> The emergence of gay affective fellowships in major urban centers, that enable men to meet men as fully identified personae, indicates a new stage in the institutionalization of gay life, as gay people occupy new spaces and adopt forms of association shared with mainstream society . . . My Israeli upbringing did not prepare me to easily accommodate with the divulging to strangers the

intimacies of daily life, with love in particular, nor, the language used to do so . . . Therapeutic attitudes as a major perspective on life, which have been adopted in recent decades by the middle-class mainstream, were frequently woven into the discussion of the SAGE Circle. That language is not part of the Israeli cultural baggage, where therapy is generally reserved for those with severe emotional problems and usually kept secret. (Shokeid 2001a: 24–25)

The weekly SAGE meetings engaged a stable group of participants with no fewer than twenty regulars, among them a strong core of members who took care of the smooth running of the group's activities. The subject of the weekly discussion convened by one of the members was chosen at the end of the first round of the sharing of issues raised by the attendees. These discussions and often friendly debates engaged in issues of gay partnership, family relationships, personal economic and health problems, retirement and relationships at the work place, etc. At the end of the evening meeting most participants continued together for dinner at a nearby restaurant, talking about personal and public matters.

The SAGE Circle was one of several of the hundred-plus voluntary groups that held meetings at the Greenwich Village Center, opened in 1983 by gay and lesbian activists, in a decaying 150-year-old labyrinthine school facility located in a busy residential area (on West 13th Street). Many of these groups were extensions of national organizations (SAGE included). The diverse cohort of groups that I observed in the late 1990s and early 2000s were composed of bisexuals, the spiritual Radical Fairies, men attracted across race, the macho Leathermen, the tender Bears, the affectionate Gentlemen, Gay Fathers, sufferers of sexual compulsiveness, and other groups catering to specific ethnic and cultural interests, sexual proclivities, or personal addictions (alcohol, drugs, and so forth).

The Sexual Compulsive Anonymous (SCA) groups

An example of the warm and open relationships among participants in the voluntary associations I observed is represented by an SCA member who shared his feelings with me, and also with attendees at a public meeting: "We know we are addicts and we are not going to give up our sexual compulsion, but we help each other, listening and sharing. We have many friends here and have a great time together." Without doubt, the SCA meetings at various locations and institutional settings (the Center, churches, etc.) provided the stage that enabled its many participants to openly narrate their most intimate and painful experiences in an endless and often risky search for anonymous sex. Without shame or guilt, they shared with their fellow "addicts" their despairing sexual behavior, its emotional and daily existential consequences that seemed to ruin their lives. For example, Saul, a youthful looking man in his mid-30s, inspired sympathy with his somewhat humorous, self-mocking style and his streak of optimism. He hated tearooms (public toilets in gay terminology) he said, they were "boring," but celibacy was even more boring and consequently he could not keep away from these boring places. On another occasion he confessed he was disgusted with his own compulsion to have predictably humiliating sex, ending on his knees in a dark room begging for affection from men who were "shut off" from any emotion. "I am probably crazy," he concluded, "but I am happy I can share the shit with you."

My conclusion in that case contradicted the clinicians' dismissal of these gatherings as a curing tool (e.g., Quadland 1985; Baum and Fishman 1994); it is not the anticipated cure of sexual behavior that keeps these groups going. A "cure" in the clinical sense, I argued, is contradictory to the production of *communitas*, which emerges as the major achievement of SCA group activities. The SCA fellowship offered its members, younger and older (mostly men but also a minority of women), a vast field of social activities beyond the scheduled meetings dedicated to the "ritual" of sharing. Participants might join one group or more in the repertoire of SCA weekly meetings. There they developed networks of close friends, who became a major source of social support, offering a safe escape from loneliness and its destructive consequences. These meetings were usually crowded, with no fewer than twenty participants representing various socio-economic circumstances, including a core of regulars in each group who took care of its administration (Shokeid 2002).

The existential conditions of gay people in contemporary urban environments were succinctly described by Bech (1997: 98): "The city, with its crowds and mutual strangers, is the place where the homosexual can come together with others; and—at the same time and for the same reasons—it is the place that confirms his loneliness."

However, Bech's observations about the "place where the homosexual can come together with others" mostly referred to the scene of gay sociability and institutions that seem to represent venues characterized as sites of "anonymous sex" (bars, baths, parks, and other venues). In my view, the SCA organization, as well as other groups presented here, emerged as a response to the predicament of the loneliness Bech described as a major feature of gay life in metropolitan cities. Like all other organizations I observed (national or local), its emergence was the outcome of the initiative of dedicated individuals active in the gay/lesbian community.

Blacks and Whites Together

My observations of an interracial—black and white—gay men's association
(Men of All Colors Together, MACT), revealed the scene that allowed men
attracted to another race to express their sexual proclivity and choice of
mates in a safe space free of the prejudices involved with that infatuation
(apart from the groups at the Center with exclusive ethnic membership).
Attracted to an interracial sexual relationship, white and black men alike
carry in the popular imagination the offensive view of a shameful sexual
taste, fascination with the black man's fabled genital endowment in particular. These humiliating stereotypes were bluntly confronted in the
association's anniversary publication, such as "the mythical notion of our
group as a social club dominated by older white men seeking sex with
younger black men." Instead, a veteran white member told me at a board
meeting: "People join because they are physically attracted cross-racially,
but later they discover there is something else that relates to rights and
other things."

Like most other groups on my list, the MACT is a national organization.
The weekly meetings with twenty to forty attendees, the majority of the
regular participants in their thirties and forties who seemed to represent a
lower middle class, were dedicated to various social, cultural, and political
issues related to the lives of the membership as black and white citizens
of the United States. Exciting in particular were the meetings dedicated to
a discourse on gay relationships and sexual topics, such as the myth and
reality of male genitalia.

As reported by the participants, the organization went through a
gradual change from the political agenda that had initiated this forum
in 1980. In its early days the membership was mobilized in particular to
address racial inequality in daily life in the US. However, with the changing circumstances of blacks in US society the association's agenda and
activities turned into more pleasurable, entertainment-oriented social
gatherings. Even so, the uninhibited yet friendly discourse evident at the
weekly meetings revealed no less the persistent schisms and racial tensions prevalent in US society. Black and white participants expressed their
disappointment at the unexpected manner in which even their attending
friends sometimes responded to situations involving racial expressions
and prejudices. Nevertheless, open discourse proceeded in a friendly
atmosphere that encouraged warm relationships among the participants,
who met for other outdoor activities too (dinners after meetings, weekend
retreats, an annual Hudson River cruise, birthday parties, and more). That
friendly ambience often initiated the more intimate bonding for sex and

for a lasting conjugal partnership between white and black individuals (Shokeid 2010).

The Bisexual Circle

The bisexual circle I observed was not an extension of a national organization but a local group initiated and advertised by a core of interested individuals. The group was hosted, like all the others, at the Center, which also publicized them in its monthly newsletter and on the daily list of activities posted at the entrance to the building. The core group of regulars consisted of a few women and men, widely diverse in age and mostly college graduates, who had some prior experience as heterosexuals (mostly divorced at that stage) or as gays and lesbians. They were exploring and trying to validate their "true" sexual identity, whether gay/lesbian, heterosexual, or both.

At the weekly meetings they related their past and present sexual experiences and considered their options for future relationships, whether with the same or with the other sex. They discussed the theories and stereotypes concerning humans' sexual nature, expressing bitterness at the stigma associated with the status of people who declare their "dual attraction." They openly shared with the members intimate information about their relationships with both genders, often delivered in a professional style. Rose, a veteran member, concluded her story of changing relationships with men and women: "I had moved along the Kinsey scale from heterosexuality to lesbianism, back and forth. What is the definition fitting me?"

Similar to the observations during the SCA meetings, I was impressed by the bisexual circle participants' lack of inhibition narrating in public intimate and painful experiences, often in the company of strangers. It was equally striking to observe the audience's willingness to listen to these often-repeated stories. Here too a few participants established close relationships, though mostly with same-sex partners.

My conclusion seemed to repeat my observations among the SCA participants. They were not really "cured" in terms of proving their "true" sexual (bisexual or gay/lesbian) identity. They remained wrestling with this dilemma, although they often spoke about a recent same-sex choice of partner who seemed much easier to encounter in real-life situations. I came to believe that the bisexual circle offered some participants an easier way into the land of gay/lesbian institutions, which they might not have dared enter if they had to take that step without the comfort and safety of these afternoon gatherings at the Center's premises as a sort of "neutral no man's land" (Shokeid 2001a).

The Bears

At the Bears' meetings, the association offered younger and older gay men of diverse background a warm reception free of the mainstream gay code of the trim body and trendy dress fashions. They had usually a "rough" appearance with beards and often heavy body frame (small paunch included), as described by Harris (1997: 105–6): "The Bear phenomenon represents one of the most violent assaults that gay men have made to date against the over-groomed bodies of urban homosexuals. The bear is a man who allows himself to age in public, refusing to reverse the ravages of time by burying them beneath Max Factor foundation bases, face-lifts, Grecian rinses, and hair replacement systems."

The Bears meetings at the Center were mostly devoted to discussions about the next events of parties and outdoor activities, such as exclusive bar meetings for the membership or weekend retreats that promised opportunities to meet with old and new friends and encounter mates for sex and partnership. Those events were marked by a tangible erotic atmosphere, allowing participants to openly express their sexual infatuations, and act upon their dreams with few inhibitions. On a dinner cruise I attended at the association's national annual meeting in Chicago, I enjoyed long conversations with Fred, a Jewish academic from a southern city in his late forties. In response to my query about the attraction that recruited 1,400 men to come along, he told me: "These people, many of them are old and not beautiful in ordinary terms. They enjoy coming here because of the reassurance they will discover here that they can be loved and desirable!" (Shokeid 2015: 149)

Gay Fathers Circle

The Gay Fathers Association assembled men who had children from an earlier married life. The weekly meetings enabled them to express their difficulties, obligations, and expectations as absentee parents. Sharing their experiences of separation from their children (who usually remained in the custody of the ex-spouse), revealed a wide spectrum of feelings—guilt, pain, anger, and hope. The participants offered each other legal advice as well as practical and emotional support. However, the atmosphere at meetings was usually relaxed and often jovial. The participants informed the group about their life and work, including intimate details of their love experiences. The group gatherings offered opportunities for the development of close friendships and a safe scene for meeting with mates for sex and partnership.

The Gentlemen

The Gentlemen Circle was initiated by an imaginative gay man in New York, a behavioral sciences professional. The group participants, who seemed to be of all ages, were trained to express physical affection toward their fellow attendees regardless of age and physical appearance. That activity was performed at the weekly meetings through a series of exercises that directed participants to caress their partners lightly and affectionately. These short intervals of delicate physical contacts allowed the participants to experience the close nonsexual affectionate touching they often missed in daily life. However, the meetings started and ended with a round of "sharing" that enabled all participants to express their feelings about the event as well as relate their recent experiences as gay people. Naturally, these affectionate communications opened the possibilities of developing networks of close friends and occasionally leading to a lasting intimate relationship. This New York-based innovation in the field of gay voluntary associations proved a most successful contribution to the Center's activities, offering unconditional intimacy to men lacking the courage or the looks to pursue their desires at other gay venues. The inventor of this social activity transformed the shady premises and the oppressive erotic atmosphere at the anonymous sex venues into an affectionate experience in a safe and a well-lit space (Shokeid 2015).

The Viability of Associations and the Style of Discourse

However, not all emerging associations remained viable or survived for many years. Membership of the association of blacks and whites seems to have dwindled in recent years. This was probably due to the emergence of new associations catering to blacks and other gay ethnic constituencies, as well as the changing social climate in US society relevant to interracial relationships. The Gentlemen Circle was abandoned with the withdrawal of its creator and the departure of the group's core of members who for a while continued to conduct these meetings in his absence. A similar fate awaited the Gay Fathers association, with the changes in gay life when fewer younger closeted gay men marry and have children under the pressure of mainstream society. But these developments only mirror the creative forces and the potential audiences that energize the emergence of various affectionate voluntary associations in contemporary US gay society.

Most important, the groups I introduced above did not represent support groups led by professionals intended to help endure sudden acute traumatic personal emotional afflictions such as imminent death, mourning the loss of loved ones, problematic relationships in the family, and so on. These voluntary associations run by dedicated lay individuals seemed to serve as substitutes for, or an expansion of, the field of gay institutions that catered to the gay constituency before and after the eruption of "gay liberation." I refrain from the stereotypical assumption that these organizations serve to replace the loss of family and community among gay people. I consider that supposition outdated when applied to contemporary heterosexual or homosexual urban people.

The construction of the "community" as a major social institution in Americans' lives recalls a real or an imagined world of preindustrial villages and of idyllic suburbs, far removed from the existential conditions of modern living in a metropolitan environment in particular. As succinctly stated by Putnam in *Bowling Alone* (2000: 402), "Americans are *right* that the bonds of our communities have withered, and we are *right* to fear that this transformation has very real costs" (emphasis added). In any case, gay people today have new options to build their families as couples and parents (e.g., Weston 1991: Lewin 1993, 2009), to inhabit city enclaves and control municipal neighborhoods (Newton 1993; Faiman-Silva 2004). The gay synagogue and gay churches exhibit similar features of social gatherings resembling voluntary associations that offer a safe space for meeting friends and engaging with intimate partners, enjoying affectionate relationships, and entering into zestful discourse on existential issues, thereby expanding the plethora of gay/lesbian institutions in a metropolitan environment.

All the organizations I observed offered opportunities to meet with partners for a loving and sexual relationship, but these were not pick-up venues like most other anonymous sex establishments that draw men often stripped of their clothing, but no less stripped of their social identity. Hiding the participants' social identity naturally diminished their personal resources, skills, and other qualities that could affect the nature of interpersonal attraction and sustain long-term relationships. A young gay man told me that he loved attending the Center's activities because its atmosphere was free of the compelling erotic sensation and the pressure to engage in sex. He defined the Center as "a gentleman's dream."

Although those associations' gatherings did not assume the structure and strategy of support groups, the style of discourse at meetings did exhibit a therapeutic mode of interaction. The "innocent" foreign observer was struck by the participants' eloquent narratives relating sensitive intimate emotive experiences presented in a sort of professional style. Although expressing personal emotionally taxing issues, the narrators exhibited a restrained—almost "pedagogical"—delivery, and seemed open to their listeners' comments. Undoubtedly, not a few participants had engaged earlier in their lives in personal therapy or were currently meeting regularly with an analyst, their "shrink." I was proudly informed sometimes about participants who postponed an appointment with their therapist in order to attend a meeting at the Center. I was gradually convinced that many attendees had been accustomed to a therapeutic approach, a manner demonstrated during their discourse on their own as well as their friends' personal confidential matters.

The mode of discourse I treat as characteristic of the "therapeutic culture in America" has a long tradition in writings exploring the early success of Freudian psychoanalytic theories and therapy. As suggested by Rieff, "Freud is America's great teacher who introduced the psychological man of the twentieth century" (1990 [1960]: 8). "As a movement, psychoanalysis was fortunate enough to achieve a counter-transference in America" (Ibid. 12), and in daily life, "to become a psychological man is thus to become kinder to the whole self, the private parts as well as the public, the formerly inferior as well as the formerly superior" (Ibid. 5). Or, as suggested by Steadman Rice (2004: 113), "the therapeutic ethic is constructed around the conviction that human nature is intrinsically benevolent, positive, and constructive". Another outsider, Illouz (2008), commented recently: "Psychoanalysis [in America] enjoyed not only the authority of a prestigious medical profession but also wide popularity among the 'lay' public" (Ibid.: 35), "the therapeutic discourse has become a cultural form, shaping and organizing experience, as well as a cultural resource with which to make sense of the self and social relations" (Ibid.: 56), ". . . making private selfhood a narrative to be told and consumed publicly" (Ibid.: 239).

However, the publicly presented intimate narrative sessions I observed were not akin to the popular TV "strip" talk shows, addressed to anonymous audiences such as the programs of Oprah and other presenters (e.g., Kaminer 1992; Plummer 2003). The gatherings at the Center were not anonymous confession encounters (reminiscent of the "anonymous sex" scene). Most attendees were regulars—familiar with their fellow presenters, and a notion of emotional mutuality dominated these gatherings even when new, unknown visitors came along.

Gay Life in Israel

I move now to the second section of the chapter. Like many other developments in US society and culture, these changes in gay social circumstances
and terms of sociability have had an impact and a circulation elsewhere in
the European and European-origin world. Though gay life has exhibited
a parallel history of liberation in many European countries, the process
and pace of change in Israel has taken a different course. As suggested by
observers of Israeli society, it is a nation torn between its grounding in
the modern, industrialized, democratic world and the stronghold of the
conservative Orthodox Jewish establishment (for example, the rabbinical
courts' jurisdiction has a monopoly on intimate personal issues such as
marriage and divorce as well as Jewish burial). A gay Israeli researcher
concluded: "Consequently, local gay men are situated in a unique position
where, among other issues, they aspire to be part of the [Western] gay and
lesbian community while confronting unrelenting pressures from traditional religious and heavily family-oriented norms and values" (Kama
2005: 172).

Only in 1988 did the Knesset repeal the British Mandate's rule making
homosexuality a criminal offense, and new liberal legislation was set
in motion comparing Israel favorably with other Western European
and North Atlantic countries. But the major step for gay rights and gay
visibility in mainstream society was taken only in 1993, when a group
of homosexuals addressed a Knesset committee on social affairs. The
leading spokesman was a professor of chemistry at Tel Aviv University
(Uzi Even), a man in his early fifties. His impressive appearance, which
was also shown on television, left a strong impact on many people who
for the first time watched a gay man announcing his sexual preference in
public. While it took a group of angry drag queens in a New York bar in
1969 to ignite the movement for gay rights in the US, a masculine-looking
reputable academic seems to have been the more appropriate hero for an
Israeli Stonewall twenty-four years later.

Thereafter, change in the public life of gays and lesbians in Israel
advanced apace. The gay researcher quoted above emphasized the "adoption of American elements by local (Israeli) value systems." In particular,
he mentioned the "demedicalization" and "depathologizing" of homosexuality, the infiltration of the US gay liberation movement of the late
1960s into Israeli lesbian-gay sensibility, and the adoption of the US model
of community mobilization through media professionals (Kama 2000: 155).
The shadowy existence of gay public activities was manifested in the sole
Israeli national gay and lesbian organization (founded in Tel Aviv in 1975),
which for many years carried the unobtrusive title The Society for the

Protection of Personal Rights—SPPR (Agudah). Only in 1995 did it advertise its true identity: The Israel Association of Gays, Lesbians, Bisexuals, and Transgendered—GLBT Israel. Probably indicative is the absence in Tel Aviv of a gay residential or entertainment concentration, a Christopher or a Castro street, typical of US metropolitan cities.

My witnessing of gay life in Tel Aviv revealed major changes that took place over ten years. My first observations in 1993 portrayed the invisibility of gay life in the public arena (Shokeid 1995). In 1998, however, a transgendered person, Dana International, won the Eurovision song contest for Israel. A crowd of several hundred young gays and lesbians, as well as others, who joined the impromptu happening in Rabin Square, Tel Aviv's main public space, spontaneously celebrated the good news that night. The international gay rainbow flags were happily hoisted on poles usually used for national and city flags. Male couples kissed in front of the television cameras, to be screened some days later on newscasts. Dana International, a provocative and outspoken person, visited the Knesset and was received by the minister of tourism who served also as deputy prime minister. Dana announced her commitment and devotion to the Israeli gay community.

Two weeks later a fund-raising event to support the battle against AIDS attracted a big crowd, estimated at 3,000–4,000, mostly young gays and lesbians who took over part of Independence Park, Tel Aviv's major beachfront park and until recently the major after-dark cruising and socializing site in Israel (e.g., Fink and Press 1999). Dana's winning song "Diva" was performed repeatedly throughout the afternoon on a stage built for the occasion. I attended in the company of Prof. Uzi Even and his partner (a former SPPR director). They were aware of the dramatic change that had taken place since Uzi Even first publicly announced his homosexuality. The late 1990s also witnessed the emergence of a few more stable gay venues in Tel Aviv. I could not avoid comparing the two heroes of gay public life in Israel who had emerged in a space of five years: the solid professor beside me and the provocative transsexual singer (Shokeid 2003). In June of that year (1998) the first gay parade was inaugurated in Tel Aviv. At last the bells of New York's gay cathedrals were sounding sweet music on the shores of Zion.

The Failure of Gay Associations in Tel Aviv

Without doubt, the position of Israeli gays and lesbians changed dramatically, beyond the expectations of all observers considering the apparently family-oriented and small Israeli society. Israeli gays and lesbians won the same equal legal rights that homosexuals have been granted in most advanced liberal societies (gay marriage excluded). In the late 2000s Tel Aviv also acquired the reputation of a gay-friendly city, alluring to gay tourists. However, my recent observations reveal that efforts made by the emerging gay institutions (the Tel Aviv municipality-supported Gay Center and the veteran SPPR/GLBT Israel) to engage Israeli men in voluntary associations, following the US model, have been unsuccessful. The few social groups meeting at these sites are mostly coordinated by professionals. Those include a forum of older gay men (over the age of sixty) who gather for weekly meetings and who have initiated a theater project. Another bi-weekly activity offers support and advice to gay and lesbian parents. A similar bi-weekly support group is available to transgendered people. Informal bi-weekly meetings are advertised for young gay men and bisexuals. The municipal gay center offers inexpensive psychological counseling and medical services to gays and lesbians, as well as a variety of lectures and other public events. Most significant is the failure to initiate support groups for HIV and AIDS patients

This last disclosure is confirmed by another observation comparing Israeli and US gay men, emerging from a study of narratives told by AIDS patients and shared with a virtual community in internet support networks (Bar-Lev and Tilinger 2009). In these silent though evocative communications, the authors claim that Israeli Hebrew speakers have adopted descriptive terms typical of US gay discourse. At the same time, however, these narratives reflect different cultural codes—the Americans expressing the individual's solitary heroic journey, as against the Israelis striving to present themselves as participants in a collective battle. In their love stories too, the Israelis' expressions appeared to confirm the national ethos of the brotherly love and dedication of combat troops on the battlefield versus the more romantic, erotic engagement in the Americans' confessions.[2] In any event, Israeli gay men seem to consider the internet virtual association an accommodating vehicle and a suitable social arena for expressing their cravings for an affectionate society.

However, of considerable success has been the IGY, the Israel Gay Youth organization, initiated by LGBT Israel (formerly the SPPR or Agudah). The site and the organization gained public exposure and overwhelming support following the murder of two participants and the injury of many others in August 2009 by an unidentified armed masked man shooting indiscriminately during an IGY evening meeting at the LGBT premises in Tel Aviv. That traumatic event resembling a terrorist attack reminded gays and others of the homophobic prejudices and violent hatred that still endanger Israeli gay people even at the heart of "liberal" and "gay-friendly" Tel Aviv.

The Israeli field of gay voluntary associations is undoubtedly far more limited than the US field of gay associations. But this is true also of the wider sphere of voluntary associations in mainstream Israeli society, except for political and civil agendas (mostly "leftists" such as Peace Now, Women in Black, Checkpoint Watch) as well as feminist, or various philanthropic concerns (such as organizations defending legal rights and supporting the welfare of foreign labor and refugees). However, secular Israelis are enthusiastic consumers of various educational programs, usually a series of semi-academic popular lectures that seem the closest to voluntary gatherings of strangers, representing participants often of an older age and of similar socio-economic background.

Gay New York/Tel Aviv: Realities Apart

The gay voluntary associations I observed in New York assembled participants who very rarely might have known other attendees prior to these meetings. The much smaller Israeli society, and its close-knit social construction even in the major urban centers, do not generate a landscape of many strangers available for communal interaction on intimate issues, which seems typical of the membership of contemporary voluntary associations in gay urban US society. Moreover, Israeli-Jewish "sentimental education" does not support the culture of a therapeutic language. Israelis are known inside and outside the country for their *dugri*—"straight talk"—conversational style (Katriel 1986). That linguistic mode of communication is deemed somewhat rude, lacking the "niceties" of therapeutic discourse. Moreover, Israelis are reluctant to admit that they need or actually resort to the help of psychological therapists. In public discourse that service is considered proper for seriously disturbed individuals, although its application has greatly increased in recent years. Dr Freud would have found his services mostly secretly admitted in the land of his tribal compatriots.

An intriguing comparison between Israeli and US gay men was suggested to me by a leading gay activist in Tel Aviv:

> The American gay man is lonely, the Israeli gay man, however, is never lonely! He has nearby close family and friends, homosexuals and heterosexuals, whom he can meet on a regular basis. They are part of his unbroken chain of major associations—from school, the army, college, and work—and who are readily available when needed.

He thus interpreted his own and others' lack of interest in joining voluntary/support groups composed of strangers. The popular image, whether real or imagined, of voluntary associations as substitutes for the loss of family and community among gays in US metropolitan cities does not suit the Israeli case. A society small in its geographical-physical layout, and socially close-knit, cannot permit anyone, heterosexual or gay, to "disappear," cutting off all ties of family and other relationships.

In New York I observed four gay religious (national) organizations: Jewish, Catholic, Protestant, and Afro-American. In Tel Aviv, however, one local liberal Jewish Orthodox congregation (Kehilat Yachad Tel Aviv—Congregation Tel Aviv Together) founded by a creative heterosexual couple welcomes gays and lesbians. The services represent mostly a mainstream Orthodox orientation, though women take a more visible role in liturgy and social life. A gay regular congregant defined to me the synagogue's direction as "Orthodoxy stretched to the limits," meaning taken to the borders of leniency in its accommodating *halacha* (the body of Jewish religious laws). Although LGBT participants constitute a major constituency of the congregation (about 40 percent according to gay congregants), there is no visible sign in its public presentation and ritual of the involvement of homosexuals, except for its advertising an egalitarian ideology and its welcoming of all sectors and religious orientations in Israeli society. I assume the accidental "innocent" visitor may not identify the presence of gay congregants.

Nevertheless, the political alliance and Israel's continuing dependence on US support; the close ties with US Jews; Israelis' traveling habits; their strong attraction to US popular culture and its scientific world—none of these can be kept separate from the "circulating" impact of the various facets of US socio-cultural therapeutic presentation.[3] There is no need to repeat yet again the popular cliché that the era of globalization is almost coeval with the impact of Americanization. The title of an article by an Israeli sociologist (Ram 2003) encapsulates that concept: "The Big M: McDonald's and the Americanization of the Motherland."[4]

The circulation of the US metropolitan ethos of an individual's freedoms and his/her "license" and skills in the open manifestation of intimate discourse does encounter some "obstacles" on its world voyage. Dominant sectors in Israeli society representing the orientation and symbols of cosmopolitanism are anxious to preserve their self image as partaking in the ever-expanding world culture of modernity. However, Illouz (2008), who studied the diffusion and globalization of therapeutic cultural models, conducted observations at some Emotional Intelligence workshops in Israel and interviewed participants, concluded skeptically:

> It is doubtful whether this workshop can single-handedly transform the emotional makeup of its participants. But such workshops should nonetheless

interest the sociologist because they point to the formation of what I would like to call a "global emotional habitus" (Ibid.: 220).

As mentioned earlier, gay Israelis enjoy most legal rights as in other liberal Western European and North Atlantic societies, and in recent years Tel Aviv in particular has gained a reputation as an attractive site for international gay tourism. Nevertheless, the social, demographic, and cultural makeup of this composite society based on conflicting cultural traditions and ethical beliefs may not easily be transformed to emulate in daily life the multiplex patterns of US voluntary associations and its therapeutic model of social interaction. The gay groups I observed in New York have developed within a particular social-demographic framework and in the context of a distinct cultural tradition dominant beyond the boundaries of gay life. It has been the "hotbed" for the emergence of social groups (religious congregations included) and relationships dedicated to various personal-sexual proclivities and innovative social agendas. In conclusion, I reiterate the wonder of a distinguished predecessor, the Dutch historian and traveler Huizinga (1927), at the US *Illusiongemeinschaft*, which is germane also to the dawn of the twenty-first century.

Moshe Shokeid is Professor Emeritus of Anthropology at Tel Aviv University. He has conducted ethnographic research in various locales, including Atlas Mountain immigrants in Israeli farming communities, Arabs in Jaffa, Israeli immigrants in Queens, and gay institutions in New York City. Major publications include *The Dual Heritage* (Manchester 1971, Transaction 1985), *The Predicament of Homecoming* (with S. Deshen, Cornell 1974), *Distant Relations* (with S. Deshen, Praeger 1982), *Children of Circumstances* (Cornell 1988), *A Gay Synagogue in New York* (Columbia 1995, Pennsylvania 2003), *Three Jewish Journeys through an Anthropologist's Lens* (Academic Studies Press 2009), and *Gay Voluntary Associations in New York* (Pennsylvania 2015).

Notes

1. "The Extended Case Method" treated each case observed in the field as a stage in an ongoing process of social relationships between specific persons or groups engaged in a social system and sharing a culture (e.g., Van Velsen 1967; Burawoy et al. 1991).
2. See Kaplan (2003) for his study of gays in the Israeli military.

3. Some innovations resembling features adopted from the American domain of voluntary associations that also seem to promote a local genre of therapeutic discourse have been recently observed. In particular, the case of CHOSHEN (The Gay and Lesbian Center for Education and Change), an organization founded in 2001 by a group of volunteers dedicated to educating the public about the process and circumstances of developing gay and lesbian identities (Cooper 2007). Its members' strategy of presenting their agenda and endearing their audiences (in high schools, army units, police departments, and other places) carries an evocative narrative revealing the visiting speaker's personal experiences on his/her journey of coming out of the closet. The talk is followed by group discussions that engage presenter and attendees in an intensive dialogue about intimate personal issues. The impressed observer commented: "It is uncommon in Israeli culture to speak about personal sexual experiences among strangers; the domain of sexuality is restricted in this culture to the private sphere" (Ibid.: 72).

4. The first McDonald's branch opened in 1993 in the first of Israel's popular large malls on the outskirts of Tel Aviv. The chain presently operates more than 130 restaurants around the country.

References

Altman, Dennis. 1986. *AIDS in the Mind of America*. New York: Doubleday.

Bar-Lev, Shirly and Efrat Tilinger. 2009. "'Life Is Not What You Lived Out but How You Remember to Tell Its Tale': Gay Men Perform AIDS Stories Online." [In Hebrew.] *Israeli Sociology* 11: 191–216.

Baum, D. Michael and James M. Fishman. 1994. "AIDS, Sexual Compulsivity, and Gay Men: A Group Treatment Approach." In *Therapist on the Front Line: Psychotherapy with Gay Men in the Age of AIDS*, 255–274.Washington DC: American Psychiatric Press.

Bech, Henning. 1997. *When Men Meet: Homosexuality and Modernity*. Chicago: The University of Chicago Press.

Bellah, Robert N., Richard Masden, M. William Sullivan, Ann Swidler, and Stephen M. Lipton.

———. 1996 [1985]. *Habits of the Heart: Individualism and Commitment in American Life*. Berkeley: University of California Press.

Bersani, Leo. 1988. "Is the Rectum a Grave?" In *AIDS: Cultural Analysis/Cultural Activism*, ed. D. Crimp, 197–222. Cambridge, MA: The MIT Press.

Bolton, Ralph. 1995. "Tricks, Friends and Lovers: Erotic Encounters in the Field." In *Taboo: Sex, Identity and Erotic Subjectivities in Anthropological Fieldwork*, ed. D. Kulick and M. Wilson, 140–67. New York: Routledge.

Brodsky, J.I. 1993. "The Mineshaft: A Retrospective Ethnography." In *If You Seduce Straight Persons, Can You Make Them Gay? Issues in Biological Essentialism versus Social Constructionism in Gay and Lesbian Identities*, ed. J.P. DeCecco and J.P. Elia, 231–51, New York: Haworth.

Burawoy, Michael, et al. 1991. *Ethnography Unbound: Power and Resistance in the Modern Metropolis*. Berkeley: University of California Press.

Cooper, Yoni. 2007. *The Patterns of Identity Building at the Advocacy Organization of the Gay and Lesbian Community in Israel*. [In Hebrew.] Unpublished MA thesis, Hebrew University, Jerusalem.

Delph, W.E. 1978. *The Silent Community: Public Homosexual Encounters*. Beverly Hills, CA: Sage.

Faiman-Silva, Sandra. 2004. *The Courage to Connect: Sexuality, Citizenship, and Community in Provincetown*. Urbana: University of Illinois Press.

Fink, S.F. and J. Press. 1999. *Independence Park: The Lives of Gay Men in Israel*. Stanford, CA: Stanford University Press.

Ginsberg, Faye D. 1989. *Contested Lives: Abortion Debate in an American Community*. Berkeley: University of California Press.

Gluckman, Max. 1963. *Custom and Conflict in Africa*. Basil Blackwell: Oxford.

Harris, Daniel. 1997 *The Rise and Fall of Gay Culture*. New York: Hyperion.

Huizinga, Johan. 1972 [1927]. *America: A Dutch Historian's Vision, From Afar and Near*, trans. H.H. Rowen. New York: Harper & Row.

Humphreys, L. 1970. *Tearoom Trade: Impersonal Sex in Public Places*. Chicago: Aldine.

Illouz, Eva. 2008. *Saving the Modern Soul: Therapy, Emotions, and the Culture of Self-Help*. Berkeley: University of California Press.

Kama, Amit. 2000. "From *Terra Incognita* to *Terra Firma*: The Logbook of the Voyage of Gay Men's Community into the Israeli Public Sphere." *Journal of Homosexuality* 38: 133–162.

———. 2005. "An Unrelenting Mental Press: Israeli Gay Men's Ontological Duality and Its Discontent." *The Journal of Men's Studies* 13: 169–84.

Kaminer, Wendy. 1992. *I'm Dysfunctional, You're Dysfunctional: The Recovery Movement and Other Self-Help Fashions*. Reading, MA: Addison-Wesley Publishing Company.

Kaplan, Danny. 2003. *Brothers and Others in Arms: The Making of Love and War in Israeli Combat Units*. New York: Haworth Press.

Katriel, Tamar. 1986. *Talking Straight: "Dugri" Speech in Israeli Sabra Culture*. Cambridge: Cambridge University Press.

Leap, William. 1999. *Public Sex/Gay Sex*. New York: Columbia University Press.

Levine, Martin. 1979. *Gay Men: The Sociology of Male Homosexuality*. San Francisco, CA: Harper & Row Publishers.

Lewin, Ellen. 1993. *Lesbian Mothers: Accounts of Gender in American Society*. Ithaca, NY: Cornell University Press.

———. 2009. *Gay Fathers: Narratives of Family and Citizenship in America*. Chicago: The University of Chicago Press.

Newton, Esther. 1993. *Cherry Grove, Fire Island: Sixty Years in America's First Gay and Lesbian Town*. Boston, MA: Beacon.

Plummer, Ken. 2003. *Intimate Citizenship: Private Decisions and Public Dialogue*. Seattle: University of Washington Press.

Putnam, D. Robert. 2000. *Bowling Alone: The Collapse and Revival of American Community*. New York: Simon & Schuster.

Quadland, C. Michael. 1985. "Compulsive Sexual Behavior: Definition of a Problem and an Approach to Treatment." *Journal of Sex & Marital Therapy* 11: 121–32.

Ram, Uri. 2003. "The Big M: McDonald's and the Americanization of the
    Motherland." [In Hebrew.] *Theory and Criticism* 23: 179–212.
Rieff, Philip. 1990 [1960]. "Reflections on Psychological Man in America." In *The
    Feeling Intellect: Selected Writings*, ed. Jonathan B. Imber, 3–9. Chicago: The
    University of Chicago Press.
———. 1990 [1961]. "The American Transference: From Calvin to Freud." In *The
    Feeling Intellect: Selected Writings*, ed. Jonathan B. Imber, 10–15. Chicago: The
    University of Chicago Press.
Shokeid, Moshe. 1988. *Children of Circumstances: Israeli Emigrants in New York.*
    Ithaca, NY: Cornell University Press.
———. 1995. *A Gay Synagogue in New York.* New York: Columbia University Press.
    Augmented edition in 2003, Philadelphia: University of Pennsylvania Press.
———. 1995. "Gay Life in Peripheral Metropolitan Cities: The Case of Tel Aviv."
    In *The City: Today, and the Day Before*, ed. G.E. Karpimska, 193–98. Lodz:
    University of Lodz.
———. 2001a. "'Our Group Has a Life of Its Own': An Affective Fellowship of
    Older Gay Men." *City & Society* 13: 5–30.
———. 2001b. "'You Don't Eat Indian and Chinese Food at the Same Meal': The
    Bisexual Quandary." *Anthropological Quarterly* 75: 63–90.
———. 2002. "Sexual Addicts Together: Observing the Culture of SCA Groups in
    New York." *Social Anthropology* 10: 189–210.
———. 2003. "Closeted Cosmopolitans: Israeli Gays between Center and
    Periphery." *Global Networks* 3: 387–99.
———. 2010. "Erotics and Politics in the Agenda of an Interracial Gay Men's
    Association in New York." In *The Anthropology of Values: Essays in Honor of
    Georg Pfeffer*, ed. P. Berger, R. Hardenberg, E. Kattner, and M. Prager, 215–34.
    Delhi: Pearson.
———. 2015. *Gay Voluntary Associations in New York: Public Sharing and Private Lives.*
    Philadelphia: University of Pennsylvania Press.
Steadman Rice, John. 2004. "The Therapeutic School: Its Origin, Nature, and
    Consequences" In *Therapeutic Culture: Triumph and Defeat*, ed. J.B. Imber,
    111–36. Chicago: The University of Chicago Press.
Style, J. 1979. "Outsider/Insider: Researching Gay Baths." *Urban Life* 8: 135–52.
Tocqueville, Alexis de. 1956 [1835]. *Democracy in America*, ed. Richard D.
    Heffmen. New York: Mentor Books.
Van Velsen, J. 1967. "The Extended Case Study Method and Situational Analysis."
    In *The Craft of Social Anthropology*, ed. A.L. Epstein, 129–49. London: Tavistock.
Weston, K. 1991. *Families We Choose: Lesbians, Gays, Kinship.* New York: Columbia
    University Press.
Wuthnow, R. 1994. *Sharing the Journey: Support Groups and America's New Quest for
    Community.* New York: Free Press.

Part II

From the Inside Out?
Reflections on an International
Anthropology of the US

Chapter Six

Who Cares?
Why It's Odd and Why It's Not

Geoffrey White

When I first read Virginia R. Dominguez and Jasmin Habib's introductory essay for their project on the foreign anthropological study of the US, I expected to find an emerging area of scholarship that marks a further step in the de-Orientalizing of anthropological practice. This collection does that but it also does much more. The questions asked, and the quandary evoked among others in the profession about the place of this work in the discipline, have implications for the way we think about anthropology as a whole.

The first item for consideration is the remark referenced in the opening of their essay quoting a panel discussant asking, "Does the future of anthropology include the US as a field site (except as "anthropology at home")?" It is in fact that parenthetical qualifier that signals a deeper disciplinary quandary. "We" (anthropologists) have known for decades that a major shift began to take place in the discipline during the 1980s when a growing proportion of American anthropology dissertations began to focus on the United States (something evident in the American Anthropological Association's annual statistical summaries of the field). And yet, inevitably, this fact of anthropological practice did not come with a change, at least not a broad change, in the kinds of stories the discipline tells about itself. The growth of "anthropology at home" did not come with any kind of consensus about the value of cross-cultural research and the fundamental tensions of "insider/outsider" knowledge construction that continue to define anthropology in the popular imagination (and in so many department self-descriptions, recruitment priorities, and so forth). The question posed by Dominguez and Habib, then, should help us pause and reflect on the stakes of positioning and of itineraries of research—questions discussed exhaustively in anthropology, but brought into focus in distinctive ways by this set of essays.

In their Introduction, Dominguez and Habib consider the possibility that critics will see this project as "fetishizing" fieldwork and respond with a strong argument that fieldwork "still" matters. The fieldwork question, it seems to me, is crucial to the set of issues that converge in this volume. If we are inquiring into the absence of the US as an "Other" in the research of non-US anthropologists, we might begin by asking about the paradigms that frame their objects of research as "Others," whether cultural "Others" or something else. Although Dominguez and Habib are clear that the questions posed here are not about studying the US "on cultural grounds," anthropological ways of framing problems often draw upon notions of enduring difference—differences that justify, if not demand, long-term, boundary-crossing research capable of unpacking densely interconnected relations and structures. Why, then, have these anthropological impulses not motivated more (field)work on the United States from outside?

It is not coincidental that one of the primary critiques of anthropological investigations of Others is that, in pursuing its object of investigation, the discipline creates a "savage slot" (Trouillot 1991). In the savage slot, difference is not only difference; it is difference that is already located in existing hierarchies of knowledge and power. In many of anthropology's traditional locations, the production of conventional anthropological ethnographies had the effect of reproducing those hierarchies in the discourse of science. Even if the term "savage slot" is now used to characterize any act of research as, potentially, an act of domination, its tribal roots are in the historical prototype for anthropological work on cultural difference: the small-scale, face-to-face, oral communities that first entered the anthropological record (and, for many in the West, history itself).

Even as ethnography has shifted to multi-sited research and developed a taste for flows, border-crossings, and interconnections, it has kept an anxious eye on the importance of sustained engagement with a specific social milieu for particular kinds of insight and intervention (Borneman and Hammoudi 2009, cited by Dominguez and Habib; and see Clifford 1997). Yet, in some national anthropologies, the hangover from anthropology's savage past tends to obfuscate the potential for the power of ethnography and sustained fieldwork to investigate other sorts of Others, whether Wall Street brokerages (Ho 2009) or evangelical churches (Luhrmann 2012). For many American anthropologists who turn their ethnographic eyes to subjects closer to "home" in the United States, it appears that their US-based work emerges as second or third projects, marking a middle phase of careers begun with a more traditional non-Western European, North American, or foreign project—projects in which they developed their fieldwork skills, later adapted in the US context. Dominguez and Habib give numerous examples. Many more could be cited.

I suspect that attitudes toward the question of cross-cultural and transcultural research reflect broad generational differences but are not limited to them. The image of anthropology as a mode of scholarship built on the study of "Other" (non-Western) communities by (mostly) Western European or North American scholars has long been exploded by the combined forces of decolonization and globalization—the former often inverting the moral and political valences of research, and the latter deterritorializing and destabilizing the very idea of "the field" (Clifford 1997; Gupta and Ferguson 1997). If my institutional experience is any indication of the reigning ambiguities, some of my colleagues remain adamant that the experience of studying outside one's own linguistic/cultural communities is a core value of the field, a defining feature of anthropology. At the same time, my department, cognizant of our place in a public university in colonized islands of Oceania, has affirmed the value of "indigenous anthropology," and is working to build programmatic support for Native Hawaiian students and scholars working in their own communities. In short, in the Pacific Islands region, with a host of new nations and ongoing anti-colonial struggles, the politics of insider/outsider research practices are constantly in the spotlight, while research on the United States, except in the context of Native Hawaiian studies, distinctly is not.

Perhaps for this reason, as I read through the essays in this collection, I was reminded of a little-known film that raised issues about the role of anthropology in small Pacific communities and, in a larger way, the place of "insider/outsider" knowledge production as a critical feature of anthropology. The release of *Anthropology on Trial: Papua New Guinea* shown on the *NOVA* television series in 1983 created a stir in Pacific anthropology circles, but otherwise went mostly unnoticed in anthropology. Beginning with a number of articulate criticisms of the work of Margaret Mead (who worked off and on in Papua New Guinea from the 1920s through the 1950s), the film went on to suggest that anthropology was changing as it (1) took stock of the importance of addressing local needs and working collaboratively with host communities, and (2) began to balance the directions of research with projects done by "Others" in the United States. The film constructed an image of a field in transition, moving beyond the paradigm of white ethnographers working in the Malinowskian tradition in command of the episteme of research and scholarship, reproducing colonial hierarchies. To drive this point home, the film concluded with an unusual twist by focusing on a Papua New Guinean doctoral student studying the United States. The final scenes of the film follow the work of Wari Iamo, a Papua New Guinean supervised by Laura Nader at the University of California Berkeley as he pursues a dissertation project in Oakland, California.

I take a moment to replay parts of a conversation between Nader and Iamo in the film that begins with a comment from Nader about the importance of Iamo's project, as a Papua New Guinean studying the United States.

Nader: You know, what you are doing is really pioneering, Wari. Because although anthropologists have gone all the way around the world, to all kinds of societies, very few anthropologists from other societies have come to study us. And the US is probably the most understudied culture in the world. And we did have people like de Tocqueville. We're still quoting de Tocqueville, a Frenchman who came to the United States to study us and observe our customs and see what made Americans tick. After all, we're a very important force in the world, and so forth. It isn't that insiders couldn't have made the same points that de Tocqueville made, but they don't. Because you have to have, you have to stand slightly outside to be able to see the things that he saw, that were great and were problematic and so forth in our society. You come from New Guinea and you look at something that, in a way, is incredulous to someone from your community. There are people in this society who don't have a house to live in, who don't have a home. How does that happen? And are there functional equivalents. And how does this society deal with the fact that there are homeless people?

Iamo: There is still one point being made, whether by Americans or by Papua New Guineans, that we still are the ones who know more about our own cultures. So an American will claim that, "yes it's true that an outsider can come and see my society objectively and say more things about it, but still I'm in control or master of it because I know the nuances of the language, I know the culture, and I know the facts."

Nader: I think what we're coming to is a realization that there are different ways of knowing and different ways of understanding. And that outsiders and insiders looking at human society trying to understand the complexity of human culture . . . It's nothing so simple as what the physicists study. And you can't simplify it. Because if you simplify it, you lose it. And we're doing the best we can, when you have outsiders and insiders looking at the same culture and working together.

While this conversation is obviously relevant to this collection's concern with the study of the US by non-US anthropologists, it comes across today as somewhat dated and even utopian. As late twentieth-century

Who Cares? Why It's Odd and Why It's Not

147

(American/US) anthropology confronted its own Orientalizing practices, one of the rhetorical moves to recuperate the field's romantic vision of knowledge in the service of humankind was to hold up examples of "them" studying "us"—as articulated well by Laura Nader. In that regard, the film captured the zeitgeist of an era in which practitioners generally believed that such studies would naturally increase as the field globalized, according to the anthropological logic of outsider knowledge production.[1]

Yet the number of such studies has always been vanishingly small, as noted by Dominguez and Habib. Indeed, Wari Iamo's primary interests always remained focused on his own society and national context, Papua New Guinea (Iamo and Simet 1998). He did not publish from his doctoral work in the United States (Iamo 1987), but rather returned to research administration and politics at home. In that respect, his subsequent career fits the dominant pattern for Pacific Islander students, including anthropologists, trained in the United States (and Australia and New Zealand) in the last few decades, nearly all of whom have focused their research on their home societies.

The proclivity of indigenous and postcolonial scholars to focus cultural research "at home" is part of a larger pattern that I have observed at the East-West Center, a federally funded research organization in Hawai'i that for over fifty years has provided graduate scholarships to students from Asian and Pacific countries as well as the US. Whereas the Center's stated mission is to strengthen relations between the United States and Asia and the Pacific by supporting cross-cultural and international research, the subjects of master's and doctoral projects done by its scholarship students from Asia Pacific and the US have focused almost entirely on Asia and the Pacific. While the rhetoric of "East-West" is in theory reciprocal, in practice it was almost always Western European or North American scholars studying the "East" (geographically west of the United States). In this institutional space, the vast majority of topics pursued by Asian and Pacific students with East-West Center scholarships focused on issues at home, while nearly all of the US students pursue studies focused on Asia and the Pacific. The gaze of area studies, as practiced in this particular US institution, has, historically fixed its gaze squarely on America's "Others." Despite the mutuality implied by the hyphen in "East-West," the absent unmarked West reflects institutional lacunae much like those noted by Dominguez and Habib.

The example of the East-West Center as a post-World War II US institution with roots in Cold War strategic thinking also serves as an important reminder of the larger institutional and infrastructural factors that must factor into any complete response questions about the stark asymmetries in anthropology's "gaze." The resources that flowed into US anthropology in the late twentieth century were in no small measure related to the emergence of US "area studies" in the Cold War environment following World War II. The dominant political and economic position of the United States in the postwar world order translated into an unparalleled base of support for the academic disciplines that could inform strategic thinking and development studies. In this respect, social science disciplines in the US academy were without peer in the levels of federal funding and foundation support for Americans learning, studying, and analyzing foreign cultures. Anthropology thrived in this environment in ways that are only now becoming visible as the logic of Cold War knowledge-making and the strategic value of long-term fieldwork style research have diminished in the eyes of policymakers.

The contrast between the brute asymmetry and inequality evident in post-World War II area studies (evident in Cold War institutions such as the federally funded East-West Center) usefully remind us that the significance of insider/outsider positioning for research is not a brute fact but rather constituted from particular historical moments and in specific institutional arrangements that make certain kinds of cultural knowledge valuable, relevant, and interesting. Whereas Laura Nader's earlier vision saw anthropology as a set of universalizing practices that can travel through time and across cultural space, irrespective of colonial or imperial histories, the essays in this collection remind us otherwise. One of the primary strengths of these essays is their critical reflexivity about their own complicated boundary-crossing that, in nearly every case, is articulated in terms of multi-sited, transnational research carried out in a comparative frame.

In point of fact, even the classical example of "them" studying "us" in America, Alexis de Tocqueville's *Democracy in America* (1835), was also written more as a transnational comparative ethnography than a foreign commentary on America for Americans. Tocqueville's project, published first in French for French audiences (*De la Démocratie en Amérique* 1835), observed the conditions of equality in America out of an interest in long-term social transformations in France associated with the end of monarchy and the decline of aristocratic privilege. Ironically, then, de Tocqueville's example is more akin to the examples of contemporary ethnography gathered here than the portrait of a Papua New Guinean graduate student walking the streets of Oakland in the early 1980s.

At about the same time that *Anthropology on Trial* appeared, the first wave of anthropology's own reflexive critique was emerging with *Writing Culture* (Clifford and Marcus 1986) and Marcus and Fischer's *Anthropology as Cultural Critique* (1986). Rather than calling for more non-Western European and North American anthropologists to study the "West," however, Marcus and Fischer argued that the important and neglected contribution of anthropology's cross-cultural paradigm is to bring cultural critique back home, adding ethnography to a form well-established in sociological and literary genres of writing.[2] Although setting out issues that remain relevant to contemporary transnational studies of the sort included in this collection, the move in the 1980s toward reflexive writing remained oddly centered in the United States, addressed to US anthropology and its self-critical moment.

In this respect, the essays in this volume invert the travel narratives presumed in earlier challenges to US anthropology and bring critical ethnography to the United States from various "homes" outside (Canada, Israel, Sweden) and they do so in much more complex genealogies than envisioned in the 1980s. All of these authors have spent significant periods of time living in the United States prior to the specific projects addressed in their papers for this volume. And they themselves are on the move, transiting between home and "field," as are, in most cases, their subjects. The field is not so much a bounded national or cultural space as a set of relations and networks that represent transnational connections and flows. Here are some of the things these authors have to say about their own positionality and transit narratives:

Samimian-Darash: "After I completed my research on Israeli preparedness for biothreats, I moved to the US, where I conducted multi-sited research on science and security in 2010–12 . . ."

Wulff: ". . . this is an ethnography of how the Unites States is observed by outsiders . . . I conducted fieldwork for six months in New York consisting of participant observation and interviews. In addition, I interviewed returnees in Stockholm; some were the same individuals as in New York, some were not."

Shokeid: ". . . my ongoing dedication to fieldwork sites in New York and my fascination with Americans' habits of association arise no less from my comprehension of the United States' exceptionality, as compared with my Israeli home society and culture in particular."

Habib writes as a Canadian of Jewish/Palestinian parentage who, after spending "several periods of living in the US," finds that ". . . [American Jewish] dissenters' relationships to Israel . . . [are] based on an awareness of a particular framing of or identification with Jewishness and Israeliness . . ."

Hannerz: describes his most recent study as ". . . transnational and multi-sited, on news-media foreign correspondents"; [and, furthermore, assumes readers] "are mostly at home in America—people familiar with its national scene, and its prominent personae, at present and in that more or less recent past when I have been coming and going, entering and leaving."

Without claiming that these projects are in any way representative of the diversity of work being done in the United States by foreign anthropologists, these examples do indicate that foreign-based ethnographic research in the US today is avowedly transnational and multi-sited. Why do these patterns emerge in the foreign study of the US (given that a significant proportion of all anthropology today is designed in similar fashion)?

I would like to suggest that there is a connection between the nature of research design for these studies and the particular social, political, and historical conditions for conducting ethnographic work in the US today. Most of these authors recognize the heavily saturated nature of cultural commentary and critique in and on the United States—a presence in the world, especially through its hegemony in global entertainment industries, which evokes constant comment, response, criticism, mimicry, resistance, and so forth. When saturation is complete, the US is no longer interesting (or even noticed) as a cultural space; its ubiquitous presence becomes the unmarked context for everything else. Thus when travelers actually do gain more in-depth experience with a specific locale, such as Swedes in Manhattan, the locale ceases to be the United States. It becomes another case of marked difference.

In particular, the issue of cultural saturation poses a challenge of "ethnographic authority" for foreign ethnographers working in a terrain that is already extensively mapped. In an environment where homegrown ethnography by US-based anthropologists and sociologists is already densely produced and where cultural criticism in literary, journalistic, and electronic media is everywhere, what is the added value of research by foreign-based scholars whose supposed advantage of "outside perspective" is counter-balanced by lesser degrees of local knowledge?

Judging from the example of Wari Iamo in *Anthropology on Trial*, establishing authority and gaining an attentive audience in the US are not easy matters. When the film portrays Iamo in the field, interviewing a lawyer about issues of homelessness, the viewer is treated to an acute illustration of the difficulty of "studying up," of working across competing professional knowledges. The film follows Iamo as he enters a lawyer's office and begins a line of questioning that implies kin relations in the US come with less obligation than in Papua New Guinea. Rather than reply to his question, however, the lawyer questions Iamo's premise that Americans do not value kinship, offering a mini-lecture about American bilateral kinship and the values of descent, signaling his own superior knowledge, both as an American and as a family (divorce) lawyer:[3]

Iamo: The degree of kinship, to what degree it's practiced here, I don't know, but there is some . . .

Lowy: [interrupts] Some degree? Wari, my god.
Iamo: I mean, to a certain degree there is kinship, no one can deny that there is
          kinship here.
Lowy: [exhaling and looking down] Okay [pause] Wari, the idea that somehow
          kinship is not as strong in our society is, I think, an erroneous idea. It's
          different. That is, we have a bilateral kinship system, certain descent
          principles. People come to me all the time to make wills. [Leaning forward
          with earnest tone to ask, rhetorically:] Who do you think they leave it to?
          Strangers? [Camera, zooms in on the lawyer, shifts to Iamo, now silent, then
          back to the lawyer.] They leave it to their children. They leave it to their
          grandchildren. People come in this office and argue over who should get
          what. Heirlooms. [Iamo: mm mm.] I promised a certain ring to a certain
          grandchild. Kinship is very, very important.

The challenges for foreign ethnographers, it seems, have as much to do
with being taken seriously as disrupting hegemonic or colonial practices.
The authors in this collection, all of whom occupy middle to senior academic positions in well-developed non-US institutions, bring sophisticated
strategies to their research that, to one degree or another, anticipate critical responses from their subject populations; in some cases taking such
views as objects of research. These challenges are no doubt one reason
that none of the essays in this collection are first projects. All of them
have evolved from longer genealogies of association and fieldwork—a
depth and length of engagement that are in fact still somewhat unusual
in anthropology (where the "second project" of professional careers finds
Western European and North American researchers switching field sites,
from one non-Western area to another, or from a non-Western society to
the US or Europe [Marcus 1998]). In addition to the sheer fact of developing cultural competence, however, the kinds of research design evident
in these projects consistently draw on comparative interpretive strategies
that produce implications cutting in both directions, toward the United
States and toward "home."

Questions of ethnographic authority are inevitably connected to ethical
issues associated with the politics of cultural representation. What are
the stakes involved with research by "outsiders"? Who cares about claims
to cultural knowledge or insight? For which audiences are these multi-
sited, transnational studies relevant or valuable? Such questions always
mark the edges of fieldwork, where "the field" entails self-conscious
boundary-crossings that raise questions about who is representing whom,
to what ends, for what audiences. Stated in this way, questions about the
conditions for twenty-first-century ethnography of the US look radically
different than those that might have been posed thirty years ago. To the
extent that the United States is not only a nation-state but a global cultural

"empire," writing about the US is not only for US audiences, but potentially of interest to audiences "at home" outside the United States. Some
examples:

> Habib: "…there is one important feature that strikes me as equally important to
> think about and through: the fear of speaking out and being castigated by non-
> Jews. This never came up in my discussions with Jewish activists in Canada.."
>
> Wulff: "New York's nightlife is a special scene when it comes to classlessness,
> yet it is interesting to consider this quality in the American context, and to
> what extent it is actually more American than Swedish."
>
> ". . . time in Manhattan was quite different from Swedish time, again mostly
> because of the fast pace."
>
> "The circulation of the US metropolitan ethos of the individual's freedoms and
> his/her "license" and skills in the open manifestation of intimate discourse is
> encountering some "obstacles" on its world voyage."
>
> Samimian-Darash: "My analysis is enabled by my particular positioning as a
> non-US researcher and by a particular anthropological mode of inquiry. "

The transnational and comparative character of these papers also suggests
a different set of challenges for the politics and ethics of fieldwork than
one finds in debates about ethnography in colonial and postcolonial societies. In the contemporary Pacific, the politics of research are sharply drawn,
just as the boundaries of indigenous communities and cultural rights are
increasingly subjects of public and policy debate. But what, in comparison, are the stakes of and for representing the US? Whereas the work of
an individual scholar can have a significant impact on the representation
of small-scale communities, marking and directing the print-mediated
reality of such societies for decades, there is little likelihood of that in
the work of individuals in American Studies, wherever they are located.
There, it seems to me, questions about the politics of ethnographic work
and the kinds of cultural analysis/critique it is capable of generating are
framed quite differently because of the overtly transcultural and comparative posture of current research—work that from the beginning addresses
phenomena that are not, in the first instance, located in bounded, national
domains, but rather of interest precisely because they entail transnational
connections and entanglements.

In sum, these essays lead us well beyond the puzzle of the absence of
a foreign anthropology of the US. Rather, they open up a critical window
on to the premises of twenty-first-century anthropology, suggesting that
the promise of the 1980s critique to "bring anthropology back home" is
only just now beginning to be addressed in complex circuits of global
ethnographic practice.

Geoffrey White is Emeritus Professor of Anthropology at the University of Hawai'i. His current research focuses on World War II in the American national imagination. His most recent book, *Memorializing Pearl Harbor: Unfinished Histories and the Work of Remembrance* (Duke, 2016), explores the social and emotional dimensions of national memorial practices.

Notes

1. Thus, foreign born anthropologists such as Nigerian-American John Ogbu or Chinese-American Francis Hsu were held up as examples of the advantage of the ethnographer's (partial) Otherness in studying the US.
2. This, of course, was not entirely new. One need only think of Margaret Mead's project in Samoa, building an argument about the cultural determinants of adolescent sexuality based on implicit contrasts between her portrait of a more relaxed Polynesian ethos and the "sturm and drang" of sexual maturation in European societies. Her subsequent career as one of the United States' most public of public intellectuals, confidant in wading in to all manner of public debate, editorializing for a US-based reading public through her *Redbook* column, museum exhibits, and articles, established a still-exceptional example for an anthropological voice in US cultural criticism.
3. The irony of this reframing of Iamo's fieldwork interview is that the lawyer, introduced only by name, in fact held both a PhD in anthropology(!) (Berkeley 1971) and a JD in law (Stanford 1978). While this is an ironic extreme in which the professional knowledge of interest to the ethnographer turns out to intersect with the same anthropological field of knowledge that he brings to the conversation, the fact of specialized professional knowledges that potentially compete with anthropological discourse is more likely to be a problem for ethnographers in the United States than in many, more "traditional" settings for fieldwork.

References:

Borneman, John, and Abdellah Hammoudi. 2009. *Being There: The Fieldwork Encounter and the Making of Truth.* Berkeley: University of California Press.

Clifford, James. 1997. "Spatial Practices." In *Routes: Travel and Translation in the Late Twentieth Century World,* 52–91. Cambridge, MA: Harvard University Press.

Clifford, James and George Marcus, eds. 1986. *Writing Culture: The Poetics and Politics of Ethnography.* Berkeley: University of California Press.

Gupta, Akhil and James Ferguson. 1997. "Discipline and Practice: 'The Field' as Site, Method, and Location in Anthropology." In *Anthropological Locations: Boundaries and Grounds of a Field Science*, ed. A.Gupta and J. Ferguson, 1–46. Berkeley: University of California Press.

Ho, Karen Zouwen. 2009. *Liquidated : An Ethnography of Wall Street*. Durham, NC: Duke University Press.

Iamo, Wari. 1987. "In Search of Justice and Shelter in Mix-Town, U.S.A." Ph.D. diss., University of California, Berkeley.

Iamo, Wari, and Jacob Simet. 1998. "Cultural Diversity and Identity in Papua New Guinea: A Second Look." In *From Beijing to Port Moresby: The Politics of National Identity in Cultural Politics*, ed. V. Dominguez and D. Wu, 189–204. Amsterdam: Gordon and Breach.

Luhrmann, T.M. 2012. *When God Talks Back: Understanding the American Evangelical Relationship with God*. New York: Alfred A. Knopf.

Marcus, George E., ed. 1998. *Ethnography through Thick and Thin*. Princeton, NJ: Princeton University Press.

Marcus, George E., and Michael M.J. Fischer. 1986. *Anthropology as Cultural Critique: An Experimental Moment in the Human Sciences*. Chicago: University of Chicago Press.

Tocqueville, Alexis de. 1956 [1835]. *Democracy in America*, ed. Richard D. Heffmen. New York: Mentor Books.

Trouillot, M.-R. 1991. "Anthropology and the Savage Slot: The Poetics and Politics of Otherness." In *Recapturing Anthropology*, ed. R. Fox, 17–44. Santa Fe, NM: School of American Research.

Chapter Seven

Power and Trafficking of Scholarship in International American Studies

Keiko Ikeda

Let me begin with an anecdote. A student who has just returned from a Study Abroad program has come to my office, and is excitedly reporting to me about her wonderful experiences in the United States. She had gone to study at an American Studies program with a proposal to research US music firsthand. As our conversation moves to talk about the progress of her research, she tells me, "Oh, by the way I changed the focus of my MA thesis. I hope you don't mind." She continues. "The professor I worked with in the US suggested that I should include more about Japan." "Oh, boy," I think to myself. "Not again."

I feel deep gratitude to, and sympathy for, US professors who earnestly try to help Japanese students who come to them from a different academic culture. I completely understand that one way to help them overcome their linguistic and academic weaknesses is to encourage them to draw on cultural knowledge that US scholars may not have. However, when we send our students off to US campuses, it is for the purposes of doing American Studies. So, I sigh to myself and ask the student: "Is that what you really want to do?" This little drama repeats itself nearly every time one of our students in the American Studies program comes back from a year in the US. Is there any lesson we can draw from this?

I first explored this for a symposium titled "Communicating with Multicultural America: The View from Kyoto." I am not sure precisely what theme was intended then, but I imagine that the organizers of that symposium aimed to underscore the importance of promoting communication between the United States and Japan and including different perspectives from other parts of the world on US society where, I believe, multicultural-ism is the rule of the day. Yet here I would like to try tackling these ideas from the perspective of how concepts and scholarship travel across the Pacific, and what forces may be working to shape and control such move-ment. By taking up the case of the current state of internationalization in American Studies, I want to explore how the situational positioning of "Other" vs "us," "foreign" vs "native," and "Japanese" vs "American" emerges and works in the production and circulation of knowledge, as we engage in various international collaborations.

I have been working for some time with Professors Virginia Dominguez and Jane Desmond, the strongest proponents of a "critical international-ism" that urges the development of egalitarian collaborations of American Studies scholars around the world in a way that aims to produce new formulations and paradigms (see Desmond and Dominguez 1996). Many of the observations I present here are derived from my experience in that context, but I believe that what I have to say has wider implications for international projects in the social sciences and humanities. Although I now teach and work in Kyoto, my contribution here is not a view from Kyoto. Nor is it from the "Japanese perspective" so often referenced in international symposia. As it happens, I spent most of my academic life in the United States as an anthropologist studying US cultural practices (see, for example, my 1999 book titled *A Room Full of Mirrors: High School Reunions in Middle America*). That was before I moved to Kyoto. I feel I am an insider and an outsider simultaneously in the academic cultures of both the US and Japan. A better metaphor to describe my position, then, may be that it is a view from a seat on a transpacific flight, an in-between state where I contemplate the ways things are in the United States and Japan. This disclaimer is important, as I hope to show here that distinctions and their meanings, often taken for granted in cross-cultural interactions, such as "Japanese" vs "American," "outsider" vs "insider," or "native" vs "foreign" are arbitrary and simplistic constructs produced and reproduced through shifting landscapes of relational exchanges. Some of us do indeed study the United States, even when we mostly live outside the US, but perhaps some of us are in and out of the US and we try to encourage our students to become specialists on the United States. Yet part of the ques-tion is how many of us do so, and how it is that more of us do not.

The field of American Studies has transformed itself dramatically in recent decades. Propelled by the end of the Cold War and the growth of postcolonial consciousness in the US academy, one of the most notable developments has been the effort to de-center "America" in American studies, drawing on shifting positions of power in every domain of the production of knowledge. Conceptualized variously as "post-nationalist American Studies," "transnational American Studies," and even "intercultural American Studies," the emerging visions and practices I acknowledge here seek to find meaningful ways to situate "America" in relational terms, and in a global context.

Out of this revisionist movement has come a genuine reflection on, and reconsideration of, the part of US scholars in all this, including the ways they interact with scholars outside the United States. I am not the first to argue that US American Studies in the past was characterized by self-complacent parochialism, and foreign scholarship on or about the US was peripheralized. Particularly influential in changing this old paradigm was the idea of "critical internationalism" set forth by Jane Desmond and Virginia Dominguez in the *American Quarterly* in 1996. There they argued that critical internationalism was more than internationalization. I appreciate their words in describing this idea, namely, that it refers to "a conceptual orientation that resituates the United States in a global context on a number of terrains simultaneously: in terms of scholarship that gets read, written, and cited and, most importantly, in the ways scholars conceive of new directions for formulating research" (1996: 475). And I appreciate how, following their call, Janice Radway, then US American Studies Association (ASA) president, argued for the egalitarian inclusion of foreign perspectives in American Studies in her 1998 Presidential Address to the US ASA. "It would be necessary," she said, "to ensure that international scholars and scholarship occupied something more than a token position within it. At the association's conference, in the pages of its journal, and in the notes of scholars who associate themselves with the field, the work produced by scholars living and teaching outside the United States ought to figure crucially in arguments about the nature of this country's history and cultures" (Radway 1999: 19).

Indeed in the last ten years, we have seen a flowering of various international initiatives in American Studies. We have seen the creation of new academic associations, such as the International American Studies Association (IASA), which is not headquartered in the United States. We have seen the establishment of exchange programs with American Studies programs and organizations outside the United States. Today, more articles by non-US scholars are included in American Studies journals. The journal *Comparative American Studies*, launched in 2004, is managed by an international editorial board, of which I am a member.

These are all welcome changes. But increased opportunities for interactions and collaborations can give rise to yet new problems for us all to consider. To be sure, problems arising from post-revisionist internationalism are not as overt as those in the days when the power relationship often described as between "center" and "periphery" was assumed to be self-evident. These new problems are more subtle, and can go unnoticed because of the highly developed multicultural sensitivities that frame many international projects. Nevertheless, in the various ways international projects are conceptualized and carried out, I find what Donald Pease called "disciplinary unconsciousness" (Pease 1990). It is something that seems to still operate today, much as it did when American exceptionalism was taken for granted.

It is important to point out that the current push for internationalization in American Studies was produced and shaped by the forces of multiculturalism that arose from particular historical experiences within US society. Growing out of the US Civil Rights movement that transformed the ways we see diversity and difference in the United States, multiculturalism and an arguably postcolonial accompanying "political correctness" are not necessarily timeless or universal. But in the internationalist discourse in US American Studies, we see tendencies to extend ideas and idioms central to US multiculturalism applied to others outside the United States in problematic ways that affect or shape the relationship of scholars outside of the United States to those who normally live in the United States.

Consider an example. A Japanese colleague of mine, a prominent feminist scholar, told me of the perplexity she experienced when asked to attend a conference to represent "women of color," which is an idiom of empowerment, popularly used in minority politics in US multiculturalism. But when such an idiom is imposed in an international context, and is used—and it often is—to describe the women of other societies, it raises a problem. To label women as "women of color" is to imply that there are women without color. "Women of color" are, as the name suggests, what linguists call a "marked category." Colorless women, by virtue of not actually being called that, are the "unmarked category." The unmarked category is unmarked because it is taken for granted and presumed to be dominant. The marked category requires marking precisely because it deviates from what is taken for granted. In terms of real-life social practice, this terminology may actually describe the relationship between US women of European descent and US women of non-European descent. But when transported or transposed uncritically to the international domain, such terminology, inversely, introduces that power hierarchy and inserts it into a different relationship. Within Japan, for example, the unmarked category is "Japanese," and social hierarchy is not defined by skin color but by other things, so to suddenly be labeled a "person of color" by someone who is not Japanese is jarring and rather disorienting. In the discursive practices of multiculturalism, "Otherness" is accorded an esteemed position. Similarly, in the revisionist projects of internationalization, the foreignness of the insights international scholars bring to the discussion is seen to be a source of inspiration and innovation. Moreover, the Otherness of foreign scholars is often romanticized and amplified, to the extent that it recreates, unintentionally, boundaries between "Us" and "Them," the "Outsider" and the "Insider" or, in the case of transpacific projects, "Japanese" and "American."

What is ironic here is that the concept of national homogeneity, the very notion that multiculturalism wanted to negate domestically, resurfaces and is used to characterize the view of foreign scholars. Situated as the "Other" vis-à-vis US scholars, they tend to be categorized by their national origins. Many articles by foreign scholars published in American Studies journals in the last ten years carry such titles as "Such and Such from a German Perspective," or "Such and Such from "a Korean Perspective." Many international symposia look like an academic Olympiad, with every participant presumably representing the view of her nation.

Such ethnicization or nationalization of foreign scholars can run counter to the pursuit of egalitarianism in academic exchanges. The ethnic or national marker "otherizes" foreign scholars, placing them in marked categories, and thereby forces them to assume a marginal position vis-à-vis US Americanists, who belong to the unmarked, and thus presumably, dominant category. Such power relationships, Sheila Hones and Julia Leyda observe, tend to make non-US Americanists feel that "to speak and be heard internationally they need to produce a self-reflective narrative in the manner of a native informant, or take up an allegedly objective 'outside perspective'" (Hones and Leyda 2005: 1029). It is not a coincidence that this observation was made by scholars studying the US who are based in Japan. As they observe, "much US-based writing about 'international' or 'global' American Studies not only essentializes existing borders and subject positions, but also works to naturalize the idea that the US-based Americanist position is simultaneously domestic and universal, while American Studies as practiced elsewhere is by contrast foreign and located" (Hones and Leyda 2005: 1019).

In the internationalist inclusion of "foreign scholars," then, non-US scholars are encouraged to embrace their positioning as foreign within the norm of US American Studies practice. Furthermore, for them to be fully incorporated within US American Studies circles, they have to learn, at least, to imitate or even to internalize, the ways scholarship is practiced in the United States. The style of narrative (or, in other words, the strategies used) for speaking and writing, the methodological premises to formulate research, and the accepted etiquette of academic interactions are mostly dictated by culturally specific conventions. Though often unacknowledged, this very fact poses critical problems in editorial decision-making and the peer review of international journals. The editorial dilemma is how to get "uniquely formulated" foreign scholarship communicated to an English-speaking audience, without the risk of it all appearing rather naïve, childish, or irrelevant. It poses an existential dilemma, too, if we de facto require foreign scholars to capitalize on particular differences while asking them to become "naturalized citizens" of the US academy.

The kind of segregation I observe may be a byproduct of US multiculturalism when it is put into practice. One extreme kind of such segregation takes place when non-US scholars are grouped together in panels organized by the US American Studies Association's Committee on International American Studies, or in panels with titles such as "Teaching American Studies Abroad." I would note, however, that such segregation, or ghettoization, if you will, is by no means unique to American Studies conferences held in the United States. It would be too easy to point a finger at one set of scholars alone if that were the case, but it is not. In conferences in Japan, we find a similar segregation of US and Japanese scholars. In this case, however, the power positioning of the two groups is reversed in a somewhat twisted way: US scholars are seen to be privileged with an authority springing from their native knowledge and an advanced scholarship that is deemed to provide a model for American Studies in Japan. This teacher-disciple relationship is a legacy of the early days of Japanese American Studies. That is something that began in the aftermath of World War II when Japan looked up to the US as a model and inspiration in building an advanced democratic nation following the defeat of imperial Japan in that war.

But this seeming privilege accorded US scholars is, in fact, a double-edged sword, and this volume argues for that unfortunate fact and seeks to change it. There are many possible examples but consider this one. Every year, as part of their internationalization efforts, the US American Studies Association sends their president and delegate to the Annual Meeting of the Japanese Association of American Studies. The ASA Presidential Address is programmed as a special event, and presentations by other US scholars are grouped together—segregated, if you will—into English-language workshops. On the surface, this would seem to enshrine American Studies scholarship by US scholars, elevating them to a position above those of the Japanese. Yet those US scholars often lament that they are afforded few opportunities to engage in discussions with Japanese scholars, whose papers are generally delivered in Japanese. Elevated, yet secluded. Here, again, the boundary is drawn between "us" and "them."

It is self-evident that academic communities and associations are formed in the contexts of particular cultures and histories. The nature of the relationships they form with the outside world is, not surprisingly, a product of such particularities and such particularities inform the questions that drive scholarly inquiry. Incongruences, then, in the contexts in which problem-consciousness is formed can lead to misunderstanding and ideological conflict. In the field of Japanese American Studies, for example, we find a tendency to speak of the United States as if it were an organic entity with a will of its own. In her presidential address to the Japanese Association of American Studies, Professor Hiroko Sato, long engaged in American Studies in Japan and a noted historian for some four decades, noted how the perspective of Otherness (that is, seeing themselves as outsiders) leads to a monolithic view of the United States. In contemporary American Studies, Sato commented:

> To conceive of the United States as a unified and homogenous country seems to be outdated—and hence something to be rejected. However, looking at the country from the outside, as most of us are doing, we cannot help regarding the country as a single unit, especially because the country is so overwhelmingly powerful in the world politically and financially as well as culturally. I myself cannot escape from the idea of one "America," though I am well aware of the plurality of society in the United States. (Sato 2001: 5–6).

I find a similar and very strong tendency in American Studies in China and Korea. It is a disciplinary unconsciousness produced by each nation's geo-political position vis-à-vis the United States. Looking at the US from different shores, and trying to understand what the US means to Japan, Japanese scholars for the most part uncritically subscribe to a similar narrative strategy. But this view of a homogeneous, monolithic United States is the very ideology being deconstructed by American Studies scholars in the United States today. Nevertheless, as we have seen in the case of internationalization projects in US American Studies, "otherization"—no matter who is doing it and where—inevitably leads to homogenization and nationalization.

Here I have focused on how the increased interaction emerging from revisionist projects of internationalization paradoxically generates some of the very problems that they aim to overcome. But I see reason for hope. Increased interactions in various academic domains involving scholars from around the globe are inevitably forcing us to become more aware of the culturally specific assumptions and premises that shape the academic cultures to which we belong. We now have more information about academies outside the United States and Japan, and various exchange programs of faculty or students provide participants opportunities to experience firsthand the different ways that scholarship can be formulated and practiced. And these exchanges are no longer unidirectional, from the alleged "periphery" to the presumed "center," or from Japan to the United States. They are increasingly bilateral, as in the case of our own program in Japan, in which we host US students from American Studies programs in the US who want to study in Japan. The academic world is becoming more globalized than ever before, and more US scholars are teaching and working outside the United States. Their cross-cultural experiences will contribute tremendously to generating reflection and an awareness that what is taken for granted in the United States is only one of countless ways scholarship may be conceived. It is this kind of "academic bilingualism," taken from a genuine critical examination of our own "disciplinary unconsciousness," gives me hope that we could really develop a truly egalitarian internationalism.

Yet let me return to the anecdote with which I began: an experience not from fifty years ago, nor even twenty years ago. Remember that I wrote that a student who has just returned from a Study Abroad program in the United States showed up at my office, and began to report, with obvious excitement, about her wonderful experiences in the United States. And remember that she had gone to study at an American Studies program and had a proposal to research US music firsthand. As our conversation moved to talk about the progress of her research, she told me, "Oh, by the way I changed the focus of my MA thesis. I hope you don't mind." She continued. "The professor I worked with in the US suggested that I should include more about Japan." "Oh, boy," I thought to myself. "Not again."

Keiko Ikeda is Professor of Anthropology and former Dean of the Graduate School of American Studies at Doshisha University in Japan. She has served as Director of the International Institute of American Studies at Doshisha from 2010 to 2013, a leading center of American Studies in Asia. Among her publications is *A Room Full of Mirrors: High School Reunions in Middle America* (Stanford 1999). Over the past several years, she has organized several international symposia on US-Japan cultural interactions, which led to the production of "On Another Playground: Japanese Popular Culture in America "(DVD, Asian Educational Media Service).

References

Desmond, Jane C. and Virginia R. Dominguez. 1996. "Resituating American Studies in a Critical Internationalism." *American Quarterly* 48 (Sept.): 475–90.

Hones, Sheila and Julia Leyda. 2005. "Geographies of American Studies." *American Quarterly* 57(4): 1019–32.

Ikeda, Keiko. 1999. *A Room Full of Mirrors: High School Reunions in Middle America.* Stanford, CA: Stanford University Press.

Pease, Donald. 1990. "New Americanists: Revisionist Interventions into the Canon." *boundary 2* 17 (Spring): 1–37.

Radway, Janice. 1999. "What's in a Name? Presidential Address to the American Studies Association, 20 November 1998." *American Quarterly* 51(1) (March): 1–32.

Sato, Hiroko. 2001. "Looking at the United States from Two Dimensions of 'Otherness,'" *The Japanese Journal of American Studies* 12: 5–14.

Afterword

The Sounds of Silence
Commissions, Omissions, and Particularity in the
Global Anthropology of the United States

Jane C. Desmond

In a recent conversation with a colleague from Seoul, over a big slice of
birthday cake, we were informally discussing our current research and
our students in our respective anthropology departments. Hers, she said,
were often not that interested in her primary topic of research and area of
expertise: the contemporary United States. I was truly surprised, given the
large presence of the US military for the past sixty years in South Korea,
the massive US Army base on prime real estate in the middle of Seoul, and
America's continuing and very public role as a counter to China's increasing dominance in the Pacific region. Surely "they" would want to know
more about "us." We were so clearly a part of "their" daily lives!

The United States can appear, as my colleague Hyang-Jin Jung then
explained to me, to be both largely irrelevant and overly familiar to the
academically accomplished and largely comfortably middle class, young,
urban South Koreans who populate her courses, the same group presumably from which future professional anthropologists might emerge. That
presumption of familiarity, a seductive lure of partial knowledge and
stereotypes, is largely gained through the circulation of US-produced
mass media, a sort of "everybody knows," when everybody does not.
This conversation came back to me a few days ago as I was rereading the
essays and provocations in this book, which asks why so few anthropologists, living and working outside of the United States, do fieldwork in and
research on the US.

Knowledge, as we know so well in theory, yet sometimes forget in fact, is produced from somewhere. Haraway and others have underlined the power of the concept of "situated knowledges" (Haraway 1988). Emerging especially with reference to previously undervalued knowledge produced by less empowered communities, like feminists or racialized and minoritized communities, this concept argues that angles of vision, lived experience, and social formations are both key constraints on, and enabling factors for, the production of knowledge. Although Haraway's original emphasis was on the discursive realm of "science," by extension, this notion applies not only to disempowered communities, and not only to scientific communities, but to all communities of knowledge producers, including elites. In this case the concept of "situated knowledges" can reference the world of highly trained scholars who embrace anthropology as their home discipline. In what follows, I want to unspool this concept as it might apply to the provocations of this book.

If we start from the assumption then that all knowledge is produced from somewhere, part of our challenge is articulating where that "somewhere" is when it also includes a complex set of "somehows." Knowledge production resides in intellectual paradigms with specific intellectual histories, and in local, national, and transnational intellectual communities. It is comprised too of publishing practices, writing genres, transnational exchange programs, funding schemes, international conference collaborations, training programs, and places of employment, with their specific conventions and expectations. This model embraces both the material and the immaterial realms that form the "habitus," to invoke Bourdieu's useful formulation, which we engage in as scholars, researchers, and teachers (Bourdieu 1984). This habitus, complex as it is, is in no way simply some unmarked "global" realm of imagined contemporary, cosmopolitan, intellectuals. It is instead very particular both to individual scholars and to communities of scholars. No matter how mobile we are, how trans- or multi-nationally situated we are, how connected we are to multiple communities through cyberspace, no one is simultaneously and equally everywhere. The particularities of our lives and our work communities profoundly shape what we care about, how we formulate, conduct, fund, and disseminate the results of our research, who reads our research, and the effects that research might have.

The essays in this book make the power of this particularity apparent. They do so both as demonstrations of the complexity of the habitus (multiple habituses)—the situatedness I sketched above—and in the unpredictable, and often illuminating, results of their findings and arguments, especially when read with and across one another. In some cases new insights emerge for a particular researcher through explicit or implicit comparisons across national borders and back again. For example, Darash's new understanding of the composite of US security and science, built, she argues, on claims of globality and an arena "outside culture," arose in part because it was markedly different from the issues as they played out in the Israeli context.

All the cases in this book reflect multi-sited lives of long commitment to more than one place, community, and set of questions. However, each of these authors also lives a professional life anchored—often for decades—in a home university in a home country/region that is not the United States. This multiplicity reveals a generative potential for new understandings not only of phenomena, communities, and practices, but also of how anthropologists craft their object of study in fluid ways over time when they sustain a multiplicity of research commitments "at home," wherever that may be, and in and with the United States and its cultural imaginaries of "America." Note, for example, that Shokeid writes/has written about issues in both Israel and the United States, as has Darash. White, a specialist on the Solomon Islands, also writes about memory and memorialization, including in the US at Pearl Harbor and most recently in France. Wulff publishes on writers in Ireland and on transnational ballet labor networks, in addition to the work on Swedes in New York. Habib works with refugee and Diaspora communities in Canada and the US, as well as with First Nations communities in Canada. Ikeda teaches US students about "America" in Kyoto. Dominguez is a specialist on Israel and on the US, embracing large questions of peoplehood. And my Korean colleague Hyang-Jin Jung, specialist on the US, also publishes on the performativity of politics in North Korea (for a partial sample of this multiplicity see, for example, the following: Samimian-Darash and Rabinow 2015; Dominguez 1986 and 1989; Habib 2004; Ikeda 1999; Shokeid 1982; Jung, 2007 and 2013; White 2016; Wulff 1998).

This multiplicity is not necessarily the same as doing "multi-sited ethnography," which more often refers to tracking related flows—of, say, commodities or practices, across space and in multiple communities, instead of hewing to the "traditional" notion of long-term immersion in just one place and community. Those multiple sites are usually seen as connected together in one larger project but, for the contributors in this book, their lives include multiple ongoing projects, some of which may in themselves be multi-sited (see Hannerz' work on foreign correspondents, for example, in Hannerz 2004), but many of which do not connect directly, rather they run along parallel lines. For example, Habib's work with First Nations communities in Canada and Jewish tourism to Israel may both be projects that engage broadly with notions of belonging, but the projects are not conducted in obvious relation to one another.

These multiple, ongoing passions and commitments, such as Hannerz's multi-decade "in and outness" of being with the United States, reflect not simply their anthropological training but also the particular habitus of these scholars and their local/national university settings, what is valued there, what is urgent on the ground locally, and what their (domestic as well as international) colleagues and students care about. This complex mix of movement and sustained locality helps produce some of the "de-naturalizing" perception that anthropology as a discipline has traditionally valued.

Part of the power of the local, the "from somewhere" in the larger sense I opened with, is the issue of "use value." I thought about this issue a lot early on in my training in American Studies in the United States, and especially when I began to develop an intense engagement with colleagues from around the world. For whom does the knowledge we produce have meaning?

In his essay in this volume, White reminds us of a poignant scene in a little-recalled 1983 film titled *Anthropology on Trial: Papua New Guinea*. In the film, we see Wari Iamo, then a graduate student from Papua New Guinea conducting doctoral research in anthropology at the University of California at Berkeley. His fieldsite was the United States, specifically the San Francisco Bay area, and his dissertation focused on homelessness. How can such a thing like homelessness happen in such a wealthy country? Perhaps US residents feel less familial obligations to take care of all their members? At one point in his fieldwork, the film reveals Iamo being subjected to a performance of nativist paternalism by a Bay Area lawyer he was interviewing, who lectures Iamo on the strength of bilateral kinship systems in the US. Clearly, the lawyer implies, Iamo, the "outsider" simply does not understand.

Such a scene, no doubt inflected by presumptions of racializing primitivism, of "third-world-ism" on the part of the lawyer, devalues the notion of "outsider knowledge," but I doubt this type of paternalism is what ultimately led Iamo to turn away from further work on the United States after successfully completing his PhD at Berkeley in 1987 (Iamo 1987). As White notes, he is not alone among scholars in anthropology from the Pacific Islands who chose to develop academic expertise on their home regions. What is different for Iamo, however, is that he started out as an expert on the US, and then never undertook or published any further work on that topic after returning home to Papua New Guinea. Instead, he focused his educational expertise on Papua New Guinean issues (and public service), instead of teaching, say, courses on the anthropology of the US back in Port Moresby. Although I have never had the opportunity to ask him, I suspect that other needs were more pressing. Other types of questions needed answers and may have been more valued "back home" both by himself and others.

It may be that in Papua New Guinea the United States, despite being a world hegemon in so many ways and despite the legacy of its central role in World War II in the Pacific, is, on a daily basis, largely irrelevant. Anthropological knowledge forged in US-based fieldwork may seem to have little use and hold little intrigue. To the extent that knowledge about "America" is desired, it can be accessed in the form of circulating cultural products, consumed as locally desired, and charged with local meaning.

Pushing this notion of relevance further, we would probably not be surprised if in Papua New Guinea there were no anthropologists who are experts on, say, Sweden, or Canada. (Japan would be another matter given the past history). But the reason those absences would not surprise us is not that Sweden or Canada are somehow not "interesting," but rather that it seems easy to see why they might not be seen as "important" there. But how, an international anthropology of the US initiative would seem to ask, could the US *not* be important? Surely, we might think, understanding the elephant in the room of the world is important to everyone/everyplace where the elephant might decide to throw its weight around, as friend or foe, through ideas, commodities, investment, foreign intervention, or mass media conglomerates. But this is not the case, and it is not the case in two ways.

First, local contexts may dictate that other types of knowledge are more pressing and, second, to the extent that knowledge about the US is deemed important, it is being produced, often at frantic paces, in other disciplines.

Work on the US is produced by experts around the globe, often in the fields of literature and political science and, secondarily, in disciplines like history and economics. The global American Studies community, reflected in organizations like the non-US based International American Studies Association, of which I am a past president, rarely attracts anthropologists to its biannual world congresses (Desmond 2014). Rather, it is sustained by specialists in literature, media studies, and political science. There are many reasons for this configuration, and specific political and economic histories to the development of such fields of expertise after World War II including the role of the US State Department. I, and others, have written about them elsewhere (Desmond 2001). Ikeda charts some of the pitfalls of navigating this community in any sort of bilateral ways. In addition, new historical scholarship calls for triangulating national histories of relationships, embedding the US relationship with communities abroad into an ever more complex context that includes multiple nations (Cuthbertson and Saunders 2014).

But clearly, as Habib and Dominguez assert in this book's introduction, time and money are not the only impediments shuttling scholars of the US outside the US into other disciplines, into non-anthropological modes of producing knowledge. In those cases where such non-anthropological work flourishes, like Italy, Great Britain, India, Japan, China, and elsewhere, there is not a lack of interest, a sense of irrelevancy, or such a presumed familiarity that academic work on the US seems uninteresting. Perhaps it is the *type* of work that anthropology can produce that seems uninteresting (a reason that could be hard for anthropologists to embrace), or perhaps, as White suggests in his reference to Trouillot's "savage slot" idea (Trouillet 1991), the formulation of anthropological research in a particular region or nation (and national traditions of, and funding for, research still do matter) does not allow for the US to come into view as a prospective fieldsite.

Sometimes the goal is just different. Some colleagues in China have explained to us that the goal of some of their research is less to expand the understanding of cultural complexity in the US than it is to look at the US as a test site for portable "best practices" in a variety of arenas that might then be retooled for use in China to address an issue there. This is a different, more direct, and applied sense of "use value" reflecting as well some Chinese state funding priorities and, while I do not know if it is widespread or not, it bears noting and further research. Anthropological fieldwork may not be seen as the most efficient or effective way to gain the desired knowledge. Of course, this type of "habitus" for scholarly production affects the formulation of research questions, methods, and dissemination and impact, as is always (but always differently) the case.

So far I have suggested that the absence this volume charts may be due to presumed irrelevancy, to disinterest, to faux familiarity, to other pressing local needs, or to the local or national practice of developing knowledge about the US through disciplines other than anthropology. That knowledge reflects, at least to some extent, either the home configurations of what "proper" anthropology is, or a desire for other types of understanding than that which fieldwork-based anthropology excels at producing—the intense focus on complexities of lived experience in particular social formations that are always in motion. So perhaps the primary beneficiary of additional anthropologists focusing on the US while embedded in professional intellectual lives largely elsewhere, is/ would be the consuming public (academic or not) *in* the US.

As has been made abundantly clear in this volume, the goal, if anthropologists chose to pursue it, of fostering more work on the US by anthropologists abroad is not to "fetishize the foreign" (Desmond 2004) as the source of distinctive national viewpoints. Ikeda makes abundantly clear some of the politically and intellectually impoverished ways this type of segregation (her word) can unfold. Rather, it is to insist that the intellectual, material, and historically shaped contours of where, how, why, and with whom we work makes a real difference in the questions we ask, the publics we seek, and the ways that knowledge gets produced. These multiplicities are generative of new research questions and new insights, as the work in this volume demonstrates. This may be especially so when those locations of professional life are *themselves* multiple, as is the case in so many of the work lives of the contributors in this volume who, like Hannerz, are constantly in and out. Such combinations of multiple situatedness, enduring over time, yet in shifting dialogic formations may, as White proposes, have implications not only for the anthropology of the US but also for transforming anthropological practices more widely.

In this respect, this volume is a provocation. It asks us to think about larger questions of presences and absences, of how anthropologists around the world construct (and are constructed by) not only their field-sites but their work lives. It demands an attention to the combination of particularity and complexity, of materiality and the immaterial that structure intellectual work and scholarly communities. In short, it suggests a call for a new disciplinary self-reflexivity, a study of the global presences and absences, passions and possibilities, rejections and active ignorings that anthropologists bring to bear in their mappings of the contemporary world.

Jane Desmond is Professor of Anthropology and of Gender and Women's Studies at the University of Illinois at Urbana-Champaign, US, where she directs The International Forum for US Studies: A Center for the Transnational Study of the United States. Author of *Staging Tourism: Bodies on Display from Waikiki to Sea World* (University of Chicago Press, 1999) and *Displaying Death/Animating Life: Human-Animal Relations in Art, Science, and Everyday Life* (University of Chicago Press, 2016), she is the past president of the International American Studies Association, Salgo Professor of American Studies at Eotvos Lorand University, Budapest, and "Visiting Eminent World Scholar" at Beijing Foreign Studies University

References

Cuthbertson, Greg and Christopher Saunders. 2014. "The United States—South Africa—Germany: Reflections on a Triangular, Transnational Relationship." *Amerikastudien/American Studies: A Quarterly* 59(4): 463–80.

Bourdieu, Pierre. 1984. *Distinction: A Social Critique of the Judgment of Taste.* Boston, MA: Harvard University Press.

Desmond, Jane. 2001. "Mapping 'American Studies' Across National Boundaries: The Politics of 'Politics,' the Politics of Knowledge, and the Limits to Collaboration." *Hungarian Journal of English and American Studies* 7(1): 127–33. Retrieved 8 February 2016 from http://www. JSTOR.org/stable/41274131.

———. 2004. "As Others See Us? Fetishizing the Foreign at the Whitney." *American Quarterly* 56(4): 1051–66.

———. 2014. "Ethnography as Ethics and Epistemology: Why American Studies Should Embrace Fieldwork, and Why it Hasn't." *American Studies* 53(1): 27–56.

Dominguez, Virginia R. 1986. *White By Definition: Social Classification in Creole Louisiana* New Brunswick, NJ: Rutgers University Press.

———. 1989. *People as Subject/People as Object: Selfhood and Peoplehood in Contemporary Israel.* Madison: University of Wisconsin Press.

Habib, Jasmin. 2004. *Israel, Diaspora, and the Routes to National Belonging.* Toronto: University of Toronto Press.

Hannerz, Ulf. 2004. *Foreign News: Exploring the World of Foreign Correspondents.* Chicago: University of Chicago Press.

Haraway, Donna. 1988. "'Situated Knowledges': The Science Question in Feminism and the Privilege of Partial Perspectives." *Feminist Studies* 14(3): 575–99.

Iamo, Wari. 1987. "In Search of Justice and Shelter in Mix-Town U.S.A." Ph.D diss., University of California, Berkeley.

Ikeda, Keiko. 1999. *A Room Full of Mirrors: High School Reunions in Middle America.* Stanford, CA: Stanford University Press.

Jung, Hyang-Jin. 2007. *Learning to be an Individual: Emotion and Person in an American Junior High School* New York: Peter Lang International Publishing.

———. 2013. "Do They Mean What They Act? Surveillance, Theatricality and Mind-Heart Among North Koreans." *Acta Koreana* 16, no. 1: 87–111.

Samimian-Darash, Limor and Paul Rabinow, eds. 2015. *Modes of Uncertainty: Anthropological Cases.* Chicago: University of Chicago Press, 2015.

Shokeid, Moshe. 1982. *Distant Relations: Ethnicity and Politics Among Arabs and North Africans Jews in Israel.* New York: Praeger Publishers.

Trouillet, Michel-Rolph. "Anthropology and the Savage Slot: the Poetics and Politics of Otherness." *Recapturing Anthropology,* ed. Richard Fox, 17–44. Santa Fe, NM: School of American Research.

White, Geoff. 2016. *Unfinished Histories and the Work of Remembrance: Memorializing Pearl Harbor.* Durham, NC: Duke University Press.

Wulff, Helena. 1998. *Ballet Across Borders: Career and Culture in the World of Dancers.* Oxford, UK: Berg Publishers.

Index

A

activists, profiles of, 65–75
Adorno, Theodore, 107
adult commitments, delay of, 36–37
affectionate relationships, 129–131
AIDS, 134
AIPAC (America Israel Political Action Committee), 58
Albert, Bruce, 89
aliyah (immigration to Israel), 74
All Our Kin, 6
Al-Qaeda, 64
America, 3
American Anthropological Association (AAA), 7, 12, 79, 106, 143
American Anthropologist, 7
American culture, 31, 51-75. *See also* United States
American exceptionalism, 105, 111
American Friends of Peace Now, 58
American Quarterly, 157
American Society of Microbiology (ASM), 95
American Studies, 14, 152
    Cold War, 156
    intercultural, 157
    internationalization, 156
    post-nationalist, 157
    scholarship in, 155–162
    transnational, 157
American Studies Association (ASA), 157, 160
An American Dilemma, 105
An Inconvenient Truth, 20
anonymous sex, 124–125, 130
anthrax, 81

Anthropology as Cultural Critique, 148
"anthropology at home," 143–145
Anthropology on Trial, 145, 148, 150, 167
anti-Americanism, 4
anti-Semitism, 56, 62, 63. *See also* Jews
anti-Zionists, 58
Appadurai, Arjun, 16
artists, 33, 34
    making a living as, 34
    types of, 35
Association for Civil Rights in Israel (ACRI), 63
au pairs, 33, 34, 35
Australia, 13
authorized scientists, biosecurity, 91–94

B

Balinese culture, 108, 109, 110
Barrio Dreams, 6
Barth, Fredrik, 12
Bat Shalom, 63
Baudrillard, Jean, 3, 107
the Bears, 128
Beck, Glenn, 112
Beinart, Peter, 58
Ben-Ari, Eyal, 97
Berlusconi, Silvio, 20
Bimkom, 63
biosecurity, 79–98
    authorized scientists vs. global sharing systems, 91–94
    Dual Use categories, 82–84
    dynamic between science and security, 86–88
    and the life sciences, 81–82
    merging scientific and global, 95–96

problem of in the United States,
96–98
public preparedness, 88–91
self-regulation, 84–86
bioterrorism, 62
bisexual circle, 127–128
"Body Ritual among the Nacirema", 7
Borneman, John, 10
Bourdieu, Pierre, 3
Bowling Alone, 21, 130
Brit Tzedek v'Shalom/Jewish Alliance for
Justice and Peace, 60
Broady, Donald, 38
Brodkin, Karen, 6
BSL-3 laboratories, United States, 81
BSL-4 pathogens, 81
B'Tselem, 60, 63
Bush, George H.W., 110
Bush, George W., 81, 109

C

Canada, 8, 13, 56, 166, 168
Canadian Independent Jewish Voices, 59
Carmichael, Stokely, 106, 111
Carter, Jimmy, 103, 110
Cattelino, Jessica, 7
Center for Biosecurity, 90
Centers for Disease Control (CDC), 81
Checkpoint Watch, 60, 63, 64
China, 13, 169
Christian right, 51
circulation, 40–47
Civil Rights movement, 158
Clinton, Bill, 103, 109, 110
Codes of Conduct in the Life Sciences
(NSABB), 85
Cold War, 53, 147, 148, 156
Collier, S.J., 81
Collins, Francis, 95
Collins, Gail, 114
Communist Party, Israel, 53
Comparative American Studies, 157
conspiracy theories, 113–115
contextualization, 87
cosmopolitanism (of Manhattan), 35
costs, Other (United States as), 2–4
The Crisis of Zionism, 58
critical internationalism, 156, 157
Cronkite, Walter, 112
cross-cultural research, 145
cultural representation, politics of, 151

cultural saturation, 150
Cultural Studies, 10
Culture and Imperialism, 64
Custom and Conflict in Africa, 121

D

Dana International, 133
Davila, Arlene, 6
decolonization, 145
Democracy in America, 3, 148
Desmond, Jane, 23, 97, 156, 157
de Tocqueville, Alexis, 3, 105, 121, 122, 148
Diaspora activism, 52–59
diasporicists, 58
Dignity, 123
disciplinary unconsciousness, 158
Disordered World, 105
dissertations, 144
dissidence and the Israel/Palestine
conflict, 59–63
dissidents, Jews, 55
*Distant Mirrors: America as a Foreign
Culture*, 10
Dominguez, Virginia R., 97, 143, 144, 147,
156, 157, 166, 169
Donald Duck, 31, 40
Dual Use categories, 82–84
Dual Use Research of Concern (DURC),
83, 84, 86, 89

E

East-West Center, 147, 148
editorial decision-making, 160
egalitarianism, 109
Egypt, 13
Egypt, 60
Ehrlich, Susan, 95
election campaigns, 108–113
Empire, 57, 64–65, 73–75, 150, 151
Erasmus Medical Centre, 88
Erikson, Erik Homburger, 16, 36
Europe, 3, 33, 151
Eurorailers (*tågluffare*), 38
Eurotrash, 33
Even, Uzi, 132–133F

F

fame in New York City, 35
Fauci, Tony, 95

fear, 55–56, 64–65
fetishize the foreign, 169
field of study, choice of, 13
fieldsites
    Manhattan, 31–47
    United States as, 143–153
fieldwork, 2, 6, 164, 168
    cost of, 2
    long-term, 5
    in the United States, 15
    why it matters, 8–12
filmmaking, 35
Fink Report (2004), 82, 96
Fischer, Michael M. J., 148, 149
foreign policy, 1, 51, 57
foreign scholars, 169
Fortuyn, Pim, 115
Fouchier, Ron, 88, 89, 90, 92, 94
France, 4, 13, 148
Franken, Al, 107
Frankfurt School, 107
freedom of science, 85
Freud, Sigmund, 131, 135
Friends of Peace Now, 59, 60
Friends of the Pea, 36
Fukuda, Keiji, 95

G

Garrett, Laurie, 90-1
Garsten, Christina, 8
Gay and Lesbian Community Services
    Center, 121, 123–124
gay Christian congregations in New York
    City, 123
gay communities, 20, 21, 22
Gay Fathers Association, 128–129
gay life in Israel, 20, 21, 22, 132–133
gay organizations (United States), 120–137
    the Bears, 128
    bisexual circle, 127–128
    comparisons to Israel, 135–137
    Gay Fathers Association, 128–129
    Gentlemen Circle, 129
    MACT (Men of All Colors
        Together), 126–127
    research in, 123
    SAGE Circle, 123–124
    sexual compulsive anonymous
        (SCA) groups, 124–125
    viability of, 129–131
Geertz, Clifford, 20, 108, 109, 114

Gentlemen Circle, 129
Germany, 3, 4, 13
global anthropology of United States,
    164–170
global experiences, maturity through,
    37–40
globalization, 80, 145
global sharing systems, 91–94
Global Studies, 168–170
Gluckman, Max, 121
Gore, Al, 20
government policies, 33
graduate studies, 3
Gramsci, Antonio, 115
Grand Tour, 38
Grant, Ulysses, 113
Great Britain, 169
Greenwich Village, 121
Greenwich Village Center, 21, 122, 124

H

H5N1 (bird flu) virus, 80, 88, 89, 90, 92,
    93, 96
Habib, Jasmin, 8, 9, 13, 17, 18, 19, 97, 143,
    144, 147, 166, 169
habitus, 165
Haider, Jörg, 115
Hammoudi, Abdellah, 10
Hannerz, Ulf, 8, 9, 19, 20, 167, 170
Haring, Keith, 41
Harvey, Paul, 106, 107, 115
Health and Human Services (HSS), 82
Hebrew University, 120
Helmreich, Stefan, 6
Henderson, Donald, 94
HHS (US Department of Health and
    Human Services), 95
HIV/AIDS, 134
Hofstadter, Richard, 20, 113
homeland security, 5, 64
homogenization, 161
homosexuals, 132. *See also* gay
    organizations (United States)
hot situations, 87, 88
Howes, David, 46
*How Jews Became White Folks and What That
    Says about Race in America*, 6
Huizinga, Johan, 122
Hurston, Zora Neale, 5

I

Iamo, Wari, 147, 150, 167
identities, experimentation of, 37
identity play, 37
Ikeda, Keiko, 8, 23
Independent Jewish Voices, 58, 60
independent voters, 111
India, 13, 169
Influenza Conference Newspaper, 89
Ingelsby, Thomas, 90
intercultural American Studies, 157
International American Studies
    Association (IASA), 23, 157, 168
international anthropology, 1–23
        approach to anthropology, 15–23
        changes in, 14–15
        cost, money, and visas, 2–4
        objectifying colleagues outside of
            the US, 4–5
International Forum for US Studies, 23
internationalization, 156, 159
Interview magazine, 41
Iraq, 64
Israel, 13, 166
        access to, 53
        activists/activism, 63–64
        affiliations and attachments to, 52–59
        aliyah (immigration to Israel), 74
        biological threats, 79
        Communist Party, 53
        comparisons to gay organizations
            (United States), 135–137
        criticism of, 51–75
        failure of gay associations in,
            133–135
        gay life in, 132–133
        Jewish activism, 64–65
        legal rights of gays, 137
        profiles of activists, 65–75
Israel Association of Gays, Lesbians,
    Bisexuals, and Transgendered (GLBT
    Israel), 133, 134
Israeli Committee against Housing
    Demolitions (ICAHD), 60, 63
The Israel Lobby, 58, 72
Israel/Palestine conflict, 17, 18, 56, 59–63

J

Japan, 13, 155, 156, 161, 162, 169
Japanese (as outsiders), 158, 159

Japanese Association of American Studies,
    160
Jewish activists (United States), 18
Jewish Agency Land Settlement
    Department, 120
Jewish Federation, 57
Jewish identity, 51–59, 63, 73–75
Jewish tourism, 166
Jewish Voice for Peace (JVP), 58, 59, 60,
    61, 62
Jewish Witnesses for Peace, 59, 60
Jews. *See also* Israel
        dissidence and the Israel/Palestine
            conflict, 59–63
        dissidents, 55
        identity, 63
        Israeli activists/activism, 63–64
        Jewish activism, 64–65
        profiles of activists, 65–75
        in the United States, 51
Jews, Race and Popular Music, 73
Jews Against the Occupation, 60, 62
J Street, 58, 60
Jung, Hyang-Jin, 8, 164

K

Kaplan, Amy, 17, 54, 64
Kaplan, Robert, 108
Kawaoka, Yoshihiro, 88, 92, 94, 95
Keim, Paul, 90
Kim, Jin K., 11
Knesset Committee on Social Affairs, 22
Knesset repeal (1988), 132
knowledge production, 86–88
Kristof, Nicholas, 114
Kyoto, Japan, 156

L

LaDousa, Chaise, 6
Lane, Stanley, 84
Latin America, 13
Latinos, Inc., 6
League of Women Voters, 110
Lebanon, invasion of (1982), 53
LeMenestrel, Sara, 8
Levi-Strauss, Claude, 12
life sciences, biosecurity and the, 81–82
Limbaugh, Rush, 112
literature, 1
Little Manhattan, 45–47

Löfgren, Orvar, 38
Long Journeys *(långresor)*, 38
Lutz, Catherine, 6

M

Maalouf, Amin, 105
Mackey, Eva, 8
MACT (Men of All Colors Together),
  126–127
Maddow, Rachel, 112
Manhattan as a magnet (to Swedes), 31–47
  delay of adult commitments, 36–37
  Little Manhattan, 45–47
  looking for the unexpected, 40–43
  maturity through global
    experience, 37–40
  memories of after returning to
    Sweden, 43–45
  nightlife, 37
Marcus, George E., 148, 149
Marxism, 53
maturity through global experience
  (Swedes), 37–40
McCain, John, 113
McCarthyism, 55
Mead, Margaret, 145
Mearsheimer, John J., 58, 72
media, 108–113
media consumers, 39, 40
memories of Manhattan after returning to
  Sweden, 43–45
Meselson, Matt, 91
Metropolitan Community Church (MCC),
  123
middle class, 12
  Europeans, 33
  origins of au pairs, 34
Middle East, 51
Miner, Horace, 7
money, 2–4
Moore, Michael, 112
moratorium in Manhattan, 36–37
multi-sited ethnography, 166
multi-sited research, 144
Myrdal, Gunnar, 105

N

Nader, Laura, 146, 147, 148
Natcher, Simon, 82
National Academy of Sciences, 82

National Geographic Society, 6
National Institutes of Health (NIH), 82, 95
nationalization, 161
National Science Advisory Board for
  Biosecurity (NSABB), 80, 82, 83, 84, 85,
    86, 89, 90, 91, 94, 95
Nations Unbound, 6
Native American/AmerIndian societies, 3
Native Hawaiian studies, 145
Nature, 89, 93, 95
New Israel Fund, 58
The New Production of Knowledge, 86–88
New York City, 15, 16
  culture of, 33
  gay Christian congregations in, 123
  gay life in, 120–137
  impact of impressions on Swedes,
    39
  Little Manhattan, 45–47
  looking for the unexpected, 40–43
  Manhattan as a magnet, 31–47
  memories of after returning to
    Sweden, 43–45
New York Times, 111
New Zealand, 81
NIAID (National Institute of Allergy and
  Infectious Diseases), 89
nightlife in Manhattan, 37
North Korea, 166
Not in My Name, 58, 59
Nowotny, Helga, 87
Nye, Joseph, 115

O

Obama, Barack, 107
Occupy Wall Street, 109
Ojeda, Amparo B., 11
"On Multiple Realities", 41
opinion polls, 112
O'Reilly, Bill, 112
Orientalism, 15
Orientalizing practices, 147
Ortner, Sherry, 42
Oslo Accords (1993), 52, 60
Other (United States as), 1–23, 161
  approach to anthropology, 15–23
  changes in anthropology, 14–15
  cost, money, and visas, 2–4
  critiques of, 144
  objectifying colleagues outside of
    the US, 4–5

scholarships in United States, 5–13
    study of, 145
othering, 156–161
otherization, 161
outside cultures, 166

P

Palestine, 52, 53, 54
    Israel/Palestine conflict, 56
    refugees, 61
    research, 54
Pandemic Influenza Preparedness (PIP)
    framework, 92
pandemics, 89. *See also* biosecurity
Papua New Guinea, 145, 146, 148, 150,
    167
pathogens, 81
Patterson, Amy, 95
peace activists, 52, 54, 59–64, 67–68, 73
Pease, Donald, 158
pea soup, 36
peer reviews, 160
peregrinato academica, 38
Pfanner, Helmut, 34
Physicians for Human Rights, 63
Pickering, Lucy, 8
political culture (United States), 103–115
    conspiracy theories, 113–115
    limitations of theatricality, 110–112
    sources of stardom, 112–113
    spectacle of, 106–108
    theater states compared, 108–110
    uses of outsiders, 104–106
politics of cultural representation, 151
The Post-American World, 20, 108
postmodern monarchies, 113–115
post-nationalist American Studies, 157
post-Zionists, 58
Powdermaker, Hortense, 5
power, 144–148
public preparedness, biosecurity, 88–91
Putnam, Robert, 21

R

Rabbis for Human Rights, 60, 63
Rabinow, Paul, 84
Radio Sweden, 104
Radway, Janice, 157
"Reading America: Preliminary Notes on
    Class and Culture", 42

Reagan, Ronald, 19, 106, 107, 110
Recapturing Anthropology, 14
refugees, Palestine, 61
regulations, security, 84–86
Relevance, 167–170
research
    cross-cultural, 145
    in gay organizations (United
        States), 123
    multi-sited, 144
    Palestine, 54
    trans-cultural, 145
Reynolds, Daniel, 83, 84, 89
Rice, Steadman, 131
Ridge, Tom, 64
risks, security, 80
*Room Full of Mirrors: High School Reunions
    in Middle America*, 156
Roosevelt, Theodore, 113
Rybicki, Ed, 93

S

SAGE Circle, 123–124
Sahlins, Marshall, 6
Said, Edward W., 15, 64
Samimian-Darash, Limor, 18, 19
Sanders, Bernie, 111
SARS, 81
Sato, Hiroko, 161
saturation (cultural), 150
savage slot, 144, 169
Schiller, Nina Glick, 6
scholars, cost of studies, 3
scholarship, 2
    in American Studies, 155–162
    United States, 5–13
Schutz, Alfred, 41, 44
Schwarzenegger, Arnold, 19, 107
science, 85. *See also* biosecurity
Science, 89, 95
Science Express, 94
Scientific American, 89
security. *See* biosecurity
    dynamic between science and,
        86–88
    regulations, 84–86
    risks, 80
segregation, 160
self-regulation, biosecurity, 84–86
Seoul, South Korea, 164
Settlement Watch, 60

sexual compulsive anonymous (SCA)
groups, 124–125
sexual orientation, 37. *See also* gay
communities
Sheen, Martin, 107
Shokeid, Moshe, 8, 20, 21, 22, 42
silence, 164–170
situated knowledges, 165
social injustice, 33
Society for the Anthropology of North
America (SANA), 7, 8
Society for the Protection of Personal
Rights (SPPR), 132, 133
soft power, 113–115
Sombart, Werner, 111
South Korea, 13, 164
Springsteen, Bruce, 112
Stack, Carol, 6
Strathern, Marilyn, 87
Stockholm, Sweden, 34, 45. *See also*
Swedes
Stratton, Jon, 73
students, cost of studies, 3
Study Abroad programs, 155, 162
Sundar, Nandini, 12-13
Sweden, 168
class systems in, 42
pea soup, 36
Swedes, 31–47
dreams of New York City, 39
Little Manhattan, 45–47
looking for the unexpected, 40–43
Manhattan as a magnet, 31–47
maturity through global
experience, 37–40
population of, 34

T

"Teaching American Studies Abroad", 160
Tel Aviv, Israel, 133–135. *See also* Israel
Tel Aviv University, 42, 132
television, watching, 39
terrorism, bioterrorism, 62
therapeutic discourse, 122–131
third-world-ism, 167
Thompson, Fred, 107
Thompson, Tommy G., 82
threats, biological, 79. *See also* biosecurity
Tisch School of the Arts, 35
trans-cultural research, 145
transnational, 145, 147, 149, 150, 152, 153

transnational American Studies, 157
Trotskyism, 53
Trouillot, Michel-Rolph, 14
Trump, Donald, 19, 107
tuberculosis, 81
Turkey, 13

U

un-American attitudes
affiliations and attachments to
Israel, 52–59
criticism of Israel, 51–75
dissidence and the Israel/Palestine
conflict, 59–63
Israeli activists/activism, 63–64
Jewish activism, 64–65
United States
affiliations and attachments to
Israel, 52–59
approach to anthropology, 15–23
biosecurity in (See biosecurity)
BSL-3 laboratories, 81
changes in anthropology, 14–15
Civil Rights movement, 158
criticism of Israel, 51–75
delay of adult commitments, 36–37
dissidence and the Israel/Palestine
conflict, 59–63
as fieldsites, 143–153
foreign policy, 18, 51, 57
gay organizations, 120–137
global anthropology of, 164–170
Israeli activists/activism, 63–64
Jewish activism, 64–65
Manhattan as a magnet, 31–47
objectifying colleagues outside of,
4–5
as Other, 1–23
political culture, 103–115
profiles of activists, 65–75
scholarships, 5–13
segregation, 160
Unity, 123
University of California at Berkeley, 146,
167
University of Manchester, 120
University of Pittsburgh, 90
Upper West Side, 34
US Army, 164

V

vaccines, 90
Venicci, Christian, 83, 85
visas, 2–4
voluntary associations (gay), 120–137. *See also* gay organizations (United States)

W

Walt, Stephen M., 58, 72
Washington, George, 113
Werbner, Pnina, 55
West Nile virus, 81
White, Geoffrey, 23
WHO (World Health Organization), 92, 93

Wilders, Geert, 115
Winfrey, Oprah, 112, 131
women of color, 158
Woolgar, Steve, 97
World War II, 147, 148, 168
Writing Culture, 148
Wulff, Helena, 8, 15, 16, 17

Y

Yamashita, Shinji, 12, 13

Z

Zakaria, Fareed, 108, 109
Zionism, 53, 55, 58, 63